The human direction

James L. Peacock
THE UNIVERSITY OF NORTH CAROLINA

A. Thomas Kirsch
PRINCETON UNIVERSITY

APPLETON-CENTURY-CROFTS
EDUCATIONAL DIVISION
MEREDITH CORPORATION

New York

The human direction

An evolutionary approach
to social and cultural anthropology

This book, or parts thereof, must not be used or reproduced in any manner without written permission. For information address the publisher, Appleton-Century-Crofts, Educational Division, Meredith Corporation, 440 Park Avenue South, New York, N. Y. 10016.

711-3

Library of Congress Card Number: 74–115012

PRINTED IN THE UNITED STATES OF AMERICA

390–69884–9

For permission to cite materials from the following sources, grateful acknowledgment is made to the copyright holders.

Pages

3   Raymond Firth, *We, the Tikopia,* 2nd ed. Copyright 1957. George Allen & Unwin Ltd., London. P. 2.

9–10   Clyde Kluckhohn, *Mirror for Man.* Copyright 1949 by McGraw-Hill, Inc. Used with permission of McGraw-Hill Book Company, New York. Pp. 176–177.

11   *True, The Man's Magazine* 49 (September, 1968), p. 20. Courtesy TRUE, The Man's Magazine. Copyright 1968. Fawcett Publications, Inc., New York.

87   Robin Fox, *Kinship and Marriage.* Baltimore: Penguin Books, Inc., 1967. Diagram 40 (p. 183).

106–107   Victor W. Turner, "A Ndembu Doctor in Practice," in Ari Kiev, ed., *Magic, Faith and Healing.* Copyright 1964. The Free Press of Glencoe, division of The Macmillan Company, New York. Pp. 260–261.

130, 134, 137, 138, 139   Hilda Kuper, *An African Aristocracy.* Copyright 1947. Oxford University Press (for the International African Institute). Pp. 69, 141, 203, 204, 205, 206, 217, 218.

147–148   John A. Wilson, *The Burden of Egypt.* Copyright 1951 by The University of Chicago. Pp. 48–49. (Called *The Culture of Egypt* in Phoenix ed., 1956.) Cited with permission of the author and The University of Chicago Press.

Although there are as many ways of teaching introductory cultural or social anthropology as there are teachers of anthropology, two strategies are common. Either the instructor covers an aggregate of topics—kinship, technology, religion, language—or he presents a mélange of portraits depicting the myriad "ways of mankind." In both instances, anthropology is presented as a set of fragmented segments. While a good teacher can render such a course rewarding, he is handicapped by the lack of focus and by the absence of a framework that encourages systematic comparison and leads by logical progression toward synthesis. Students who begin the course enthusiastically often lose interest as it proceeds but fails to progress and resolve chaos into order.

The Human Direction is designed to contribute focus and system to introductory courses in cultural or social anthropology. We have tried to retain the great virtue of the orthodox strategies —diversity of exotic immersions—and at the same time organize these experiences within a broad evolutionary framework that will logically progress toward synthesis, encourage the student to compare the societies and cultures of the world systematically, relate anthropology to significant social issues, and ultimately lead to the broadest of questions: What is the future of man?

After an opening chapter aimed at sensitizing the student to the anthropological view and to certain crucial anthropological concepts, the text moves into its evolutionary analysis. Chapter 2 sets forth the main dimensions of the evolutionary scheme and asks the question: In what direction is the world evolving? The next four chapters portray, in detail, selected societies—the Australian aborigines, the Swazi of Africa, the Buddhists of Thailand, the medieval Christians, the modernizing Japanese, and others—in order to expound the evolutionary theory as well as to encourage systematic understanding and comparison of these particular societies. Chapter 7 treats contemporary America, which the student can approach with fresh insight and objectivity derived from the comparative and evolutionary perspective of the first six chapters. The final chapter briefly considers the dynamics of sociocultural evolution, and speculates about the future shape of human society and culture.

In constructing the evolutionary framework that provides the skeleton for the text, we classify all the societies of the world, past and present, in terms of a scale whose levels, following Robert N. Bellah, we label as primitive, archaic, historic, early-modern, and modern.[1] * These stages represent different levels of sociocultural complexity, of which each allows a greater potential for change and a greater degree of freedom in dealing with the environment than the preceding level. The progression from the primitive to the modern is charted along a number of dimensions: specialization of social units, functional specificity of social relations, centralization, and autonomy of religious systems in relation to social systems.

We recognize that not every society of the world fits neatly and unambiguously into any single level of our scheme. Many a so-

---

* The notes are on page 295.

ciety is at one level along certain dimensions, at another level along others. Despite the admitted difficulty of neatly classifying all societies, however, the portrayal of a number of the world's societies as cases logically ordered in a general scheme can be highly instructive. Such portrayal highlights contrasts and correlations. For example, society *A* may be classed as *archaic* in its religion because it possesses a pantheon of gods clearly distinguished from men, whereas society *B* is classed as *primitive* in its religion because it possesses not gods, but rather spirits who are not clearly distinguished from men. Similarly, society *A* may be classed as archaic in its government because it has kings, whereas society *B* is classed as primitive because it possesses elders and chiefs, rather than kings. This simple example illustrates how an evolutionary scheme can display not only contrasts between societies, but also correlations between institutions (in this case, correlations between kingship and theism, chieftainship and animism) within any single society. Alerting the student to such contrasts and correlations between and within societies is an important goal of anthropology.

Our evolutionary scheme can be viewed not only as a convenient framework for classifying societies, but also as a world history. Although there are societies (for example, some in Southeast Asia) whose histories closely follow the sequence from primitive to modern outlined by our scheme, we make no attempt to periodize the history of any one society, much less of all societies, and we do not maintain that every society necessarily develops in the sequence we outline. Rather, our scheme plots world history by dividing it into periods each bearing the label of the most advanced sociocultural pattern—primitive, archaic, historic, early-modern, or modern—achieved during that period.

Thus, prior to the emergence of the great Near Eastern civilizations, which are dated from such archaeological sites as Jarmo (6700 B.C.), it appears that there existed no societies more advanced than the primitive type; hence, the period prior to 7000–6000 B.C. is called *primitive*. During this era, the most advanced societies were those that had undergone what V. Gordon Childe has called the Neolithic Revolution.² Technologically, these societies had passed from the stage of hunting and gathering food to that of raising food and breeding stock. Although they produced food, these Neolithic communities were socioculturally primitive.

By 7000–6000 B.C., archaic society had come into being, and it remained the most advanced form of society until about 1000 B.C. Archaic societies flourished in the Indus River region of India and Pakistan, in China, and in the Near East, and (much later) in the New World. Capitalizing on the farming and stock-raising techniques developed by Neolithic primitive man, archaic societies achieved certain important advances, such as the creation of cities, writing (which was, however, restricted to a few craft specialists), and political centralization.

Two to three thousand years ago, the first historic societies appeared, stimulated by the rise of the great world religions—Buddhism, Christianity, and Islam. The central achievement of historic societies was spiritual: a more universal definition of man than that found in primitive and archaic culture. Universalistic conceptions encouraged numerous social and material developments, such as the spread of literacy to a sizable religio-political elite, the development of bureaucracy, and the creation of kingdoms and empires far more extensive than those of the archaic era.

Early-modern society appeared only some three or four hundred years ago during the time of Western religious reformation, political revolution, and industrial development. Early-modern patterns of industrialism, nationalism, and science are still spreading throughout the world. Until recently such patterns were, in terms of our scheme, the most advanced yet achieved by man.

We hypothesize the eventual appearance of a modern pattern that goes beyond the early-modern one. This hypothesis is based partly on the notion that sociocultural evolution is an unending process and partly on observation of trends and events occurring primarily in the West and especially in America. Whether current trends are true signs of an emerging pattern or are simply abortive reactions to current strains is unclear, and our speculations about the future form of modern society and culture are necessarily very tentative.

While our evolutionary scale can be viewed as a world history, every one of the sociocultural levels or types distinguished by that scale is represented by some contemporary society. That is, primitive, archaic, historic, and early-modern societies all exist in the *contemporary* world. To underline this point, a contemporary society has been chosen as a central illustrative case for each of the evolutionary levels. Although the contemporary world tolerates a diversity of societies, all of these are apparently converging into a single type, a world-wide pattern that emphasizes early-modern and modern features. At every period of world history, the trend has been for the less advanced societies to absorb, either willingly or reluctantly, the patterns of the more advanced societies. During the modern era this trend has accelerated. The less advanced societies are changing in the direction of the most advanced pattern extant more rapidly today than ever before in human history.

Implicit in our evolutionary scheme is a philosophy of history—one that tries to be flexible rather than dogmatic, suggestive rather than definitive. At various points, we alert the student to alternative interpretations, to unresolved theoretical and methodological issues, and to possible lines of speculation that go beyond this book. Since the book focuses on a process whose end result no one can predict precisely, we emphasize the open-endedness of the evolutionary process. The final chapter, on the future shape of human culture and society, is frankly speculative.

The Human Direction does not exhaust the entire field of anthropology, and the instructor will doubtless wish to incorporate supplementary materials. Many such materials—on kinship, on peasant societies, on New World ethnography, or on Old World prehistory, for example—will fit nicely into certain rubrics of the evolutionary scheme. The Suggested Readings at the end of the chapters propose sources for this kind of elaboration of the text. The book does not attempt a systematic treatment of physical anthropology, linguistics, or archaeology, and the instructor who assigns this text for a course that covers these fields as well as sociocultural anthropology will presumably treat them with the help of additional texts. A few suitable and readily available works in these fields are proposed in the Suggested Readings of chapter 1.

Certain traditional materials even of sociocultural anthropology have been omitted, and some materials not ordinarily deemed anthropological, such as Max Weber's studies of India, China, and the West, have been incorporated. With the accelerating pace of modernization and the resulting rapid transformation of non-modern societies, social and cultural anthropology is increasingly training its sights on the problems of transition to modernity, on the new nations, on the great traditions of the Near and Far East, on complex societies generally, and on our own society in particular. These trends have brought anthropology into closer touch with the other social sciences—history, political science, sociology. A text that did not reflect this movement would fail to reflect one of the most dynamic features of contemporary anthropology. Nor could a text be considered truly contemporary if it failed to consider a related and equally important movement within current anthropology: the revival of interest in the process of sociocultural evolution.

A final characteristic of this book is its emphasis on *culture,* especially religion, and its deliberately limited treatment of technology and economics. This is not meant to imply that techoeconomic factors are unimportant in sociocultural evolution, for clearly they are of great importance. But since certain anthropological schools have treated such factors as the prime movers of evolution, we strive to correct the bias by emphasizing the contribution of religion. Religion is a kind of gyroscope that sustains the stability of a wide range of social activities and institutions; it can also become the generator of widely ramifying social changes. Analysis of religion is therefore remarkably revealing of the values and operation of society and of broad-scale social change.

Recognizing the difficulties of analyzing subjective phenomena such as religion, we acknowledge the advantages of concentrating on more objective factors such as technology and economics. We are reluctant, however, to de-emphasize a fundamental facet of human life and sociocultural evolution simply because it is difficult to measure and dissect objectively. The temptation to concentrate on the easily discernible, and for that reason to assign it the status of prime mover in the evolutionary process, is great. The fallacy in such a procedure is illustrated by the following parable, recounted by the philosopher Abraham Kaplan.[3] A drunk, having dropped his keys in the gutter, proceeded to search for them on the sidewalk under a street light. A passerby, noting that the gutter was the place the drunk had dropped his keys, asked him why he did not search there instead of on the sidewalk. The drunk replied, "There's more light up here." The moral is that the place most easily lighted is not necessarily the place to find what one is searching for.

We would like to express our deep appreciation for the comments, suggestions, and encouragement of Ingrid Kirsch, Lucy Milner, Jeannette Mirsky, Florence Peacock, and Amelie Rorty, and for the scholarly assistance of Mark Leone and Martin Silverman. Professors Arthur Vidich, Robert Smith, and Robert Bellah read the manuscript, provided helpful advice, and, in the case of Professor Bellah, an orienting scheme for the entire work. We should also express our gratitude for the indispensable careful editorial guidance of Eric Valentine.

J. L. P.
A. T. K.

Contents

The human direction

1

On the study of society and culture

As Raymond Firth's ship neared the beach of the tiny Pacific island Tikopia, he saw a crowd of natives bustling about in response to his visit. Firth, a British anthropologist, later reflected:

> Even with the pages of my diary before me it is difficult to reconstruct the impressions of that first day ashore—to depersonalize the people I later came to know so well and view them as merely a part of the tawny surging crowd. . . . In his early experience in the field the anthropologist is constantly grappling with the intangible. The reality of native life is going on all around him, but he himself is not yet in focus to see it. He knows that most of what he records at first will be useless: it will be either definitely incorrect, or so inadequate that it must later be discarded. Yet, he must make a beginning somewhere. He realizes that at this stage he is incapable of separating the patterns of custom from the accidentals of individual behavior, he wonders if each slight gesture does not hold some meaning which is hidden from him. . . . He is conscious of good material running to waste before him moment by moment: he is impressed by the vastness of the task that lies before him and of his own feeble equipment for it in the face of a language and custom to which he has not the key. . . . At the same time, he is experiencing the delights of discovery, he is gaining an inkling of what is in store; like a gourmet walking round a feast that is spread, he savors in anticipation the quality of what he will later appreciate in full.[1]

Cast into the midst of this "tawny surging" crowd, the anthropologist finds himself in a world whose laws and dimensions he cannot yet fathom. Confused by the shock of strangeness, he hungers after understanding; in Firth's word, he "savors" the quality of that which he will someday appreciate and comprehend. This appreciation and comprehension will perhaps yield intense insight, similar to that of psychoanalysis, Zen meditation, or some other deep emotional/intellectual quest. But to put all of this less mystically: the anthropologist craves, even as he is absorbed in the concrete events of native life, to *formulate* a *pattern* in terms of which events can be explained. After that pattern is formulated the events appear logical and comprehensible.

The term *formulate* is important. The anthropologist in the midst of an exotic milieu does not see, hear, or touch a pattern—any more than a physicist in the laboratory sees, hears, or touches, a thermodynamic law. The pattern, like the law, is an intellectual construct rather than a perceived event. Patterns and laws are formulated to explain perceived events, and conversely perceived events furnish a basis for formulating patterns and laws. But the events he experiences are not the only basis on which the anthropologist formulates patterns. Along with his camera and notebook, the anthropologist brings prior concepts to his field experience, and these concepts influence his formulation of pattern perhaps as much as the experience itself.

Some of the concepts that the anthropologist brings to the field are specific. He may arrive with a hypothesis in mind, for example, that a system of marriage has political effects, and in the field he may collect data relevant to this hypothesis. Other concepts that he brings are more general. Some are so general, in fact, that together they comprise an *anthropological view,* a broad perspective on human behavior that most, although perhaps not all, anthropologists share as a result of their training and experience. Just as there is the historical view of human behavior, the statistical, the psychological, and the economic, so there is the anthropological view, which, when combined with these other views, yields a sharpened vision of human affairs. The purpose of this chapter is to introduce the reader to the anthropological view.

PATTERNS

A pattern is more than the list of its parts. To describe the parts that compose a pattern is not sufficient to describe that pattern; the relations between the parts must also be described. Thus, if one went no further than describing each of the four sides of a square, one would fail to achieve a description of a square; the four sides could also form a rhombus. To make clear that one refers to a square and not to a rhombus, one must define the relations between the sides. In this case, that means defining the angle of the corner formed by the joining of any two sides. To describe both the parts and their relations to each other is to describe a pattern.

Formulating patterns rather than just listing parts is one practice essential to the role of the anthropologist. The explorer, by contrast, often simply recounts the various parts of a group's life without going very deeply into the relations between these parts. From an explorer we might learn that society X lives in a marshy plain, that it grows rice, and that it enjoys the custom of polygyny, in which ideally each man possesses many wives. We would not expect to learn much about how these customs interrelate since analysis of this sort is not the explorer's purpose. The anthropologist, on the other hand, feels compelled not only to describe these separate customs but also to grope toward an understanding of the way they interlock. He might succeed in showing that the custom of polygyny allows a distribution of labor, for example, that allows rice to be grown under the particular conditions imposed by the marshy plain setting. Thus, the anthropologist would formulate a simple pattern.

Imagine that some anthropologist were to take a liking to Mae West's classic remark that the important thing is "not the man in your life, but the life in your man." If he then happened to recall the exhortation of President Kennedy that one should ask not about "what your country can do for you," but about "what you can do for your country," the anthropologist would realize that the West and Kennedy remarks follow a single pattern. Trying to formulate that pattern, he would observe that both remarks are based on the rule, "Restate a phrase or clause, reversing the position of certain words in the original statement." The anthropologist would thereby have formulated a simple pattern.

Modes of formulating patterns

The perceptive reader may have sensed a difference in the manner of formulating patterns illustrated by the example dealing with Mae West and President Kennedy, and that illustrated by the example dealing with rice and polygyny. In the rice/polygyny example, the anthropologist formulated what we call a *functional pattern*. In the West/Kennedy example, he formulated what we call a *logical pattern*. A functional pattern reveals working relations between elements of a group's life; a logical pattern reveals symbolic relations.

To describe the logical relations among the elements of a group's life, one simply shows that the various elements derive from a single principle or rule. Thus, both the Kennedy and the West remarks were derived from a single rule. Another example of a logical pattern in language concerns the rule of English grammar, "Add -*ed* to form the past tense." The child who has not learned the exceptions to this rule often applies it inappropriately by saying "comed" or "bringed" for the past tense of "come" or "bring." These errors are derivations from a rule. By formulating the rule and listing its behavioral derivatives, the anthropologist formulates a logical pattern pervading an area of American life. Such logical patterning is not restricted to the realm of language. For example, Americans are legally bound to stay on the right-hand side of the road while driving, and they also tend to stay on the right-hand side of the sidewalk while walking. These two behaviors can be derived from a single rule, "Stay on the right." [2]

The key relationship in a logical pattern is the relationship between rules and derivations. The key relationship in a functional pattern is the relationship between conditions and consequences. Thus, the anthropologist tried to show that polygyny is a social condition that prompts an agricultural consequence—rice-growing in a marshy terrain. A folk saying offers an excellent illustration of the condition/consequence relationship.

> For want of a nail, the shoe was lost; for want of the shoe, the horse was lost; for want of the horse, the rider was lost; for want of the rider, the battle was lost; for want of the battle, the kingdom was lost, and all for the want of a horseshoe nail.

This saying could be diagrammed as a chain, with each element a condition of the next element on the chain and a consequence of the previous element.

A functional chain is often circular, as in the case of a certain kind of electric circuit. When this electric circuit is activated, the switch makes contact with a magnet, but in doing so breaks the circuit. The magnet loses power and the switch moves out of contact. This, of course, again closes the circuit, with the result that the switch reestablishes contact with the magnet. Again the circuit is broken . . . and so on. Similar circular systems are found in society.

It is usually a mistake to think of a chain or circle of functionally related elements as a row of billiard balls—each imparting motion to the next upon contact. The relationships are often less direct. For example, the first American consul in Japan, Townsend Harris, was visited by a Japanese officer who asked if he could borrow Harris's horse. Harris said yes. A few days later he discovered that the horse of the Japanese prime minister, as well as the horses of all his officers, had been shod.[3] Now, introducing the horseshoe to Japan did not cause a sudden appearance of Japanese men talented at copying the mechanical inventions of the West. Men with that capacity already existed, as fully matured adults, at the time the horseshoe was introduced. But the presence of such men was functionally related to the introduction of the horseshoe. Because such talent was already present, the horseshoe could be copied; because it was copied successfully, new opportunities for developing such talent were generated; because such talent was then utilized, a favorable atmosphere for other technological innovations emerged. Thus, a system of complicated functional interrelationships must be unraveled to explain the historical process, and one must avoid the temptation to think in terms of the simple, slam-bang causality of the billiard ball example. It is not as though horseshoes were thrown at the heads of the Japanese men, thereby causing mechanical talent to spring full-blown from those heads.

No matter where they are or what they are analyzing, anthropologists tend to interpret their observations and experiences in logical patterns, in functional patterns, or in a combination of these two. Broadly speaking, when the anthropologist analyzes or synthesizes he formulates the logical or functional relationships among elements of a system.

Interpreting events in terms of patterns

As he struggles to formulate the patterns expressed by native life, the anthropologist is also trying to interpret each particular custom or event in terms of that pattern. The task is surprisingly difficult, especially since everyone, layman and anthropologist alike, tends to perceive particular events as if they were not part of the native's society and culture, but, by some sorcery, a part of the society and culture of the observer.

A Western audience looks at films depicting the behaviors of certain non-Western peoples. African Masai are shown spitting on one another; African Basuto, hissing at each other; African Bi Rom, shaking clenched fists at one another; and the Toda of South India are shown thumbing their noses at one another.[4] The audience's natural impulse is to conclude that in each case war is imminent. Yet studies of the Masai, Basuto, Bi Rom, and the Toda indicate that all the gestures depicted are meant kindly. The Masai spit on each other to express their feelings of benediction. The Basuto hiss to express respect. The Toda and the Bi Rom express friendly feelings by fist-shaking and nose-thumbing. Thus, the audience's initial intuition proves wrong. The spectator is interpreting, more or less unconsciously, the native actions as if they were Western actions.

He is ascribing familiar meanings to foreign behaviors, not realizing that the same physical act may assume different meanings in different cultures. Thus emerges the simple but important principle: *Interpret native actions in terms of native patterns.*

This principle can have some very practical consequences. Among the many reports issuing from anthropologists who served as World War II advisers to the armed forces came one from the late Clyde Kluckhohn. Discussing the American military's interpretation of Japanese behavior during World War II, Kluckhohn writes:

> Most of our top military men reasoned this way: We know that the Nazis are fanatics, but the Japanese have proved themselves still more fanatical. How can leaflets and broadcasts possibly affect soldiers who will go readily into a Banzai charge or fight under hopeless conditions in a cave, finally blowing themselves to pieces with a hand grenade? Why should the lives of our men be risked in attempting to secure more prisoners when it is obvious that Japanese prisoners will not provide us with intelligence information?
>
> The generals and admirals who argued in this fashion were highly intelligent men. In common-sense terms their picture was perfectly sound. Common-sense was not enough, for it assumed that all human beings would picture the same situation to themselves in identical terms. An American prisoner of war still felt himself to be an American and looked forward to resuming his normal place in American society after the war. A Japanese prisoner, however, conceived of himself as socially dead. He regarded his relations with his family, his friends, and his country as finished. But since he was physically alive he wished to affiliate himself with a new society. To the astonishment of their American captors, many Japanese prisoners wished to join the American army and were, in their turn, astonished when they were told this was impossible. They willingly wrote propaganda for us, spoke over loud speakers urging ther own troops to surrender, gave detailed information on artillery emplacements and the mili-

tary situation in general. In the last six months of the war
some Japanese prisoners flew in American planes within forty-
eight hours after their capture, spotting Japanese positions.
Some were allowed to return within the Japanese lines and
brought back indispensable information.[5]

Kluckhohn's explanation for the inability of Americans to predict
or understand how Japanese could so easily shift allegiance, yet
display fanatical courage during a Banzai charge, is oversimplified
(as are many anthropological sermons), but it is still suggestive.
The Americans, says Kluckhohn, were raised in the Judeo-Christian
tradition of absolute morality: the same code is demanded for all
situations. By contrast, Japanese morality is situational.

> As long as one was in situation A, one publically observed
> the rules of the game with a fervor that impressed Americans
> as "fanaticism." Yet the minute one was in situation B, the
> rules for situation A no longer applied.[6]

The Americans, perceiving Japanese behavior in terms of the principles of absolute morality, found it difficult to shake the conviction
that any soldier who responded with fanatical loyalty in one situation, as the Japanese soldier did, could assume a totally different
loyalty in another situation. The Americans perceived the fanaticism
of the Japanese in their caves as if it were an event in the life of
Americans. They did not analyze it as an event in the life of the
native himself.

Ethnocentrism and grand theory

Violation of the principle *Interpret native action in terms of native
patterns* is called *ethnocentrism*. Even the anthropologist, whose
professional creed and training sensitize him to the dangers of
ethnocentrism, never wholly escapes this bias. The field anthro-

pologist, whose task is only to record accurately what he observes, is plagued enough with the disease of ethnocentrism; the grand theorist is doomed to even more suffering. The analyst of a single society can at least try to record the behaviors of the natives in terms of their own concepts; the grand theorist, who wishes to compare many different societies, can never do so in terms of the concepts or categories of any one society. Rather, he must strain to define a single set of categories that will apply to all the societies he compares. And since his categories inevitably derive from his own society's intellectual traditions, he is even more likely to commit the crime of ethnocentrism than is the analyst of a single society.

To illustrate the conflict between the grand theorist and the field anthropologist, suppose that each is confronted with the transcript of a commercial reportedly heard over All India Radio:

> Use Jayanti Miracle Oil internally for cancer and externally for eczema. Jayanti Miracle Oil brings furniture to a high polish, removes rust stains from metal, and is an excellent cooking substitute for ghee. Use Jayanti Miracle Oil on your hair, on the floor, and in the kitchen. . . .[7]

The broadcast prompts the grand theorist to speculate excitedly that lack of specialization in Indian social roles is paralleled by their unspecialized material substance. Just as an Indian Brahman can be both priest and cook, so Indian oil can be used for both eczema and furniture. By contrast, in America roles are specialized and so is material substance. Priests specialize in being priests, cooks in being cooks, and similarly cooking oil specializes in being cooking oil, hair tonic in being hair tonic. The field anthropologist objects to such comparison on the grounds that it is ethnocentric. *Role* is a concept of Western social science, as is *specialization,* and even *priest* and *cook.* To be properly understood, the Indian must be described in terms of his own categories, rather than in terms of social science categories. "But how can you compare India and America if not in terms of some abstract category such as *role* that applies to both societies?" asks the grand theorist. Comparison of societies poses a dilemma for the anthropologist who would avoid ethnocentrism.

SILENT PATTERNS

The anthropologist does not expect to find a native word for every significant unit of the native pattern, nor does he expect to meet a native who can fully verbalize that pattern. It is the anthropologist who has the task of formulating the native pattern. Those facets of the pattern which the anthropologist formulates, but which the native cannot or ordinarily does not verbalize, are called *silent patterns*.

Formal, informal, and technical patterns

Edward T. Hall, in his engaging book *The Silent Language*,[8] suggests the distinction between *formal patterns* and *technical patterns*. If a pattern is formal, the group adhering to it feels that it defines *the way* its members, or certain of its members, should act. If a pattern is technical, the group adhering to it feels that it defines *a means* to achieve a designated goal. A group of scientists might regard precise thought as the way to think—as a custom valuable in itself regardless of any purpose that it might or might not serve. By contrast, they might regard any given mathematical technique as merely a means to achieve precision of thought, and if a new technique came along that promised to achieve this goal more efficiently than did the old technique, they would happily drop the old in favor of the new.

In all societies, including our own, ideas about time are part of formal patterns; that is, without stopping to think about it, we and other natives simply assume that time is what we have been brought up to believe it is. *Year* is a formal unit in the Western time system. For Westerners, year means 365 days plus one fourth day that is accounted for by adding an extra whole day to the year every fourth (leap) year. Although Westerners take it for granted that time is measured in years, the year once was more a technical unit than a formal one. Egyptian priests who created the year as a device for calculating the annual Nile floods perhaps saw it in a technical way since for them the year was simply a means to achieve a designated goal. Yet today the year is part of a formal pattern in the West.

Americans assume without question that time is like a straight line. Every event can be imagined as occurring between two points on this line. The age of dinosaurs lies some distance back on the line; the American Revolution is much nearer to our present position. Gestation stretches for nine months along the line, death is no broader than a point. All the events of our lives and of history or prehistory can be plotted on this one universal line we perceive as time. For those who have grown up thinking linearly it is completely natural to assume that this is just the way the universe is built.

Yet Hopi Indian tradition apparently did not include the concept of a universal time line along which all events could be located and measured. Each event had a shape of its own, unrelated to any other. Corn matured. Women gestated. Lambs became sheep. It did not occur to the Hopi to measure obviously different processes or events in terms of the constant units—minutes, weeks, months, years—that would make up a universal time line. Some claim that even today the Hopi find following a schedule or meeting a deadline difficult and unnatural. Thinking in terms of schedules requires classifying a wide variety of events by placing them sequentially on a single abstract line. In Hopi tradition the notion of such a line would be meaningless.

Americans think formally of time sequence as evidence of causality. *Post hoc, ergo propter hoc* ("after the fact, therefore because of the fact") may be a fallacy in logic, but it is very much a part of American thinking. The occurrence of one event immediately after another leads us to look quite naturally for a causal relationship between the events. Our thinking follows the billiard ball pattern: the cue ball is the cause, and when the ball it slams into moves, that is the effect. It is natural for us to think this way since the idea of *causation* is part of our formal culture, built into the structure of English grammar and elaborated in the world of science and technology. But this is not the way all men think. As early as 1890, Sir James George Frazer, in *The Golden Bough,*[9] advanced the notion that some men think sympathetically rather than causally. According to sympathetic belief, if one native were in the jungle hunting, and another native back in the village touched oil, then the hand of the hunter would turn slick on his spear. This would not be attributed to any direct causal relationship between the two events. It is not that the hand touching oil at home somehow would set up a conduction through ground or air that would eventuate in the hand getting greasy in the jungle. Rather, hand-at-home and hand-in-jungle are alike, hence in sympathy. Therefore, it is believed that one greasy hand *becomes* the other.

Americans, assuming that time is a straight line with a beginning and an end, have traditionally viewed work as an activity directed toward an end, with the proper path toward that end being the "straight and narrow." To allow oneself to stray from that path is sinful. Thus, Americans resent interruptions. Very different are the Trobriand islanders of the Western Pacific who, it is said, do not particularly mind interruptions; to them, time is not a line along which one moves, but a puddle in which one wallows.[10]

Probably the American's formal assumptions about time affect even his biological behaviors such as sleep. Americans are brought up to believe that a certain space along the daily time line, eight hours, should be devoted to uninterrupted sleep, yet observers of those tribal cultures which are not obsessed by a time line have remarked on the ability of the natives to miss sleep with no evidence of harm.[11]

Assumptions about time are good examples of formal patterns, for we naturally assume that the way time seems to us is objectively the way it is. All formal patterns carry such assumptions—they are taken to be universal truths. Precisely because we do not question them, we do not think about them, and so they are *silent patterns:* it is difficult or impossible for us to put them into words. But the anthropologist is in a position to dissect such patterns even if, as in these last examples, he is actually dissecting himself.

Informal patterns are yet another type of social pattern the anthropologist may discern. They differ from the formal in that they are less absolute a definition of the way a society's members should act, yet they resemble the formal patterns in that they are hard to verbalize, and therefore silent. To illustrate informal patterns, Edward T. Hall [12] analyzed the punctuality rules of American businessmen. He concluded that American businessmen adhere to the following informal code: being three minutes late for a business appointment is not serious enough to require comment; being four minutes late calls for an unintelligible remark; and being five minutes late requires a short apology. By contrast, Hall cites a country where an hour's tardiness is equivalent to five minutes in America, where fifty minutes equals our four minutes. The American ambassador to this unnamed country was once visited by local diplomats, who arrived at a time such that they were not so punctual as to be obsequious, yet not so late as to be insulting: they arrived fifty minutes late. The meeting did not go well, and the ambassador later remarked to his colleagues, "How can you depend on these people when they arrive an hour late for an appointment, then just mutter something?" The ambassador felt this way, Hall maintains, because he was governed by American rules of punctuality. Not warned of the native pattern, he became annoyed when, after a fifty-minute wait, he received only the muttered equivalent of the American apology for a four-minute tardiness.

Ideal patterns and actual patterns

Every anthropologist who has lived with and observed the natives of a foreign society has discovered not only that the natives have trouble describing some of their patterns of behavior but also that some of their descriptions differ markedly from their actual behavior. Certain Brazilian Indians, for example, are fond of telling anthropologists that they live in villages laid out in the form of a bisected circle, but flying over such a village shows that this is not so. The Chinese provide a more complicated example. For centuries they have claimed that they live in what anthropologists call *extended households* (households that, in addition to parents and children, include grandparents, aunts, uncles, and cousins). Even high school world history texts now dutifully report that the Chinese, before the Communist Revolution, lived in such households. But analysis of the way the Chinese actually lived reveals that only a tiny percentage of Chinese households, mainly those of the elite, were of this extended type.[13] Thus, a native stereotype of native society can mislead the unwary observer into assuming that native behavior follows a pattern that, in actual fact, it does not follow.

Linguistically codified patterns

One of the most provocative ideas about silent patterns is that a language structures the patterns of thinking and perceiving of those who speak it whether they are aware of it or not. Just as the artist and the geologist who look at the Grand Canyon may see it differently, so speakers of different languages perceive the world in different ways. Each language codifies its own distinctive perceptual pattern. A language's grammar is particularly important for such codification. This theory, still a center of debate, is most clearly illustrated by comparing English grammar to the grammars of languages outside the Indo-European family. Because the languages we are accustomed to call foreign, such as Greek, Latin, Italian, Spanish, French, German, and even Sanskrit, are all of the Indo-European family, they display grammatical patterns—and therefore perceptual patterns—that are similar to those of English. But the

Hopi and Navaho languages, spoken by Indians of the American Southwest, belong respectively to the Uto-Aztecan and Athabaskan families, and they seem to codify perceptual patterns that are radically different from those of English.[14]

Whereas English verbs change form to distinguish past, present, and future, Hopi changes form to distinguish fact, expectation, and law among events. When an English speaker sees a man running, he says "he runs" or "he is running" (both signifying "now"), but the Hopi speaker says *"wari"* ("running occur")—a statement of fact. When the runner has passed out of sight or has finished running, in English we say "he ran," "he has run," "he was running," but the Hopi would still put it *"wari"* ("running occur")—a statement of fact, if the speaker actually saw the runner. For future events, we say "he will run" (a statement of confidence in a future event) or "he shall run" (a statement of the speaker's compelling insistence that he *will* run in the future). The Hopi verb changes to *"warikni"* ("running occur I daresay"), a statement of expectation.

If an English speaker wishes to make a statement of law or regularity, such as "he runs on the track team," and even though such running could be placed in the past or the future, he would say "he runs." To express regularity, English simply uses the common present tense, but in Hopi, the verb must change its form to *"warikngwe"* ("running occurs characteristically").

In sum, English changes the verb form to express changes in tense: present ("he runs"), past ("he ran"), and future ("he will run"). Hopi changes the verb form to express changes in the epistemological state of events, that is, to indicate how sure the speaker is about the occurrence of the events in question. If the event is a fact, the speaker says *"wari";* if it is expected, he says, *"warikni";* if it is law, he says, *"warikngwe."* Hopi grammar is, therefore, radically different from English grammar: it lacks tense.

Navaho verbs, like Hopi verbs, differ from English and from other Indo-European verbs in that they do not necessarily express tense by their forms. The Navaho speaker is not compelled to indicate tense every time he utters a verb, as is the speaker of English.

But the Navaho is forced by the grammatical structure of his language to indicate other categories. For example, Navaho verbs change their form according to the shape of the object involved in the action expressed by the verb. To simulate this pattern we might pretend that the English speaker must add a different suffix or prefix to the verb *handle* whenever he refers to a different shape of object. He would speak of "handlefying" poles (objects of a long rigid type); of "handleating" snakes (objects that are slender and flexible); of "handleificating" a cup of tea (objects of the container-with-content type; of "behandling" salt (objects of granular mass); and of "behandleificating" hay (objects which are bundled). The Navaho is forced to make just such distinctions by varying his verb forms.

How strongly do a language's rules of grammar affect the way its speakers think and act? This is the controversial question which anthropologists and linguists have debated for decades. On the face of it, it is hard to believe that the pattern of categorizing the world, forced upon a person by his language, would not affect his world view. The question is, how much does it affect it? And is the effect significant enough to warrant our attention? Evidence indicates that the grammatical rules do have significant effects on world view. As anecdotal evidence, Edward T. Hall recounts experiences with the traditional Navaho that illustrate how little the "future" meant to him—so little, in fact, that schedules and promises were irrelevant to Navaho culture. The reader will recall a similar comment regarding Hopi culture. Other evidence comes from an experiment by Carroll and Casagrande,[15] based on the Navaho pattern of changing the form of a verb according to the shape of the verb's object.

The experimenters hypothesized that, because the Navaho were brought up to categorize shape of objects by choice of verb form, Navaho speakers would learn to discriminate between the shapes of objects at an earlier age than English speakers—whose grammar does not force them to make such shape discriminations. Thus, since Navaho grammar forces discrimination between such objects as string or rope (long, flexible), paper or cloth (flat, flexible), and sticks or poles (long, rigid), Navaho speakers should perceptually and manually distinguish such objects earlier than English speakers. The subjects were 135 Navaho children. Some spoke only Navaho, some spoke both Navaho and English, and some spoke only English. The experiment was conducted in the Navaho language or, when appropriate, in English. Each child was presented with a series of pairs of objects, one pair at a time. After being shown a pair of objects, the child was shown a third object and asked to say which object of the pair most closely matched the third object. For instance, one of the pairs was a yellow stick and a piece of blue rope of comparable size. The child was then shown a yellow rope, and asked whether it went better with the yellow stick or with the blue rope. Thus he could choose to match similar shapes (ropes) that fall into a single Navaho verb-shape class (long flexible object), or he could match similar colors (yellow). It turned out that children who spoke only Navaho matched objects on the basis of shape with greater frequency than did children who spoke only English. Thus Navaho grammatical categories apparently do influence the way Navaho children perceive and manipulate the physical world. This experiment, coupled with other evidence, suggests that in spite of the controversy about precisely how much impact language has on perception of the world, there can be little doubt that grammatical categories do introduce some bias in perception and action, and that this bias is greater than most people realize.

Invisible functions

Not only can natives either fail to see the patterns that guide their lives, or assert as gospel patterns that aren't actually followed, but they may also overlook ramified functions of their social patterns: the ways in which these patterns contribute to their social and personal lives. The assumption that every pattern that serves a function was deliberately designed by somebody to serve that function is known as the *teleological fallacy*. Formerly, that "somebody," who was supposed to have created the patterns and completely understood their functions was God. Benjamin Franklin argued:

> God clearly wants us to tipple, because he has made the joints of the arm just the right length to carry a glass to the mouth, without falling short of or overshooting the mark: let us adore then, glass in hand, this benevolent wisdom: let us adore and drink.[16]

Franklin's argument is that because the arm serves the function of conveying drink to the mouth, God intended it to do so and knows that it does so. Teleologists more recent than Franklin impute such intention to agents other than God. Thus some students of biological evolution have written as if the ancient lungfish deliberately developed the rudiments of hands in order that, millions of years later, the primates could use those hands for grasping trees or tools. Similarly, some historians have written as if Calvinism could not have provided the cultural basis for capitalism unless the Calvinists had intended that it do so. Teleological arguments often confuse intention and consequence, purpose and function. They assume that if X serves a function, it must have been intended that it do so. Stated baldly, the argument is unfounded, but teleological thinking is still pervasive.

Anthropologists not only reject the notion that if a pattern serves a function some agent created it for that purpose, but they also— as a task central to their discipline—endeavor to contradict the notion that the agents involved in a pattern are necessarily aware of its function. They try to reveal ways in which patterns serve functions that are "invisible" to the natives. George Herbert Mead's analysis of crime and punishment nicely exemplifies such invisible functions.[17] The cry "thief" or "murderer," says Mead, unites the community in anger against the criminal, its common enemy. Yet, the criminal does not commit the crime with the conscious intent of uniting the community against him; nor do the people who become aroused against the criminal and scream for his execution do so with the conscious purpose of uniting themselves. In fact, if the community were aware of the positive function (the community's unification) served by the crime, their anger against the criminal might cool. But if the community failed to unite in anger against the criminal, the criminal would fail to serve his positive social function. Here apparently is a case where ignorance is useful to society; if society recognized and appreciated the benefits of crime and punishment, then crime and punishment could no longer supply those benefits.

The denial that a pattern serves a social function may, in some cases, actually increase the pattern's social effectiveness. For example, some artists in Western society insist that their art has no social function: that it exists for its own sake. (Humphrey Bogart, upon being asked if he thought art should carry a moral message to influence society, replied, "You got a message? Send it Western Union.") But this very claim perhaps enhances art's ability to affect society. People are often averse to being proselytized or inundated with propaganda. Such an attempt brings up their guard, and they tend to resist the message. Artists, disarming their audience of its resistance by denying that they want to preach or propagandize, may increase their actual power to do so.

A provocative theory set forth by George Devereux suggests that the silent function of art is to express socially unacceptable thoughts or acts in socially acceptable ways.[18] According to Devereux, an art form that is socially acceptable because of its beauty, refinement, or cleverness may express with impunity socially exceptionable content. As the saying goes, "I'm willing to listen to a dirty story if it's really funny." When the artist emphasizes form, argues Devereux, he is free to claim that the content really does not matter. For example, a youth who expresses his love for a girl by writing a poem can repudiate the poem's content if it becomes embarrassing by saying that it is just a poem and not really a declaration of love. By emphasizing form, the poet is able to express content that he could not express otherwise.

And conversely Devereux reasons that if art sanctions the illicit by means of refined form and beauty, then wherever form and beauty are emphasized there is an illicit message to be found. Accordingly, Devereux suggests that brilliantly scored staccato passages for brass instruments are really the composer's method of flatulating in public. Devereux wants to unveil the animal urges that he believes are served by high culture—whether we admit it or not. If nothing else, his theory is a useful part of the anthropological outlook: it prods the anthropologist into seeking out the illicit functions that respectable natives would often prefer not to see.

Shifting from a psychological to a sociological orientation, consider this notion: many idea patterns that to the natives are formal —"the way," "God-given"—can be shown by the analyst to serve social functions that the natives do not ordinarily recognize. Natives are not brought up consciously to admit, for example, that beliefs which they hold sacred serve to support the *status quo;* yet analysis can often show that this is the case. For instance, the Hindu notion of cyclical time bolstered the position of the Indian elite, for this time concept involved belief in a cycle of rebirths according to which the status of a person—high or low—in his next life depended on how well he followed the law (*dharma*) in this life. Following the *dharma* required his being contented with the caste into which he was born. To rise from his caste in this life endangered his existence in the next; one overly ambitious might even be reborn an animal. Thus Hindu beliefs discouraged members of the low castes from competing with members of the elite castes for power and prestige. In a similar way, the Western notion of linear time may reinforce the class and society system peculiar to the West. The concept of time as moving in a straight line, made sacred in the Judeo-Christian notion of history, supports the idea of progress. And the idea of progress justifies the position of all progressives.

Like the psychiatrist, the anthropologist preaches the value of assuming, on proper occasions, an objective stance toward one's own behavioral patterns. The psychiatrist hopes to alleviate his patient's neurosis by forcing him to dredge from his subconscious those painful early experiences that presumably provoke his suffering, and to dissect those experiences coldly, as if they were specimens on a laboratory bench. The psychiatrist tries to lead his patient to a degree of objectivity that will enable him to analyze his own actions with the detachment of a man who is examining not himself but a character in a movie. In much the same way, the anthropologist would like to teach some of the natives (including himself) to view their entire society as if it were depicted on a movie screen—with all of its silent patterns and invisible functions in sharp focus.

SHARED PATTERNS

All right, girls, into your stretch nylon denims! You know the ones—the ones that look like they were designed by some leering, knuckle-rubbing old tailor with a case of workbench back who spent five years, like da Vinci, studying nothing but the ischia, the gemelli, and the glutei maximi. Next, hoist up those bras, up to the angle of a Nike missile launcher. Then get into the cable-knit mohair sweaters, the ones that fluff out like a cat by a projecting heating duct. And then unroll the rollers and explode the hair a couple of feet up in the air into bouffants, beehives, and Passaic pompadours. Stroke in the black makeup all around the eyelids, so the eyes look as though Chester Gould, who does Dick Tracy, drew them on. And then put those patient curls in your lips and tell Mother—you have to spell it out for her like a kid—that yes, you're going out with some of your girlfriends, and, no, you don't know where you're going, and yes, you won't be out late, and for God's sake, like don't panic all the time, and then, with an I-give-up groan, tell her that "for God's sake" is not cursing.

At least that is the way it always seemed, as if some invisible force were out there. It was as though all these girls, all these flaming little Jersey teen-agers, had their transistors plugged into their skulls and were taking orders, simultaneously, from somebody like the Ringleader Deejay.

Simultaneously, all over Plainfield, Scotch Plains, Ridgefield, Union City, Weehawken, Elizabeth, Hoboken, and all the stretches of the Jersey asphalt, there they went, the Jersey teen-agers . . .[19]

This passage from Tom Wolfe's *The Kandy-Kolored Tangerine-Flake Streamline Baby*—already a bit dated but still useful—vividly catches the idea of a shared pattern.

Obvious as it may be that teen-age conformists share a pattern, we are perhaps less accustomed to emphasize the sharing of patterns by creative individualists. Devotees of an author such as James Joyce, for instance, stress his uniqueness—the individuality of his twists of language and his idiosyncratic perceptions. But if an anthropologist were to analyze the patterns that Joyce has in common with the rest of his society, the great mass of shared conventions and beliefs contained in his writings would loom into prominence, overshadowing the idiosyncratic elements in his image. For instance, a rough calculation would surely reveal that in spite of Joyce's liberties with the English language, he abides by more rules than he breaks. It would be most surprising, for example, to discover that he begins numerous words with *ng*. No such words exist in English, but more important, when native speakers of English are invited to coin new sound combinations, these rarely turn out to begin with *ng*. One of the unspoken but iron laws of English is "Never start a word with *ng*," and although speakers of English do not realize that they are doing so, they learn this rule early and follow it faithfully—so faithfully that they find it difficult even to pronounce words from foreign languages (such as the Malayo-Polynesian languages) that do start with *ng*. (Pronounce the Thai word *nguang* "to be sleepy" or the Javanese word *ngamang* "to speak.") If one were to list all the rules of English grammar and of literary form, and then all the laws, morals, conventions, and patterns of thought to which any creative artist unthinkingly conforms even when he is at his most creative, one might well conclude that we overemphasize the uniqueness of genius and we underemphasize the extent to which even the thought of a genius reflects patterns that he shares with others in his society. Doubtless, in the time of Cervantes or Pope (when authors were regarded as spokesmen for society) and in primitive societies today (where artists are regarded as conveyors of tradition to such a degree that they do not even sign their works), the public was and is not so entrapped by a faddish preoccupation with the unique.

Assuming a broad view helps one see similarities between what had previously appeared as idiosyncratic behaviors: one perceives shared patterns. Jazz aficionados will emphasize the originality, the uniqueness, of each inspired improvisation. Yet a broad comparative perspective can bring into sharp relief the patterns common to all the supposedly unique improvisations. Thus all jazz improvisations are based on the Western scale of seven tones separated by equal intervals, a feature that contrasts with all Balinese *gamelan* (percussion orchestra) improvisations, since these are based on a scale of five tones separated by unequal intervals.

There is yet another way in which the jazz musician expresses a shared pattern. Consider the hero in *Young Man with a Horn*.[20] He strains to hit a note on his trumpet that has never been heard before. In other words, he is a conformist. He conforms to the American tradition that each individual should strive to transcend tradition, should strive to create something new. The mandate for change is the central unchanging value of American ideology, and the young man with the horn is simply expressing a pattern that he shares with countless other tradition-bound revolutionaries.

Just as the physicist who stands back and surveys the universe as a whole perceives similarities between swinging pendulums and orbiting planets, so the anthropologist observing a society as a whole finds similarities among parts that are missed by narrower disciplines. The problem of narrow viewpoint is nicely illustrated by the Russian story about the worker who left the factory every afternoon with an empty wheelbarrow. Since the factory guards never found anything inside the wheelbarrow, the worker was always allowed through the gate. But weeks later it was discovered that the worker had been stealing wheelbarrows.

CULTURE AND SOCIETY

We come now to two perspectives or concepts of particular importance: *culture* and *society*. *Personality* is a third concept that must be distinguished from both of these. Culture is a system of logically related ideas and values shared by participants in a social system, which in turn is a system of interacting roles and groups. Society is a particular type of social system. Personality is the system of behavioral components of an individual person.*

Returning to the crowd of natives that Firth encountered on the Tikopia beach, consider the cultural, social, and personality patterns that the anthropologist might abstract from his observations of a group of this kind. The anthropologist might treat such a group as a social system, *i.e.,* a system of interacting roles or groups. From this perspective, he would formulate the manner in which leaders relate to followers, old men to young men, men to women, members of clan *Z* to members of clan *Y*. The anthropologist might also treat the group as a cultural system, a system of logically related ideas and values: he might formulate the group's shared concepts of honesty and fair play, of good and evil, and go on to show how these ideas and values relate logically to each other. Finally, the anthropologist might depict the personality of each member of the group, laying bare the components that compose each person. He could, for example, portray the leader of the group on the beach as compensating for a sexual frustration by his domineering be-

---

* Our view of culture, society, and personality derives from Talcott Parsons's action theory as first expressed in his *The Structure of Social Action,* chapter 19, more recently in his Introduction to Part IV of *Theories of Society.*

havior. What must be remembered is that these three types of pattern—culture, society, and personality—are analytical, not concrete. They are formulated by the anthropologist. Although not themselves observable events in the group's life, they are based on the anthropologist's observation of such events. Nor are these patterns necessarily formulated by the natives, although the natives may well formulate patterns like those formulated by the anthropologist.

An important question is to what extent can a given analytical formulation explain concrete, observed behavior. We would say, for example, that one can go a long way in explaining the concrete, observed behaviors of Firth's beach group by considering it as a social system, while ignoring for the moment the idiosyncratic personalities of the individuals in the group. Obviously, varied personalities will be found in this group. Some will be boisterous, others reserved. Yet all members of the group will share certain traits. They are all there to greet Firth; they all display similar gestures in greeting; and they are all dressed similarly. Furthermore, many of the variations that do appear among the different individuals can be explained by the roles they play in the group; thus, the leader is domineering because he is the leader. And the assignment of each individual to a role often is influenced by other roles he plays in the society rather than by any unique talent he possesses; thus, the leader may have been chosen because he is the son of a chief. No amount of depth analysis of each personality within the group, by itself, would explain the group's concerted behavior. The considerable independence of the group's functioning from the functioning of any of the individual personalities that compose it would be revealed if a beach group of the same island in 1930 and one in 1940 were to display similar patterns (as is likely) even though the members have changed.

It is not only a small group, whose members are periodically collected within the sight of a single observer during a flash of time, that can be viewed as a social system; a more ramified system of social interactions can also be viewed in this way. For instance, the system of exchanges of money, goods, and services that we analytically define as the American economy can be viewed as a social system. As in the case of the beach group, the role a person plays in the American economy is not the only role he plays in life: he may be a son, father, husband, and hobbyist, as well as producer, buyer, and seller. No man, not even the dedicated captain of industry, plays a purely economic role every moment of his life. Therefore, when an economist analyzes an economy, he is not analyzing a system of total personalities. He is investigating relations among specialized roles, in this case economic roles. A social system such as the economy is thus treated as if it existed apart from the personalities who play specialized roles in it. The beach group continued to be the same group (in the sense that its patterns of interaction remained the same) even when its members changed; similarly, the American economy continues to exist through the years even though its personnel changes.

A society, like an economy, is large and ramified, but a society differs from an economy—which is a subsystem of a society—in that it encompasses all, or virtually all, aspects of its members' lives. Since a society includes economies, governments, families, schools, churches, and other subsystems, it includes the economic, political, familial, educational, religious, and other strands of the lives of its members. And because a society includes all of these subsystems, it is more self-sufficient than any one of its subsystems. The American economy, for example, cannot produce its own new members, but American society can. The American economy must recruit its members from another subsystem of American society: the family system, which has the means to give birth to new individuals; on the other hand, American society includes the family system, and is therefore self-regenerative. Although a society may recruit some of its members from outside, by adoption, conquest, enslavement, or immigration, it replenishes itself mainly from within.

Maintaining considerable control over its own territory is one way a society sustains its self-sufficiency. This does not imply that the boundaries of every society are clearly defined geographically.

Such clear-cut boundaries—marked by fences, guards, and customs officials—followed the rise of modern national states, and are not found in primitive societies. An Australian aboriginal tribe, for instance, roams about a vaguely defined territory which, for religious more than governmental or legal reasons, it regards as its own. But however loosely defined this territory is, the tribe still considers itself to be in control of its own territory.

A society's members share a common culture—a pattern of ideas and values. A shared culture allows and encourages members of a society to get along well enough so that the society is not destroyed by civil war or anarchy. But since the shared culture in itself can hardly assure harmony, society also sets forth laws, customs, and procedures which control conflict and competition. The court trial, a means to resolve conflict, is one obvious example.

What is the relationship between culture and society? The distinction between a cultural system and a social system is analytical, not concrete, which means that by viewing a single episode of behavior, such as the behavior of the Tikopia beach group, the analyst can formulate either a social system, or a cultural system, or both. The same is true of all the behavior that passed before the observer's eyes during his stay on Tikopia. All the observations amassed might form the basis for two separate books. One, *The Culture of Tikopia,* would delineate logical linkages between the Tikopian conceptions of the cosmos, of society, of beauty. The second, *The Society of Tikopia,* would illustrate the way in which chiefs relate to followers, parents punish children, clans exchange wives, and other customary social relations. Some of the same observations would appear in both books, but each book would analyze these observations from its own perspective.

Although the cultural/social distinction is analytical in the sense that it is formulated by an analyst, it is also helpful in illuminating many concrete real divisions within behavioral systems. One can say, for instance, that universities are more culturally oriented than governments, and conversely that governments are more socially oriented than universities. American universities are more oriented toward maintaining the system of ideas and values that constitute Western culture, whereas American government agencies are more oriented toward maintaining the system of social relations that constitute American society. The distinction rests in the degree or emphasis; for although each organization is both culturally and socially oriented, each emphasizes one of these orientations to a greater degree than the other.

This notion of concrete analogues to the analytical cultural/social distinction raises questions about the concept of cause and effect. Since *cultural system* and *social system* (or *culture* and *society*) are different concepts which the analyst employs in viewing the same behaviors, we cannot logically speak of the cultural system as "affecting" the social system, or vice versa. This would be like saying that the volume of a body affects its weight, for *volume* and *weight* are two different analytical perspectives on the same physical body. Similarly, it would not be logical to say that a cultural system affects an observed group of persons, any more than one can say that a physics formula fires a rocket, for the formula is an analytical formulation which possesses no physical power in itself. On the other hand, by the so-called comparative method, we can show that if statements *x, y, z* . . . *n* regarding a group's cultural system are defensible, then statements *a, b, c* . . . *n* regarding that group's social system are likely to be defensible too. In other words, by surveying numerous societies, we can show that where ideas and values of a particular type are present, social patterns of a particular type are likely to be present also. Therefore, we *infer* that certain ideas and values are necessary for the existence of a particular type of social life, and vice versa.

One reason for emphasizing the distinction between social systems and cultural systems is the tendency of members of many societies to distinguish phenomena that are more cultural from those that are more social. As will be seen later, the more radically members of a society distinguish between their social institutions and relationships and a system of symbols representing cosmic or religious (cultural) ideas and values, the more dynamic, complex, and adaptive their society and culture are likely to be.

OVERVIEW

For the anthropologist, all men in all societies, including his own, are a "surging crowd" of natives. Entering any society for field study is much like Firth's experience upon arriving at Tikopia. Embarking on his study, the anthropologist resembles an infant: he must painfully learn to make sense out of the "booming, buzzing confusion" into which he has been thrust. To his task the anthropologist brings a kit of concepts, such as *culture, society,* and *personality.* In terms of these, he sorts and classifies his observations, his raw data, and order gradually emerges. The anthropologist formulates the patterns—logical and functional—that underlie observed behaviors.

Anthropologists are especially attuned to cultural differences. They must be aware of the difference in the meaning of shaking a clenched fist for Americans and for Bi Rom, of military action for Americans and for the Japanese, and of the more subtle differences in such things as perception of space and time that are codified differently in different languages. Their awareness of these differences cautions them against ethnocentrism—the interpretation of native actions in terms of the observer's culture. More positively, it sensitizes them to the need for interpreting the native's actions in terms of the native's world view. Among other things, this implies that key statements gleaned directly from native informants are very important anthropological data.

Yet the anthropologist cannot base his formulations exclusively on the native's statements about his society and culture. The native's statements must be measured against the anthropologist's observations. The native often perceives his own society and culture as more closely approximating his ideals or his utopian visions than it really does. For this reason and also because the native is so accustomed to his way of life that he takes it for granted, an outside observer may perceive many native patterns that are "silent" to the native himself, many functions that are invisible to him.

Although the anthropologist strives to see native behavior from the native viewpoint, he must also strive to see even more in native life than the native sees.

A more compelling reason for the anthropologist to transcend the native viewpoint is that he can never stop with analyzing a single society. The ultimate aim of anthropology is to understand the entire range of social and cultural phenomena—past, present, and future. Therefore, the anthropologist must analyze many societies and their cultures. Just as he formulates patterns that explain diverse (and apparently chaotic) behaviors within a particular society, so he must formulate the patterns that give order to the diversity among societies. Such formulation requires a conceptual framework that encompasses the features of many societies and cultures and is not restricted to the features of any one society or culture. We turn now to consideration of such a framework: a theory of sociocultural evolution.

TOPICS FOR DISCUSSION

A basic fact confronted by the anthropologist is that of deep-seated cultural differences—most conspicuously, as we have seen, differences in world view and in perception of space and time. From the existence of such differences, the anthropologist must conclude that culture is not immediately given in the human biological structure and that it is not simply an induction from the encounters of individuals with the external world. And yet there is powerful evidence that mankind is fundamentally one: men are a single biological species and display basic psychic similarities. How is it possible to reconcile cultural differences with the unity of man? And what is the bearing of this question on the dilemma of the anthropologist who seeks to understand native society in native terms while of necessity remaining bound to his own culture? What assumptions must he make in order to believe that he can bridge the cultural gap between his own society and some other society?

ANTHROPOLOGICAL FIELDWORK

Tristes Tropiques (paperback, English translation, 1964) by Claude Lévi-Strauss. Poetic, philosophical, written by the anthropologist who has supposedly usurped Sartre's throne as France's leading intellectual.

Return to Laughter (paperback, 1964) by Elenore S. Bowen. A novel providing a down-to-earth portrait of field experience.

"Curt Nimuendaju, 1883–1945" (1946) by H. Baldus. Life story of an anthropologist who went native, told in an obituary of Curt Nimuendaju.

In the Company of Man: Twenty Portraits of Anthropological Informants (paperback, 1964) edited by Joseph B. Casagrande. Vivid descriptions of the anthropologist in the field.

* Full facts of publication for each work cited in the Suggested Readings are provided in the Bibliography. Information on distributors of films cited is provided in the Film Bibliography.

PATTERNING

A Course in Modern Linguistics (1958) by Charles F. Hockett. An excellent illustration of the linguistic analysis of language pattern.

Language (1921, paperback available) by Edward Sapir. Influential in the development of the concept of patterning in language and culture.

Language (1933) by Leonard Bloomfield. Provides a clear and detailed exposition of Grimm's Law, a convincing formulation of linguistic patterning which predicts patterned sound changes in Indo-European language (pp. 347 ff.).

The Silent Language (paperback, 1961) by Edward T. Hall. On the problem of inferring "silent" patterns.

Language, Thought, and Reality: Selected Writings of Benjamin Lee Whorf (paperback, 1956) edited by John B. Carroll. Provocative analysis of the relationship between the Hopi language and thought patterns.

The Navaho (paperback, 1956) by Clyde Kluckhohn and Dorothea Leighton. Analysis of the relationship between the Navaho language and thought patterns (chapter 8).

Language in Culture and Society: A Reader in Linguistics and Anthropology (1964) edited by Dell Hymes. Includes perspective of the Whorfian as well of the newer ethnoscience school which is concerned with methodologies for formulating cultural patterns in terms of the native's own categories.

"Residence Rules" (1956) by Ward H. Goodenough. An example of the ethnoscience approach and a particularly precise statement of the difference between native categories and those used for the purpose of comparing societies.

CULTURE, SOCIETY, AND PERSONALITY

Culture: A Critical Review of Concepts and Definitions (paperback, 1963) by Alfred L. Kroeber and Clyde Kluckhohn. On the concept of culture.

Sociology: A Systematic Introduction (1960) by Harry M. Johnson. On the concept of society and social systems. Provides the best simplified exposition of Talcott Parsons's ideas, on which this book bases its discussion of society, culture, and personality (chapters 1 and 2).

Personality in Culture (1967) by John J. Honigmann. On the notion of personality, especially as conceived by the anthropological culture-and-personality school. An exhaustive treatment.

HISTORY, SCHOOLS, AND PERSONALITIES OF ANTHROPOLOGY

Mirror for Man: The Relation of Anthropology to Modern Life (paperback, 1968) by Clyde Kluckhohn. Colorfully illustrates how anthropology is applied to practical problems and issues, and how different types of anthropologists do their work.

They Studied Man (paperback, 1965) by Abram Kardiner and Edward Preble. Short biographies of such significant anthropologists as Franz Boas, Bronislaw Malinowski, Alfred Kroeber, Ruth Benedict, Sir James Frazer, and Sir Edward Tylor.

From Ape to Angel (paperback, 1964) by H. R. Hays. An informal history of social anthropology with biographical information on some famous anthropologists.

Social Anthropology (paperback, 1965) by Godfrey Lienhardt. The concepts and history of British social anthropology.

Social Anthropology and Other Essays (paperback, 1964) by E. E. Evans-Pritchard. The history of British social anthropology.

The History of Ethnological Theory (1937) by Robert H. Lowie. Dated, but useful for its material on the Austrian diffusionist school.

A Hundred Years of Anthropology (revised edition, 1965) by T. K. Penniman. Valuable for its treatment of the development of archaeology and physical anthropology.

The Rise of Anthropological Theory (1968) by Marvin Harris. An entertaining, encyclopedic, sophisticated, but polemical, history of social and cultural anthropology.

BIOLOGY AND CULTURE

The Evolution of Man's Capacity for Culture (paperback, 1959) edited by James N. Spuhler.

The Human Animal (paperback, 1960) by Weston LaBarre.
"The Human Revolution" (1964) by Charles F. Hockett and Robert Ascher.

These three speculative but suggestive discussions deal with the biological characteristics of man that allow (or force) him to develop culture.

INTRODUCTORY TEXTS

History of the Primates (paperback, 1965) by W. E. Le Gros Clark. Physical anthropology.
The Stages in Human Evolution (paperback, 1967) by C. Loring Brace. Physical anthropology.
Approach to Archaeology (paperback, 1965) by Stuart Piggott. Archaeology.
Invitation to Archeology (paperback, 1967) by James Deetz. Archaeology.
Anthropological Linguistics: An Introduction (paperback, 1968) by Joseph H. Greenberg. Linguistics.

In an introductory course on general anthropology, these texts may suitably supplement *The Human Direction,* in order that the four major fields of anthropology (physical, archaeological, and linguistic, as well as sociocultural anthropology) may be covered.

FILMS

The Hunters. A compelling portrait of a Kung bushman hunting expedition in the northern Kalahari desert.
Dead Birds. A poetic interpretation of the Dani of West New Guinea.
Dynamics of Male Dominance in a Baboon Troop. Caricatures human society and thus encourages an objective view of that society.
The Baboon Troop (Amboseli Reserve). Caricatures human society.
Four Families. Dramatizes social perspective by portraying Indian, French, Japanese, and Canadian patterns side by side.

The Loon's Necklace. Depicts exotic gods and myths.

Glooscap County. Depicts exotic gods and myths.

Trance and Dance in Bali. A Balinese dance-drama-trance featuring an oedipal struggle between witch and dragon.

Bear and the Hunter. A lyrical account of a bear hunt in northern Lapland.

The Navaho as Filmmaker. A series of seven films made by the natives themselves.

The films are selected for their ability to sensitize the viewer to exotic patterning. For descriptions of other ethnographic films as well as information on reviews of films and readings pertaining to them see Karl G. Heider's *Films for Anthropological Teaching* (1968).

2

The evolution of
society and culture

The nineteenth century was certainly Darwin's in the sense that the 1859 publication of his *On the Origin of Species* gave definitive form to an evolutionary perspective that dominated the thought of many scholars of the time. Students of society were not immune to the evolutionary virus. During the last half of the nineteenth century, social evolution was a major topic of anthropological speculation.

Das Mutterrecht ("Mother Right"), which was published in 1861 after being presented as a lecture series in Stuttgart, Germany, in 1856 (three years before Darwin's book was published), was the work of a German-Swiss legal scholar, Johann J. Bachofen (1815–1887). Bachofen entertained the intriguing notion that society emerged from a state of sexual promiscuity (hetairism). Women rebelled against the humiliation they had suffered during that mythical bawdy epoch, and they established a gynaecocracy, a society ruled by women. The dominance of women was symbolized by the condition of the heavens, where female deities ruled over male, and the moon over the sun. After an embarrassing interlude when men asserted themselves by pretending to be mothers, fatherhood—the highest principle of life—came to the fore, and the final stage of patriarchy was achieved.

Drearily solid in comparison to Bachofen's scheme was the work of another jurist, Sir Henry Maine (1822–1888), who, having had first-hand experience in colonial India, based his theories on Aryan India and Europe. Maine thought that society originated as a patriarchy. He also believed that the significant evolutionary shift was from societies based on status, where the individual's social position was determined almost exclusively by the kinship status into which he was born, to societies based on contract, where a man's relations to others were determined primarily by the restricted, voluntary agreements into which he entered.

The Scotsman John McLennan (1827–1881), a lawyer like Bachofen and Maine, shared Bachofen's idea that human society began in a state of primitive promiscuity, with each person in a group mating with every other person of the opposite sex, kinsman or not. McLennan went beyond Bachofen, however, in emphasizing that all the mating or marrying occurred within a given group, a situation McLennan termed *endogamy*. McLennan thought that as society progressed men started avoiding women from their own group, marrying women from other groups instead, a situation he termed *exogamy*. He was particularly impressed by the custom of bride capture described in classical myths and in reports from travelers in the Americas, India, Siberia, Mongolia, Arabia, Africa, and Australia. Bride capture was a sign of the shift from endogamy to exogamy, and in McLennan's view stealing wives was an advance over primitive promiscuity.

For historical reasons, one of the most interesting of the early evolutionary schemes is that of Lewis Henry Morgan (1818–1881), yet another lawyer, from Rochester, New York. Morgan, whose theories were inspired by the nearby Iroquois Indians, postulated that human society had passed through three stages: savagery, barbarism, and civilization. Fire and the bow and arrow—but not pottery—were man's possessions during the stage of savagery. This stage was characterized by primitive promiscuity, reflected in the kinship terminology of savages. In one such Oceanic classificatory terminology, Morgan found that the same kinship term was applied to one's father and one's mother's brother. To Morgan this implied that brothers could mate with sisters, since if they did so a woman's child could rightfully call his mother's brother by the same term as his father. During the stage of barbarism, man possessed pottery, had domesticated plants and animals, and used a descriptive kinship terminology, with which one type of kinsman could be precisely distinguished from another. This terminology suggested to Morgan that the barbarians were more concerned than the savages about who mated with whom. Morgan's ultimate stage was civilization (which was very much like nineteenth-century Victorian society as manifested in Rochester, New York). Civilized man was literate and practiced monogamy, a state for which "Morgan had a warm reverence," believing that "the whole previous experience and progress of mankind culminated in this one institution." [1] Morgan's scheme contained many suggestive ideas and a rich store of fact, as well as the fancy cited here, but aside from its contributions to anthropology, it is of interest because it was incorporated into Friedrich Engels's *The Origins of the Family, Private Property, and the State*. The views of this conservative Victorian lawyer became part of the core of Marxist theory, with the odd result that while Morgan's ideas are virtually forgotten in America, they are still known and honored in Soviet Russia.

Questions of social evolution were *the* questions for nineteenth-century anthropology, but for the past half-century in Anglo-American anthropology the social evolutionism of Morgan and others has stood in almost total disrepute. Why this reversal? What was wrong with evolutionism? These are important questions, because underlying our presentation of anthropology is a theory that in many respects resembles those of the classical evolutionists.

"Morgan's fault," writes Godfrey Lienhardt, "like that of many would-be historians of institutions of his time, was to try to arrange all [institutions] in a universal time sequence. We must accept that there is not and can never be any historical evidence for one original form of marriage or the family, or indeed that any one original form ever existed." [2] One can certainly agree that the search for *an* archetypal form from which all subsequent society has sprung is fruitless; we simply have no way of knowing precisely what happened when humanity began. On the other hand, Lienhardt's criticism is unduly harsh and demanding, for, in principle, a social or cultural anthropologist should be able to follow a method parallel to that employed by the physical anthropologist. The physical anthropologist no longer searches for *the* fossil of *the* original human. Instead, from scattered finds of fossils, such as those of *Proconsul* (a primate that presumably existed in central Africa during the early Miocene period) or *Dryopithecus* (a primate that presumably ranged over north Africa, India, and Europe during the late Miocene or early Pliocene), he infers that the proto-hominoids who gave rise to both apes and men must have displayed one set of anatomical or physiological traits rather than another. The social anthropologist who paralleled this procedure would search not only for fossils, but also for tools and other artifacts. From these he would attempt to reconstruct the general features of the social life of man's ancestors. But, while there is nothing wrong with such a procedure in principle, in practice such reconstruction is extremely difficult because of the paucity of tangible evidence.

Another criticism leveled at the classical anthropological evolutionists is that they conceived of their postulated historical sequences as implacable natural laws: every society had to pass through every stage of the proposed sequence; no stage could be skipped, nor could the order of the stages vary. This criticism, however, is based on a stereotyped misrepresentation of the evolutionists' views. As Marvin Harris [3] has shown, the evolutionists were, almost to a man, more flexible than this. Indeed, since different evolutionists proposed different sequences, it is hard to believe that each did not suffer some doubt as to whether his particular scheme was truly *the* revelation of universal natural laws binding on all societies.

Since it is tempting to think of any evolutionary scheme, including the sociocultural, as setting forth stages through which all societies must pass, we must emphasize the flexibility of sociocultural evolution. Societies are not like biological organisms. A society does not have a genetic program which insures that its maturation will proceed in order through stages *A, B, C*. While a society's government might propose a plan for such a sequence, the society can discard the plan (and the government), but an organism cannot reject its genetic program. The concept of sociocultural evolution also differs from the concept of biological maturation in that sociocultural evolution is largely a learning process. A society can always skip stages through which other societies have passed by learning from those societies how to avoid their mistakes. Japan, for instance, learned from the West, and so skipped some of the painful stages through which the West passed in its struggle to industrialize.

The nineteenth-century evolutionists have been castigated for their ethnocentrism. They did not hesitate to classify the societies or races of mankind into lower and higher levels, devising a scale from the apelike to the godlike, with Europeans at the top. The idea was that the higher societies were not only more advanced technologically but, with their monogamy, were also more righteous. Later scholars objected, asserting that technological sophistication does not necessarily imply higher morality. Lienhardt, for example, cites a study completed in 1915 by Hobhouse, Wheeler, and Ginsberg, which attempted to correlate moral traits with economic development. They were forced to conclude, however, that economic progress

> has no necessary connection with improvement in the relations between members of a society. It does not imply greater considerateness or a keener sense of justice, and may in some ways be held to be adverse to them. . . .[4]

Certainly we agree that economic or technological advance does not necessarily lead to moral improvement, but, conversely, economic stagnation does not necessarily lead to goodness. Some who idealize the natural savage or the spiritual Easterner appear to believe so, and such a notion would clearly appeal to those who hope that the meek and poor shall inherit the earth. We do not dismiss so easily the maxim voiced by others that "last guys aren't nice," [5] that backwardness may engender frustration, resentment, and aggression. In any event, the proposition that economic progress fails to correlate with moral progress does not preclude the formulation of an evolutionary scheme. Whether moral progress is or is not correlated with economic progress, it is still both theoretically and practically possible to construct two scales, one measuring degree of moral progress according to some explicit criterion, the other measuring degree of economic progress. It is equally possible to classify societies according to how high they rank on each scale. If numerous societies rank high on one scale and low on the other, this simply suggests that scales more refined than the combined moral-economic ones used by the Victorians are required.

The defects of the Victorian evolutionary scales do not imply that all evolutionary scales are useless. The advantage of evolutionary scales, such as the modernization scale that we are about to

present, is that they permit comparison, correlation, and classification of data which would otherwise remain in disarray.

THE DIMENSIONS OF MODERNIZATION [6]

We distinguish five stages or levels of sociocultural evolution: primitive, archaic, historic, early modern, and modern.[7] The levels are
conceptualized as distributed along a scale of relative modernity.
This scale is composed of a number of dimensions which may be
characterized as follows.

Social, political, and economic organization

The more modern a society, *the more specialized are the units that
compose it*. That is, societies at the upper levels of our modernization scale consist largely of units that specialize in the various social
tasks—economic, political, religious, recreational. Conversely, societies at the lower levels of modernization consist largely of unspecialized units, each of which performs all or at least several of
these tasks rather than just one.

Consider, for example, the task of education. Modern society
contains a vast number of units that specialize in education. Not
only are there primary, secondary, and advanced schools, but there
are also dentistry, medical, and law schools, as well as schools for
recently developed specialties, such as filmmaking and computer-
programming. Americans, who tend to take all of these specialized
educational units for granted, may forget that throughout history
education has predominantly occurred within a unit not specializing
in education: the family. Where education has taken place outside
the family, it has been in similarly unspecialized units, such as the

temples or churches of historic Buddhist, Muslim, and Christian societies.

In other fields besides education, specialization also proceeds as societies modernize. In archaic Egypt, where the king was also a god, political and religious units tended to be unified, while in more modern societies, separation of church and state is generally the rule; some units specialize in government, others in religion.

The increasing distinction between units for work and units for play provides a final illustration of the trend toward specialization. The primitive both plays and works within his kin-based community, whereas modern man works in one unit, *i.e.,* a factory or an office, while playing in another. Such clear separation of work units from play units encourages the vacations that are so important to modern man; vacations take place in play units that are clearly separate from work units, and for primitives who do not make such a clear separation *vacation* is a meaningless term.

In sum, as one moves up the scale toward modern society, one finds men dividing their time among an increasing number of increasingly specialized units. As one moves down the scale toward primitive society, fewer, less specialized units are found, and people function in all of them more or less simultaneously.

As modernization proceeds, not only do units become increasingly specialized, but *social relations become to an ever higher degree functionally specific, and to an ever lesser degree functionally diffuse.* That is to say that as we move up the scale toward modernity, we find that people increasingly define explicitly what is entailed in their social relationships. Conversely, as we move down the scale toward the primitive, we find that the rights and obligations entailed in social relationships are more often considered implicit to that relationship.

A comparison of traditional China with contemporary America furnishes a good illustration of the contrast between functionally specific and functionally diffuse relationships revolving around the institution of contract. Ideally, in America, the businessman-customer relationship is kept as functionally specific as possible. The relationship is often defined by a contract, and if the contract is vague it is considered a bad contract. Even where there is no written contract, as in simple retail transactions, the obligations involved in the American transaction are, ideally, precisely delimited. Thus, when a customer buys a soft drink, his only obligation is to pay the advertised price. If he hands over a sum less than the advertised price, the buyer is liable, and the seller can repossess the merchandise. The seller's obligation is to deliver the goods as advertised. If there is a rat in the bottle, the seller is liable for restitution of the price. Thus, simple business relations in America are more often than not functionally specific.

In traditional China, on the other hand, the ideal business relationship was kept functionally diffuse. The businessman was expected to feel a great sense of responsibility for his customer. He was expected to grant extra requests, to offer special prices, and—in extreme cases—to protect the customer even at the cost of his own financial ruin. All of this diffuseness derived from the kinship, friendship, or neighbor relationship that underlay the Chinese business relationship. When business in China was between strangers, rather than kinsmen, friends, or neighbors, a *caveat emptor* attitude obtained. Seller and buyer would work as fraudulently and as ruthlessly as possible, each to maximize his own gain.

Perhaps the common knowledge that business was basically immoral explains, in part, why in so many historic or archaic societies, such as traditional China or Japan, the status of merchant was ranked lowest of all by the great moral philosophies of the times, and why it was thus necessary to link the business relationship to some diffuse relationship, such as kinship, in order to establish trust. By contrast, business in America is governed to a striking degree by a code of fair play, backed by law and the courts. Therefore, strangers can do business with confidence and even with amiability. Perhaps, because business is comparatively moral, the businessman occupies a status in modern society, both morally and socially, that would be unheard of in nonmodern societies.

As societies modernize, *markets and media of exchange become increasingly generalized.* The more modern the society, the wider the range of goods and services that each of its media of exchange (such as money) can buy, and the wider the range of choice of market partners with whom goods and services can be exchanged. Conversely, media used by more primitive societies can buy only a limited range of goods, and the markets available to these societies are rudimentary. The difference between highly generalized and highly restricted media and markets can be illustrated by Bronislaw Malinowski's description of the *kula* exchange among the primitive Trobriand islanders and the market exchange of modern society.[8]

Kula is an exchange of treasure objects and takes place largely between permanent partners. Each participant in *kula* can trade only with his permanent partners—five or six for a commoner, perhaps seventy or eighty for a chief. A man's *kula* partners come from islands other than his own, and what he gives to his partner or receives from him is prescribed by the location of the partner's island in relation to his. Thus, a man may give arm bands to his partners living on islands that lie in one direction, but he will give shell necklaces to partners living on islands in the opposite direction. Each time a Trobriander receives an object from his partner in the North, let us say, he passes it on to his partner in the South. The *kula* system, then, forms a huge ring several hundred miles in circumference. Necklaces traveling in one direction will pass arm bands coming from the opposite direction, and trading expeditions circulating around this huge ring provide great excitement and adventure for the Trobrianders.

Treasures used in the *kula* exchanges are not highly generalized media of exchange. A necklace can be exchanged only for an arm band, and an arm band only for a necklace. A necklace cannot even buy another necklace, much less food, housing, land, or labor. One is limited in what one can obtain with a *kula* object. By contrast, no matter how dreary it may seem when set beside the glitter and exoticism of the *kula* objects, modern money is a highly generalized medium of exchange. It is one of the great cultural achievements in that it is a symbol into which virtually everything can be translated and for which virtually everything can be exchanged.

Just as money is a more generalized medium of exchange than

kula objects, so the modern market organization is more generalized than the *kula* circle. The *kula* trader has only a few choices of trading partner, and the group from whom he chooses his partner was probably not his choice in the first place. He probably inherited it from a relative. And the type of object that the Trobriander wishes to trade strongly limits who his partner can be. If he has a bracelet in hand, he can trade with a partner who lives in only one direction; if it is a necklace, he must trade in the other direction. Thus, when the Trobriander sets out in his canoe with his necklaces or bracelets, he faces only a limited array of opportunities for exchange.

The trader in modern society, however, is free to choose as a partner anyone who will buy what he has to sell or who sells what he wants to buy. The field is open, he is not bound to a group of permanent partners, but only to his contractual obligations—which he enters voluntarily. Also, certain institutions in modern society insure that no man loses the freedom to seek new contractual partners. It is illegal for a man to sell himself into slavery, partly because as a slave his rights to enter new contracts voluntarily would be abrogated. Here lawful restraints insure continuing freedom of choice. It is the same, of course, with antitrust laws. As graduates of the Harvard Law School are admonished: "Administer these just restraints that you may make men free."

It is important to realize that generalized media other than money have emerged in modern society. For example, the vote, as employed in modern government, is a generalized medium. It can be exchanged for a wide range of goods and services. By "paying" his vote to the candidate of his choice, a citizen may hope to receive the kind of government he wants. Both the custom of "trading votes" and the institution of the "influence peddler" suggest other parallels between dollars and votes.

Centralization is another dimension of modernization. The more modern a society, the more centralized it is: the more tightly its parts become coordinated with one another under some central control. Such coordination and control is not just political. In the

United States the ecumenical movement and the United Fund represent increasing centralization: diverse churches and diverse charities become coordinated with one another under a central control. Similarly, centralization occurs when smaller unions are welded into one federation, and businesses merge to form larger corporations. The high stage of development of transportation and communication in the United States facilitates the centralization of its various institutions. Indeed, in all respects save the political, the United States is more highly centralized than the Soviet Union.

Obviously, in primitive societies like that of the Australian aborigines, where families are dispersed without intercommunication while wandering about seeking food, and where there is no chief or central government, the degree of centralization is low. Even in archaic societies, such as traditional China, which boasted a pony express capable of transporting the true relics of the Buddha from India to the Chinese capital in a few days over rough terrain, or in Rome with its imperial highways, centralization was not comparable to what it is today. Transportation and communications were simply too slow.

Anomalously, many contemporary primitive societies enjoy transportation and communication facilities (airplanes and radios) that are infinitely more efficient than those available to more modern societies of the past. Because of their airplanes and radios, these primitive societies are rapidly entering the sociopolitical network of the great powers, while the decisions of these powers (perhaps to form a guerrilla force backing one side in a war the native soldiers do not understand) help to transform such societies into colonial appendages. In this sense, the primitive societies are not really skipping steps in their evolution toward modernity; they are simply being assimilated into a centralized system.

The speed with which bodies, goods, and messages move about the modern world not only changes sociopolitical patterns, but apparently leads to deep and important changes in the personalities of the people involved. According to studies carried out in the Near East (Turkey, Lebanon, Egypt, Syria, and Jordan), centralization encourages empathetic capacity.[9] As a society becomes centralized, its members learn to project themselves into the role of the stranger and to imagine themselves as participants in exotic situations. This increased empathetic skill is understandable, for in societies that are *not* centralized, most people live in small, self-sufficient villages. They deal mainly with people whom they know well and who are like themselves, and with situations which are familiar. There is little need, therefore, to develop skills of empathizing with the unfamiliar.

To test the ability of Near Eastern villagers to empathize with strange people and situations, researchers asked them such questions as: "If you were made the editor of a newspaper, what kind of paper would you run?"; "If for some reason, you could not live in our [native] country, what other country would you choose to live in?"; "Suppose you were made head of your country's government, what are some of the things you would do?" The researchers were only a little less astonished at the answers they received than were the villagers at the questions they were asked. In reply to "What would you do if you were president of your country?" a Turkish villager exclaimed: "My God! How can you ask such a thing? How can I . . . I cannot . . . President of Turkey . . . Master of the whole world?" When a Shi'i shoemaker in Saida, Lebanon, was asked what he would do if he were editor of a newspaper, he first accused the interviewer of ridiculing him, then begged the interviewer to change the question. The interviewer consented, noting later that "the shoemaker was making all kinds of frantic movements with his head and hands."

But a modern, centralized society such as America requires great empathetic skill for effective operation. In social contexts ranging from the most trivial to the most vital, Americans have burnished this skill to a high gloss. The slogans *Be a defensive driver* and *Think for the other guy* illustrate the need for empathy in our complex society—for our very survival. When an American votes, he chooses in large part on the basis of empathy with a stranger; it is extremely rare for the voter to know a candidate personally. But the most remarkable talent Americans display is for empathizing with the characters of television advertising whose breath is not sweet or whose hair is diseased. Yet on precisely such empathy do American advertising and the American economy depend.

As a society modernizes it becomes increasingly *bureaucratized*. Bureaucracy proliferates not only in government but also in firms, schools, and other institutions that organize functionally specific offices with well-defined lines of authority. Indeed, bureaucratization is so essential to modern society, and so ingrained, that even those who preach against it are forced to bureaucratize if they wish to propagate their message efficiently. Whether a modern society is communist, democratic, or socialist, it depends on bureaucracies. And at premodern stages of evolution, the shift toward bureaucratization is crucial. As we shall see, the change from *kin*ship to *king*ship as a basis for social organization marks the crucial emergence from the primitive pattern.

The great early archaic bureaucracies, although undeniably magnificent creations, were smaller and less effective than some people claim. The Chinese bureaucracy, one of the most intriguing of these early bureaucracies, never, by the most generous estimate, involved more than a half million persons. Nor did it ever really manage to overcome the interference of kinship ties. True, entry into the bureaucracy depended on performance in examinations on Chinese literature, and not on one's kinship bonds to officials; and there were other devices to insure that kinship favoritism did not interfere with the workings of bureaucracy. Nevertheless, when viewed carefully and comprehensively, the Chinese bureaucracy reveals itself to have been merely an island of functional specificity in a sea of functional diffuseness. Invariably, kinship bonds intruded. Nepotism and corruption, involving favoritism for one's kinfolk, always interfered with impersonal loyalties to the bureaucracy and the emperor. Perhaps this was one reason why eunuchs and celibates played important roles in so many archaic bureaucracies; not having children they could favor, the eunuchs and celibates were not so likely to institute dynasties within the bureaucracy.

It is interesting to observe what happens when a "primitive" tribe, with a social structure based on kinship, is forced to deal with the bureaucracies of the nation in which it resides. In Greece, as J. K. Campbell [10] describes it, there is a tribe of shepherds, called the Sarakatsani, whose roving way of life frequently gets them into trouble with the Greek government. Since the Sarakatsani believes that he is too lowly to relate to so elevated a figure as a government official, he seeks an alliance with some influential person, usually a lawyer, who will act as a go-between. Since lawyers and bureaucrats meet in the hotels of Greek towns to drink coffee together, the Sarakatsani thinks that the lawyer might have influence with the bureaucrat. To bind the lawyer to himself the Sarakatsani commonly seeks to make him a spiritual kinsman. This he accomplishes by asking the lawyer to be his child's godfather, a request not easily refused. As the child's godfather, the lawyer must stand with the child at its baptism, which immediately follows the rite of confirmation, a critical rite for the Sarakatsani. During the confirmation rite the godfather, replacing the child's own parents, holds the child, names it, and at the close of the service hands the child back to its mother, saying, "I return the child to you in this life, but I shall ask it back from you in the next. Protect it well from fire, water, and all evil!" Ever after, throughout the child's life, the godfather's spiritual bond to the child is so like kinship that the child is forbidden to marry into his godfather's family, and, because of his spiritual kinship to his godchild, the godfather cannot refuse a favor asked by the parents in the child's name. The parent is now in a position to obtain favors from the lawyer—to ask him to intercede on his behalf with the bureaucracy. Thus, in Sarakatsani society, as in many similar societies, relations with the bureaucracy are conducted as much like kinship relations as possible.

Kinship and the family structure

Kinship is a subject central to anthropology. What generalizations can be made about the effects of modernization on kinship? Evidence indicates that as society shifts from primitive to modern, the importance of the conjugal bond increases while that of the kinship bond decreases: more emphasis is laid on the bond between husband and wife, and less on that between child and parent. One sign of this conjugal emphasis in modern society is that a married couple resides neolocally: husband and wife, more often than not, live apart from their parents. In contrast, primitive couples often reside patrilocally or matrilocally: either with the husband's parents and kinsmen or with the wife's parents and kinsmen.

A description of the way in which a Sarakatsani couple chooses a place to live illustrates the nonmodern society's tendency to emphasize kinship bonds rather than conjugal bonds.[11]

The first stage of the Sarakatsani domestic cycle occurs just after a man and woman marry. The wife comes to live with her husband in his parents' household: the couple begins its domestic life by residing patrilocally. At this point the husband's primary loyalty is to his kinsmen—especially to his parents and siblings. The husband acts as though he were ashamed of his wife: he insults her and sleeps with her only in secret.

The second stage of the cycle begins when the wife gives birth. The husband's behavior toward his wife changes. His insults cease. The backbreaking labor that the wife was forced to endure previously for the sake of her husband's family now diminishes. Why these changes? The wife is no longer simply a wife. She is also a mother. As such she is related more closely to her husband's family, through her blood relationship to her child, than she was before the child arrived. As a mother she is more highly regarded than she was as a wife, because it is the parent-child bond rather than the husband-wife bond that merits respect among the Sarakatsani.

Later when the wife finds herself and her child sharing the house of her husband's parents in company with the wives and children of her husband's brothers, the third stage begins. Even with only a few brothers, enough wives and children are on hand to fill the house with noise and quarrels. Each wife worries loudly about whether her child is getting a fair share of whatever the brothers jointly produce. Eventually this discord becomes so great that the loyalty the husband holds for his child takes precedence over his loyalty to brothers and parents. The husband takes his wife and children away from his parents' household, and establishes a household of his own. Clearly, this move is not for the wife's benefit; if he did not leave his parents in the early days of their marriage when she was unhappiest, why should he leave now? It is his child who is in difficulty—therefore he moves. Once more, as in most nonmodern societies, the child-parent bond carries the most weight.

In America the husband-wife bond counts more than among the Sarakatsani. Not only do American newlyweds usually set up housekeeping away from their parents for the sake of their marriage, but they also feel, in general, that if conflict arises between one's parents and one's spouse, one should take the spouse's side. In nonmodern societies, the reverse tends to be true.

Conjugal emphasis is at the core of the modern belief that marriage should be based on love, rather than on class or kinship. One ideal of the romantic love complex is that the individual should marry whomever he loves: that marriage is mainly the concern of the individuals involved. In most nonmodern societies, however, marriage is an alliance between kinship groups, such as clans or lineages. Since a healthy alliance between kinship groups is what matters most, elders from the two groups arrange the marriage. This situation is common in primitive societies, but even in historic societies, such as those of lowland Southeast Asia, parents frequently arrange their children's marriages. In Thailand and Java the young people yearn for the romantic marriages depicted in novels, films, and songs. For them opposition to parent-arranged marriage is still a burning issue, and choice of their own spouse still a highly charged fantasy.

Not surprisingly, romanticizing the husband-wife bond, and thus strengthening it, has weakened the parent-child bond. Not only does this imply that spouses will lose interest in their parents, but also that, as their interest in each other increases, they will lose interest in their children. At present, in societies such as Java, parents tend to be more interested in their children than in each other. A marriage is hardly considered sealed until it has produced children; this is indicated by symbols of fertility hung outside the wedding place and by the constant hopeful queries directed at a new wife to find out if she is pregnant. But in time the child focus should give way to a conjugal focus. Effective contraception methods will probably give impetus to this trend.

In most modern societies, kinship is reckoned bilineally, whereas in many nonmodern societies, especially primitive societies, kinship is reckoned unilineally. To reckon descent bilineally is to trace one's kinsmen more or less equally through both paternal and maternal lines. To reckon descent unilineally is to trace kinsmen through only one parent, or at least to emphasize one line more than the other. If the emphasis is on the father's side of the family, we speak of patrilineal descent; if the emphasis falls on the mother's side, we speak of matrilineal descent.*

Patrilineal or matrilineal reckoning of kinship involves the notion that only one parent is regarded as a kinsman. The other parent is considered an affine or in-law, *i.e.,* a person married to a kinsman, rather than a blood kinsman. The Trobrianders, who trace descent matrilineally, are said to believe that the "mother's husband" plays no part in procreation. The mother is the procreator. From her comes the life substance. From her blood the child is created, so the child is blood kin to her. The "mother's husband" is a kind of in-law to the child, a person who happens to be married to that kinswoman of the child termed "mother."

The Kachin of Burma, who reckon descent patrilineally, hold an opposite view. The Kachin believe that the child is created from the bone of the father. The "father's wife" is regarded as a kind

---

* Ward H. Goodenough, in his "Residence Rules," demonstrates the crudity of such categories as "patrilocal" and "matrilocal." The point could be extended to "patrilineal" and "matrilineal." For the purpose of introducing the notion of variability of patterning in kinship and for broad-scale comparison, these categories are adequate, but for technical and refined analysis of any single society more subtle distinctions would have to be made.

of in-law, a person who happens to be married to that kinsman of the child termed "father." [12]

The experience of growing up in a family founded on notions of this kind is far different from the experience of growing up in the bilineal Western family. It appears that the much discussed oedipus complex takes another course among the Trobrianders than among Westerners. The oedipus complex in the West involves father, mother, and son. The theory is that the son is jealous of the father's sexual relationship with the mother. He fears that the powerful father will castrate him as punishment for his forbidden desire for the mother. He therefore represses his sexual yearnings for the mother and enters a period of latency, during which he shows little interest in girls. According to Freud, this latency period lasts until puberty.

The Trobriand boy does not have a father in the Western sense. He spends his childhood in the company of his "mother's husband," but, as the term suggests, the man has little authority over the boy. Instead, authority is vested in the boy's kinsmen, and since the boy's father is clearly not a kinsman, it falls to the boy's maternal uncle— as his closest senior male kinsman—to exercise discipline, to punish him for childhood wrongs. The uncle is also the breadwinner; among the Trobrianders it is customary for a man to support not his own wife and her household, but his sister and his sister's household. It is the boy's uncle, not his father, who provides the yams. In effect, the Trobriand uncle serves almost all the functions of the Western father.

But with one crucial difference: the brother of the boy's mother has no access to her sexually. She is, after all, his sister, and among the Trobrianders the taboo on incest is strong. Thus, what in the West is the single role of "father," in the Trobriand Islands is split into two roles: the role of "mother's husband" and the role of "mother's brother." With the object of oedipal anger thus splintered, the Trobriand boy's conflicts are also splintered—he cannot play them out so directly against a single father figure as can his counterpart in the West.[13] Variations in patterns of tracing descent may have deep implications for human experience.

Let us turn briefly from patterns of tracing descent to patterns of residence. We contrast nuclear-family households with extended-family households. The nuclear-family household, composed of parents and unmarried children, is dominant in modern society. The extended-family household, composed of parents, their children, and these children's spouses and children, was the mode among elite groups of the past. The ancient Icelandic tale, *Nyal's Saga,* tells of old Nyal's extended-family household in which lived not only Old Nyal and his wife Bergthron, but also their three sons and the sons' wives and children. Including servants, there were fifty people in this one household.

Among the advantages of such an extended living arrangement is that a father and his sons, who own a plot of land jointly, can live on that land and farm it together; but with the advent of modernization, fathers begin to care more about hiring efficient workers to farm their land, less about building and sustaining the bond with their sons. At the same time, sons lose interest in farming. Instead, they care more about making their own fortunes. The result is that extended-family households tend to give way to nuclear-family households established by the sons in cities or other locations away from home. Wherever modernization occurs, extended-family households may be seen giving way to nuclear-family households, and with this change the emphasis on kinship bonds diminishes, while the emphasis on conjugal bonds increases.

It cannot be too highly stressed that kinship, in all its aspects, thoroughly pervades nonmodern society. The Sarakatsani, for example, choose their friends mainly from among their kinsmen; in one survey, seven out of ten reported that they regard a "cousin" as their best friend. Nonkinsmen, on the other hand, are generally perceived as enemies, current or potential. A Sarakatsani traveling through hills inhabited even by his fellow tribesmen would not spend the night with "friends" who were not kinsmen. Not only friends but also co-workers are kinsmen or affines; "companies" of cooperating shepherds are composed of brothers and brothers-in-law, never of nonkinsmen. Generally, Sarakatsani mistrust non-kinsmen, and expect nonkinsmen to betray them. Conversely, kins-

men are expected to display total loyalty to one another. Campbell
says of the Sarakatsani: "Where kinsmen betray one feels horror,
as with treason in our own society." [14] The remark is revealing,
since it suggests that for the Sarakatsani the family is the object of
highest loyalty, just as the nation is for modern man. It is logical,
then, that a Sarakatsani without family is as lacking in honor as
a modern man without a country. Having no family and no honor,
the bastard child is deemed hardly human, and is left on the mule
path to die.

Social differentiation, mobility, and change

In concluding these remarks on the characteristics of social modernization, let us outline three broad social factors. These factors,
derived in part from those already mentioned, are *social differentiation, social mobility,* and *social change.*

Social differentiation (the separation of social units from one another) issues in part from the growing specialization of units that
accompanies modernization. With modernization societies come to
be composed of increasingly numerous units differentiated from
one another by their specialties. At the early stages of modernization, this differentiation is mainly along class lines. From virtually
classless primitive society emerges the archaic pattern which distinguishes the elite that specializes in religio-political functions and
the masses who specialize in manual labor. The archaic stage is
followed by the historic when religious elite and political elite form
separate classes, both distinguished from the masses. We call the
primitive pattern one-class, the archaic two-class, and the historic
three-class. During later stages of modernization, society divides
into a great number of political, occupational, religious, and other
factions that cut across class lines. For this reason, with the advent
of early modern society, we stop viewing social differentiation in
such simple terms as class.

Social mobility is the movement of individuals between the strata of a society. Often a society's myths and ideology depict a higher rate of social mobility than actually exists. For instance, although the "American Dream" expresses the ideal that any man with the will can find a way up the social ladder, some commentators believe that the *actual* rate of movement between strata in America is declining. In any event, it is still a fact that with modernization both the idealized rate of mobility and the actual rate tend to rise: not only do people think they can rise (or fall) faster in the social milieu but they actually can. One reason for increased mobility is that modernization weakens the bond between the individual and the group into which he was born; it becomes easier for him to move away from that group and up (or down) into a new group.

Finally, the more modern a society is, the more rapid is its overall rate of change. This point relates to the argument that fast-changing societies adapt best to a fast-changing environment and that among all types of societies, the modern is the fastest to change.

A major reason why modern men are more ready to change than nonmodern men is that modern men put less emphasis on tradition and more on rationality, *i.e.,* on efficient relation of means to ends. Modern men don't always act rationally, but they do feel a greater need to justify their actions on rational grounds. A Trobriand islander might farm quite rationally, efficiently exploiting available resources to produce bountiful yam harvests, but if asked to explain why he did what he did, he would likely reply: "Because this is the way we have always done it." On the other hand, the modern farmer, if asked to justify his method of fertilizing, might well reply: "Because this method produces a high yield per acre"—in other words, because method X is the most efficient, or rational, way to achieve the end he seeks. Since the modern farmer professes loyalty to the canons of rationality, he is bound to feel some pressure to keep searching for more efficient methods to achieve the desired goal of high productivity. Thus, even if he is a rural conservative, he is constantly goaded to change. The

Trobriander justifies his practices by phrasing them as outgrowths of a tradition that, in his view, was laid down by his ancestors and has never changed. The Trobriander's ideology gives greater sanction to lack of change than the modern man's ideology, and on this ground alone we would expect the overall rate of change in modern society to be greater than in Trobriand society.

It can be said that all of the traits we have called modern speed social change. Take, for example, centralization. The more centralized the society, the more quickly change spreads through it. This is true not only of political, economic, and communications centralization, but also of what we might call "ethical centralization" —the development of a single ethic that applies to all situations. The relation between ethical centralization and the speed of social change can be illustrated by comparing the Judeo-Christian and Oriental religious traditions.

The monistic Judeo-Christian tradition decrees that its God and Law should be followed under all circumstances. To be Christian on Sunday, but not on Monday, is deemed morally exceptionable. To be Jewish at one hour, Buddhist at another, is not encouraged. Furthermore, most Jews or Christians would find it strange to be Catholic at home, Protestant in the office, and Jewish at play. Patterns like these are common in the Orient, however. Javanese do not feel uncomfortable professing Islam in some situations, animism in others, and a kind of Buddhism in still others. Thai are not worried about acting, in various situations, as Buddhists, animists, or Brahmanists. Many anthropologists call such Southeast Asian patterns syncretic since they blend many traditions, but the traditions are not so much blended as distributed carefully and selectively among diverse situations. Situationalism rather than monism is the pattern not only in Southeast Asia, but also in East Asia. As noted earlier, the Japanese apparently does not experience the same discomfort the Westerner might feel if called upon to apply an ethic in situation A that contradicts the ethic appropriate to situation B. Perhaps in Japan this ethical situationalism encourages an unevenness of change. Japan has demonstrated a striking ability to industrialize rapidly while retaining customs alien to the industrial milieu, whereas in the monistic West, industrialization has brought sweeping changes in all spheres of life. It could be argued that the West's ethical monism fostered an attitude that change in any situation ought to be generalized to all situations, but that Japan's ethical compartmentalization helped to prevent change in one area of life from spreading into other areas.

Religion and ideology

In the ideological and religious facets of modernization, we note the trend toward a *universalistic* ethic which decrees that men must be judged on the basis of merit or skill, rather than on the basis of some immutable status assigned to them at birth. Not kinship, race, sex, or caste, but deeds are what count in a universalistic ethic. Where such statuses count more than deeds, we speak of a *particularistic* ethic.

If we move from an archaic and particularistic society, like that of ancient China, to an early modern and relatively universalistic society, like that of nineteenth-century Britain, we observe a rise in the tendency to hire and fire on the basis of what a man can do, rather than on the basis of who he is in terms of kinship. In Britain and America the continuing trend toward universalism is reflected in the changing laws and attitudes regarding race, women's rights, and poverty. Another example of the trend toward universalism is provided by the developing nations. Many of these nations were formerly archaic or historic kingdoms, organized on the basis of particularism; the status into which one was born determined one's life. Colonialism, with its racist and elitist tendencies, helped perpetuate particularism, but at the same time it propagated the Western notion of universalism. Thus, colonialism sowed the seeds of its own decline.

Today, in many of the developing nations, the act of becoming modern is strongly bound up with the notion of universalism. An interesting symptom of the shift toward universalism in one developing nation, Indonesia, is displayed in the themes of its folkplays or *ludruk*. In *ludruk* of earlier derivation, the villain could never lose if he came from a high class. The hero, if lowborn, could never win. In more recent *ludruk,* however, the characters are punished on the basis of what they do rather than who they are. This is only one of many signs of a growing Indonesian universalism.[15] But it should also be noted that, more often than not, the developing nations still cling to one form of particularism: their nationalist ideologies will cause a man to be evaluated more favorably if he is of the home nationality than if he is foreign, even if the native and the foreigner are equal in merit and skill.

Ancient China furnishes an excellent illustration of a large-scale society that operated largely on a particularistic basis. According to Chinese ideal and expectation, kinship considerations always came first. Even an attempt to assassinate the emperor could be forgiven if the would-be assassin could prove that he did so to avenge a genuine wrong done to his father or another ancestor. Nepotism was no cause for embarrassment. In fact, if a traditional Chinese was caught *not* favoring his relatives for jobs, it was distinctly embarrassing. From the Chinese viewpoint, not to give preference to relatives was inhuman and bestial (in the China of today, cultural revolution on the mainland is eliminating many of the old particularistic ideals). While American politicians or businessmen are often nepotistic, they are commonly defensive about it and often criticized. Thus, although there are still particularistic practices in America, our ideals are generally universalistic.

There is a second broad ideological trend that accompanies modernization. The more modern the society, the less will its members believe that their society exercises control over their cosmos, or ideal system. The less modern the society, the more they will perceive or believe such control exists. With the advent of early-modern society, the cosmic came to be perceived not only as separate from the social, but also as taking control over the social.[16] This trend becomes clearer by examining, briefly for now, the following three stages:

1. *Primitive level: exemplified by the Australian aborigines.* The aborigines perceive little separation between the cosmic world, which they express by myth and ritual, and the actual world, in which they live. They imagine that their cosmic world, "The Dreaming," is populated by their own ancestral kin who live in "everywhen." These kin merge the social present with the cosmic past, and the cosmic thus mixes intimately with the social.

2. *Historic level: exemplified by Thai Buddhists.* The Buddhists perceive a radical discrepancy between the ideal world and the real world. In fact, they claim that the real world is not real, but simply an illusion from which men should flee. It is the Thai Buddhist attitude that the real world should be left behind by retreat into monastic seclusion. The monk, therefore, becomes a prestigious person and plays a central role in Thailand.

3. *Early-modern level: exemplified by the early Calvinists.* Like the Buddhists, the Calvinists perceived a radical discrepancy between the cosmic world, the "Kingdom of God," and the actual world, the "Kingdom of Man." But, unlike the Buddhists, they did not favor fleeing from the world to escape its imperfections. Rather, they were beset with a compulsion to reform the world in the image of the cosmic.

In this schematic overview, the shift from the primitive Australians to the historic Buddhists is accompanied by a rise in the perceived discrepancy between the actual social order and the imagined cosmic order. The Calvinists, like the Buddhists, perceived the discrepancy, but they also added another dimension—a compulsion to reform the actual to conform to the image of the cosmic. Hence, the Calvinists possessed a powerful stimulus to change society, a stimulus that the aborigines and Buddhists lack. Like *technological* modernization, *ideological* modernization helps society to change and adapt to altering environments.

Technology

A society is technologically modernized to the extent that it employs tools and inanimate power sources. Power resources include everything from gravity, wind, and water to electricity, steam, and nuclear energy. Tools run the gamut from primitive digging sticks to modern electronic computers. All societies make use of some tools and some inanimate power sources; yet it is obvious that the differences between those used by primitive, archaic, historic, and modern societies—and the ways in which they are used—are great.

Technological modernization, as defined here, is not simply equivalent to industrialization. It includes the application of mechanization to farming as well as to industry. Indeed, for modernization the mechanization of farming is as crucial as industrialization. America's high standard of living is due as much to its unique agricultural efficiency as to its industrial efficiency. Since factories are more symbolic of modernization than are farms, developing nations tend to emphasize industrialization more than agricultural mechanization, an emphasis which is sometimes unfortunate.

THE DIRECTION OF WORLD HISTORY

The more modern the society, the greater is its capacity to change rapidly in order to exploit a rapidly changing environment. A society's environment includes not only its natural surroundings but also its man-made physical setting, its social surroundings formed by other societies, and its psycho-organic milieu (the bodies and personalities of its members). All of these environments, especially the last three, are changing at an accelerating rate, and if a society is to make fullest use of them, its own rate of change must accelerate. Modern sociocultural patterns—partly because they encourage high technological development, which in turn makes possible a quick, effective response to such upheavals as floods, war, and population explosion, and partly because they encourage a general flexibility and capacity for rapid change—maximize a society's ability to adapt.

Assuming the above argument is true, consider the principle of natural selection that has emerged from studies of biological evolution. This principle maintains that over time a population tends to display more and more the traits of its most adaptive members, since it is these who are most likely to survive and reproduce their traits. Since the less adaptive members tend not to survive and reproduce, their traits disappear over time. An analogous principle may operate for societies. The most highly adaptive societies at any period of history will be the ones that survive and reproduce—by disseminating their patterns. Therefore, these patterns become more and more widespread, while the patterns of the less adaptive societies become less common. In our own time, the early-modern and modern patterns are increasingly prominent, while during the past six or seven thousand years the trend has been away from the primitive pattern. According to one estimate, only six percent of the world's people still live in primitive societies. This trend reflects the greater adaptive capacity of the modern pattern and the lesser adaptive capacity of the primitive pattern.

Having made the analogy between natural selection in biological evolution and in sociocultural evolution, we must emphasize that this is only an analogy. Analogies are meant to suggest hypotheses, not to prove them.[17] The applicability of these statements to biological evolution is no proof that they are equally applicable to sociocultural evolution. Sociocultural statements must be judged on their own terms. Indeed, certain criteria employed by students of biological evolution would be inappropriate for the analysis of sociocultural evolution. For instance, the rate of biological survival and reproduction among members of a population can by no means be used to predict the rates of survival and reproduction of the sociocultural patterns which that population follows. The birthrate in nonindustrial societies today is much greater than the birthrate in industrial societies, yet the industrial pattern is the one that is surviving and spreading.

Sociocultural evolution appears to be moving in a different direction from biological evolution. Biological evolution is often likened to a branching tree, with more and more branches appearing as evolution proceeds. Thus, insects have branched out (undergone adaptive radiation) to such a degree that today some 600,000 insect species exist. By contrast, sociocultural evolution appears to be converging into a single "species." The trend seems to be one in which all societies will eventually assume the early-modern or modern pattern.

A second difference between biological and sociocultural evolution is that men's motives and plans play a more important role in the sociocultural process than in the biological. Since the principle of natural selection was originated to explain the evolution of all animals, it does not consider motive and plan as possible causes. The principle of natural selection recognizes only that if by accident, mutation, or other process a more adaptive trait or pattern appears, that trait or pattern will tend to be perpetuated. No assumption is made about how the trait or pattern originated, and the biologist is particularly wary of talking as if the organism in which a given trait or pattern originated had planned it that way. The virtue of this position (which avoids the teleological fallacy) is plain, but at the same time we must take into account the observation by Redfield [18] and others that the more modern the society, the greater the capacity of its members to control their destinies—to move in the direction of consciously established goals. Hence, when an overwhelming number of today's developing societies say they yearn to modernize, we cannot ignore this yearning in predicting the direction in which the world's societies are likely to move. Of course, modernizing societies mourn the loss of their traditions, but at the same time many recognize that in the face of population pressures and other environmental threats, modernization is the only way to survive. Not only the objective observer but also the natives of the societies involved recognize the adaptive advantage of modern patterns.

Arguments such as this have inspired Marion J. Levy, Jr., in his *Modernization and the Structure of Societies,* to brand the modern pattern a "universal solvent." Levy claims that when a non-modern society comes in contact with a modern society, the non-modern society inevitably modernizes, whereas the modern society never "demodernizes." Levy believes that this occurs because every society, no matter how spiritual its values, contains some individuals who want the material advantages which modern patterns produce. The process of modernization need not occur all at once. Perhaps only part of a society is affected at first. But modernization is like a dye which, upon touching one thread, is slowly absorbed until it changes the color of the whole cloth. Adopting modern technology to gain material advantage soon results in changes in family structure, government, and other institutions. According to Levy, only romanticists could believe that part of a society can modernize while the rest remains entirely intact. Although societies such as Japan apparently do segregate modernizing sectors and traditional sectors for a time, it is doubtless true that such segregation cannot endure forever. Eventually all societies will thoroughly modernize.

Although this view of world history, according to which all societies will eventually conform to the modern pattern, may be crude, it seems better founded than the idea that there is no discernible direction to the transformations of today's societies. Modernization theory calls into question the belief that every society is developing along its own unique path according to its own unique genius.

Today's stagnating societies might still be happily stagnating in 3000 A.D. But with the onrush of modernization fewer and fewer backwaters in which to hide will remain. Modernization tends to integrate all regions of the world into one system. The few primitive societies found today remain primitive partly because they have been able to retreat into the jungles, deserts, or mountains and avoid the advance of modernity; but as modernity pushes further these havens too will be lost. Indeed, just as the pace of technological innovation has accelerated steadily since human history began,[19] so the process of sociocultural change itself has accelerated. As the world becomes more nearly a single system, changes in one sector instantly excite changes in the other sectors. Exotic societies, therefore, may be doomed.

OVERVIEW

Evolutionary theory tries (1) to formulate features common to all societies, and (2) to study the differences among societies in terms of these features. Such dimensions of modernization as centralization and specialization achieve both these objectives. They serve, on the one hand, to delineate and label processes common to all societies and, on the other, to define scales along which societies can be ranked and compared. All societies are to a degree undergoing processes of specialization and centralization. Because some societies have carried these processes further than others, we can ask how much greater is the degree to which one society has centralized or specialized in comparison with another.

Evolutionary theory also tries (3) to understand how each society functions, *i.e.,* to understand the principles in terms of which each operates. This objective is partly attained by delineating the functional relationships between processes such as centralization and specialization (for instance, we can state, as a generally valid principle, that the more specialized units a society has, the more centralized it must become in order to integrate its units). The objective can also be approached by classifying the world's societies into types, such as "primitive," "archaic," "historic," "early-modern," and "modern," and delineating the distinctive principles and patterns governing the operation of each type of society.

In its emphasis on formulating the principles according to which societies operate, evolutionary theory differs from conventional world history. From world history one learns the chronological sequence of the world's events, but not the principles governing the function of each type of society. For this reason, knowledge of conventional world history is not sufficient for making an accurate prediction of the future. Could one predict that an engine is about to explode merely by knowing the history of its use? Knowing its history would be helpful, but one would also need to analyze the engine's current condition and the principles of its operation. To predict a system's future, one must know not only the chronology of events that have resulted in its current condition, but its current condition and operating principles as well.

Evolutionary theory also tries (4) to plot the broad trends in the world's development. Thus, we have argued that all societies are moving toward modernization, a trend that involves many dimensions. A number of these dimensions might be summarized as different facets of a single broad trend, a trend toward a more complex and extensive society. With increased complexity (including increased differentiation and specialization of units and increased separation of cosmic and social orders), a society becomes more flexible in relating to its various environments. It is, therefore, able to adapt to a wider range of environments—conquering not only the land, the oceans, and space itself, but ultimately such environments as the human body and personality. The ability of complex societies to adapt to a wide range of environments encourages them to move into the environments of less complex societies. The result is either that the more complex societies assimilate (or destroy) their less complex neighbors or that the less complex societies assimilate the more complex patterns. Thus, all the world's societies are moving toward a uniform pattern of high complexity. Ultimately, all of these societies may unite to form a single complex and extensive society—a world society.

TOPICS FOR DISCUSSION

An evolutionary approach to anthropology has a number of advantages. It enables the anthropologist to encompass the entire range of social and cultural diversity within a single coherent scheme, to recognize processes of change responsible for the diversity, past and present, of social and cultural forms, and to perceive relationships that might otherwise be overlooked. Unfortunately, the evolutionary approach also poses problems which the student should consider along with the advantages. It forces the anthropologist to measure and compare societies in terms of standards not necessarily held by any one of them. It thus violates the doctrine of cultural relativism: that a society should be evaluated only in terms of the standards held by that society. Many anthropologists favor relativism rather than evolutionism. Has the pace of change and centralization in the contemporary world affected the viability of a relativistic perspective? The student must consider the issues involved in choosing one point of view rather than the other.

The evolutionary approach raises one fundamental question: What dimensions should be selected as constituting or defining modernity? Some prefer to give emphasis to technological dimensions, others to ideological ones. Some identify modernity with a particular institution, such as an industrial economy or a nation-state; others regard it as a quality of mind and an attitude toward the world. The selection of any dimension presupposes a conception of what modernity is. The student should be aware of the implications of selecting one set of dimensions rather than another.

NINETEENTH-CENTURY SOCIAL EVOLUTIONISTS

Social Anthropology (paperback, 1964) by E. E. Evans-Pritchard.
Chapter 2 provides a succinct summary of the ideas of some of
the early evolutionists.
The Rise of Anthropological Theory (1968) by Marvin Harris. The
most recent comprehensive history of anthropological theory.

A number of evolutionary classics have recently become available in
paperback and might be consulted for an insight into the intellectual
atmosphere in which the evolutionists worked. Note particularly the
following:

Ancient Society (originally, 1877; paperback, 1963) by Lewis Henry
Morgan.
*Ancient Law: Its Connection with the Early History of Society and
Its Relations to Modern Ideas* (originally, 1861; paperback, 1963)
by Sir Henry Maine.

RECENT SOCIAL AND CULTURAL EVOLUTIONISTS

Man Makes Himself (paperback, 1956) by V. Gordon Childe, a
seminal archaeologist.

What Happened in History (paperback, 1946) by V. Gordon Childe.

Social Evolution (paperback, 1951) by V. Gordon Childe.

The Primitive World and Its Transformations (paperback, 1953) by Robert Redfield.

Primitive Social Organization (paperback, 1962) by Elman R. Service.

The Theory of Culture Change: The Methodology of Multilineal Evolution (1955) by Julian H. Steward.

The Evolution of Culture (paperback, 1959) by Leslie A. White.

Societies: Evolutionary and Comparative Perspectives (paperback, 1966) by Talcott Parsons.

Human Societies: A New Introduction to Sociology (in press) by Gerhard Lenski.

American Sociological Review (June, 1964). This issue contains several seminal articles on social evolution, including the source for the scheme of the present book, Robert N. Bellah's "Religious Evolution."

DIFFUSIONIST THEORY

Writings of the *diffusionists,* who frequently argued against the evolutionists, usefully supplement evolutionary writings. Rather than formulate stages of development applicable to all societies of the world, the diffusionists sought to show how cultural patterns and inventions that emerged in one society spread to others.

Anthropology (1948) by Alfred L. Kroeber. Provides fascinating and readable examples in chapters 11 and 12.

The History of Ethnological Theory (1937) by Robert H. Lowie. Furnishes summaries of diffusionist theories.

Configurations of Culture Growth (1944) by Alfred L. Kroeber. Offers semi-diffusionist portrayal on the grand scale, of the rise of civilizations.

THEORY OF MODERNIZATION

Modernization and the Structure of Societies: A Setting for the Study of International Affairs (paperback, 1969) by Marion J. Levy,

Jr. Volume I, part I, chapter 1, summarizes much of Levy's theory of modernization, to which the present authors are strongly indebted.

"Social Patterns (Structures) and Problems of Modernization" (1967) by Marion J. Levy, Jr. Furnishes a brief and lucid summary of Levy's theory of modernization.

KINSHIP

Kinship and Marriage (paperback, 1967) by Robin Fox. Well-written exposition of current anthropological thought on kinship.

African Systems of Kinship and Marriage (paperback, 1950) edited by A. R. Radcliffe-Brown and Daryll Forde. A classic statement on the theory of kinship and marriage is found in the introduction.

Matrilineal Kinship (1961) edited by David M. Schneider and Kathleen Gough. General synthesis and theory on matrilineal kinship.

The Elementary Structures of Kinship (1969) by Claude Lévi-Strauss. A provocative synthesis.

Marriage, Authority, and Final Causes (1955) by George C. Homans and David M. Schneider. A vigorous attack on Lévi-Strauss's synthesis.

Structure and Sentiment (1962) by Rodney Needham. A vigorous defense of Lévi-Strauss by a rebutting of the attackers.

Social Structure (paperback, 1965) by George Peter Murdock. Statistically synthesizes a massive amount of data to produce a crude but seminal theory of kinship very different from Lévi-Strauss's.

The Human Animal (paperback, 1960) by Weston LaBarre. A suggestive and thoroughly readable psychoanalytically oriented theory of the biological, psychological, and cultural ramifications of the family pattern.

Psychological Anthropology: Approaches to Culture and Personality (1961) edited by Francis L. K. Hsu. Traces psychological implications of family patterning. See especially Hsu's and Whiting's articles.

World Revolution and Family Patterns (1963) by William J. Goode. Lucid and extensive analysis of kinship in relation to modernization.

"The Family" (1956) by Claude Lévi-Strauss.

"The Future of Kinship Studies" (1965) by Claude Lévi-Strauss.

"The Structure of Unilineal Descent Groups" (1953) by Meyer Fortes.

Schism and Continuity in an African Society (1957) by Victor Turner. One of the best analyses of a matrilineal society.

The Nuer (1940) by E. E. Evans-Pritchard. Classic analysis of a patrilineal society.

Kinship and Marriage Among the Nuer (1951) by E. E. Evans-Pritchard. Extends the classic analysis of patrilineal society.

The Javanese Family: A Study of Kinship and Socialization (1961) by Hildred Geertz. Analysis of the bilineal family in a complex modernizing society.

Honour, Family, and Patronage (1964) by John K. Campbell. A powerful and impressively written analysis of the bilineal family system of a tribal ethnic minority in contemporary Greece.

The Family Revolution in Modern China (paperback, 1968) by Marion J. Levy, Jr. Outstanding analysis of changes taking place in a family-centered, unilineal, large-scale society.

American Kinship: A Cultural Account (paperback, 1968) by David M. Schneider. A succinct but sophisticated exposition of the patterning of American kinship.

The Developmental Cycle in Domestic Groups (1958) edited by Jack Goody. A collection of articles analyzing the dynamics of family life in several societies.

ECONOMICS

Economic Anthropology (paperback, 1965) by Melville J. Herskovits. An extensive if naive treatment of the role of culture in primitive economic life.

Primitive Polynesian Economics (1939) by Raymond Firth. A classic of economic anthropology.

Peasant Marketing in Java (1962) by Alice G. Dewey. An informative study of small-town economics.

Peddlers and Princes: Social Change and Economic Modernization in Two Indonesian Towns (paperback, 1963) by Clifford Geertz. Compares the role of Javanese Muslim traders and Balinese Hindu nobles in Indonesian economic modernization.

The Gift: Forms and Functions of Exchange in Archaic Societies (paperback, 1967) by Marcel Mauss. A classic analysis of the cultural implications of exchange among primitive and archaic peoples.

Social Anthropology (1963) by Paul J. Bohannan. Contains a good summary of primitive economics.

POLITICS AND GOVERNMENT

African Political Systems (1940) edited by M. Fortes and E. E. Evans-Pritchard. The classic British social-anthropological view of tribes without rulers. See especially the introduction.

Tribes Without Rulers (1958) edited by John Middleton and David Tait. Treats six African "stateless" societies.

Bantu Bureaucracy (paperback, 1965) by Lloyd Fallers. Applies some of Max Weber's categories in a careful analysis of a nonmodern governmental system.

Political Systems of Highland Burma (paperback, 1965) by Edmund Leach. Brilliant analysis of the dynamics of political and social change.

The Politics of Modernization (paperback, 1965) by David Apter. A turgidly written—yet brilliantly argued—analysis of the major changes occurring as tribal and other nonmodern societies modernize. It builds on more restricted anthropological studies of tribal politics.

LAW

The Law of Primitive Man: A Study in Comparative Legal Dynamics (paperback, 1968) by E. Adamson Hoebel. Provides a general theory of law in primitive society.

Justice and Judgement Among the Tiv (1957) by Paul J. Bohannan.

The Judicial Process Among the Barotse of Northern Rhodesia (1955) by Max Gluckman.

The Ideas in Barotse Jurisprudence (1965) by Max Gluckman.

The Cheyenne Way: Conflict and Case Law in Primitive Jurisprudence (1941) by Karl N. Llewellyn and E. Adamson Hoebel.

TECHNOLOGY AND SOCIOCULTURAL CHANGE

Power and Privilege: A Theory of Social Stratification (1966) by
    Gerhard Lenski. Broad correlations of technological changes with
    sociocultural changes extending from primitive to industrial
    society.
*The Theory of Culture Change: The Methodology of Multilineal Evo-
    lution* (1955) by Julian H. Steward. Correlation of technological
    and sociocultural change primarily at the primitive level.
Medieval Technology and Social Change (paperback, 1962) by Lynn
    White, Jr. Fascinating analysis of a historic case.
The Rise of Anthropological Theory (1968) by Marvin Harris. Lists
    numerous works that correlate sociocultural evolution with techno-
    environmental development and presents extensive and lively
    argument in favor of emphasizing the latter factor.

FILMS

Although modernization is too broad a process to film *in toto,* several
films dramatize specific confrontations that flow from modernization.

The Exiles. Portrays the night life of three young Indian men who
    have left the reservation to live in Los Angeles.
Fincho. Depicts the penetration of Western technology and capitalism
    into a remote Nigerian village.
Trobriand Islanders. Might be of interest since the Trobrianders are
    used as illustration in this chapter.

3

Primitive society and culture

THE AUSTRALIAN ABORIGINES

Examples of primitive society and culture, the Australian aborigines were branded by early anthropologists as the most backward of peoples.* Although they are only hunters and gatherers possessing a simple set of tools—basically, the digging stick, the boomerang, the spear, the spear thrower, the stone axe, the fire-making stick, the wooden or stone chisel, and the stone knife—the aborigines have managed to survive in a desert that has strained the endurance of well-equipped European expeditions. The aborigine's sensitivity to natural signs and seasons is the basis of his survival ability. The aborigine does not place equipment between himself and nature; he approaches his surroundings in a direct manner that yields him a precise and intimate knowledge of nature. He is a man to whom the rising of Orion early on a June morning reveals that dingo pups are being born in secluded places and may be sought for food, to whom the yellow flowers of the wattle tree signify that magpie geese will be flying along certain routes where they can be stunned by thrown sticks. He can track wallabies, scrub turkeys, or men with an uncanny skill.

Despite his knowledge of nature, however, the aborigine has never practiced agriculture or animal husbandry. Because of primitive technology and the absence of agriculture, the aboriginal population has never been great—even though aborigines have probably roamed the Australian continent for more than ten thousand years.

* Although many contemporary aborigines have settled near missions and ranches as hired sheepherders, or have taken other jobs (the current bantamweight boxing champion of the world, Lionel Rose, is an aborigine), some still follow a mode of life similar to that of the past, and we shall write as if all did. That is, we shall follow the anthropological convention of writing in the ethnographic present.

Aboriginal culture is of course much more complex than we portray it here. Considering both the complexity of the society and the diversity of anthropological interpretations, we have chosen mainly to follow the generalized synthesis of A. P. Elkin, *The Australian Aborigines*.

It has been estimated that when the first British colonists appeared in 1788, fewer than 300,000 aborigines (divided into about 500 separate tribes) existed. A recent census counted only about 50,000 full-blood and 40,000 mixed-blood aborigines. On the basis of technology it is certainly legitimate to classify the aborigines as primitive. It is equally legitimate on the basis of their social organization, although aboriginal social patterns are quite complex and ingenious.

Social organization

Anthropologists have commonly classified the aborigines into tribes ranging from 100 to 1,500 members. Each tribe usually has its own language or dialect, its own territory, its own customs, and its own name. Not every tribe possesses a name, however, and some tribes, such as the Murngin of northeast Arnhem Land, are vague about their territorial boundaries. A reason for this vagueness, which is characteristic not only of the aborigines but also of other primitive groups, is a low degree of bureaucratization and centralization. Indeed, the aborigines lack a king or even a chief. Authority among them is vested in elders of patrilocal groups. A tribe—which seldom if ever functions in concert except on ceremonial occasions—is basically a confederation of these patrilocal groups, and the bonds that unite the groups are those of myth or ceremony and of kinship or marriage.

Aboriginal notions of owning a territory differ fundamentally from modern concepts of ownership. In contemporary Western societies land can be bought, rented, or sold. Land is *alienable*— it is an object to be disposed of by the owner in whatever fashion best suits his purpose. By contrast, the aborigine is not so much master of his land as his land is master of him. Aboriginal tribal territory "owns" the tribe as much as the tribe owns the territory. So strong is the bond between a tribesman and his tribal territory that it can never be severed. Its power issues from the mythical significance of the land itself. A tribe's territory is rich with memories of heroes and ancestors who dwelt in the mythical "Dreamtime." Tribal mythology associates each detail of the landscape with some adventure or some creation of its heroes and ancestors: at this pile of stones an ancestor rested while on a journey, at that waterhole a hero created a new rite of fertility. Each site and each hero possesses and is possessed by a particular tribe. Since the aborigine is born into his tribe and thus cannot sever his bond to it, neither can he sever his bond to the land and its myths. Because tribe, person, myth, and land are joined in one enduring relationship, wars of territorial conquest have no meaning in aboriginal society.

Intertribal relations, too, are sanctioned by mythology. An aboriginal coalition of tribes is not a nation, for it possesses no central government or leader. Meetings among tribes, when they occur, are arranged and managed by the elders of the various tribes. (The kind of centralization in which there is an intertribal chief is found in archaic societies such as those of the Near East, Africa, Asia, and Polynesia.) Intertribal meetings among the aborigines are important, for it is at these gatherings that customs are exchanged and myths jointly celebrated. Thus, a number of tribes in northeastern South Australia convene to celebrate the adventures of mythical heroes known as *mura mura,* in whom they collectively believe; by such celebration the well-being of each tribe will be assured. But no single tribe can "own" the whole mythical cycle; each tribe can be responsible for only a particular portion or phase. One myth, for example, is reported to be "seven hundred miles long"—a tale of heroic adventures ranging over a territory seven hundred miles in length. The telling of such a myth requires the cooperation of all the tribes residing within this area. Since each tribe "owns" part of the seven-hundred mile adventure, the whole story can be told only if all tribes are present.

More important to the aborigine than his tribe is his patrilocal group, for in this group he spends most of his time. The group is also patrilineal, tracing its ancestry through males descended from particular ancestors who lived within a particular locale; an aborigine's grandfather, father, brother, son, and grandson—all would be proper members of his patrilocal, patrilineal group.

Comparing the role of kinship in aboriginal society with its role in American society will demonstrate the great importance of kinship to the aborigine. Most Americans do not bother to trace their kinship network beyond the most immediate family, perhaps including first or second cousins. Among aborigines—where the patrilineal, patrilocal group is the main unit of social life—relationships will be carefully traced throughout the community and even beyond the borders of the tribe. All social relations among aborigines must be kinship relations; an aborigine does not know how to act toward a stranger until he has discovered how the other is kin to him. It has been said that if such kinship could not be discovered—or fabricated, as when a European is adopted as brother—the stranger would have to be killed. There is simply no way for an aborigine to deal with a nonkinsman.

In modern society, individuals tend to relate to one another *universalistically* (on the basis of what each can do), rather than *particularistically* (on the basis of kinship). Most modern relationships are governed by such considerations as "This person is selling what I want to buy," or "This person can flunk me," or "This person must be treated politely because all people should be treated politely." Most primitive relationships, such as those among the aborigines, are guided by a single consideration: "This person is kin to me in a particular way, therefore, I must treat him in a particular way."

The principle that each kinship relationship is associated with a particular set of rules specifying how the kinsmen should interact is revealed in avoidance customs. Aborigines taking food at a mission station will face in all directions, instead of sitting face to face and chatting as Americans might do under similar circumstances. Some will sit back to back, neither speaking to nor looking at one another. Or sometimes the group will split into two segments with no conversational exchange. These arrangements conform with precise rules stating that persons related in certain ways must avoid one another. This avoidance does not signify hatred or dislike, but rather the great respect one kinsman holds for the other. Thus, the aboriginal man must avoid his mother-in-law because "She is the greatest friend I have, for she has provided me with a wife." Similarly, a man must demonstrate respect for his wife's mother's brother by avoiding him, because, by custom, it is he who helps arrange the marriage of the man's niece. Nor are such avoidances restricted to in-laws. In some tribes, brothers and sisters, once childhood has passed, must face in opposite directions when they converse—a custom linked to the taboo against incest.

Although these avoidance customs spring from diverse conditions and serve varied functions, all of them work chiefly to preserve the intricate aboriginal kinship network. In the modern community, where people are usually unrelated, a fight between kinsmen will not throw the entire community into turmoil; but in the primitive community, where kinship is pervasive, a fight among kin could be disastrous. By decreeing that relatives with a high potential for tension between them must avoid each other, these customs help stabilize the primitive community.

Just as aboriginal kinship determines avoidances, it also determines alliances, especially by marriage. Moderns tend to view marriage as a matter of individual choice based on romantic love; but for aborigines, it is kinship more than affection that determines the marriage partner, and thus determines which families become bound together as in-laws or affines. The marrying couple have little to say about their own marriage. Kinship rules often specify the kinship the two mates should or must hold to one another; hence a mate selection is limited to persons who fall within the proper kinship category. The marriage will probably be arranged by senior kinsmen of the couple's local groups. Infant betrothal is common. One set of relatives may promise a daughter to the son of another set even before the two spouses-to-be are born; under these circumstances the wishes of the spouses count less than the kinship bonds between the two in-law groups. Since the groups are already kin, the marriage is a handy way of perpetuating and strengthening the existing bond. In some respects aboriginal marriage resembles a system common to European royalty: the son of one king marries the daughter of another king who is already a relative of the first, thereby strengthening the ties between the two royal houses and between the nations they rule. However, not all Europeans marry in this way, while traditionally *all* aborigines do.

It has recently been suggested that the many complex types of aborigine marriage systems should be understood as variations of a basic pattern of sister exchange between groups. From this perspective, marriage among the aborigines is interpreted as an attempt by men of two or more groups to marry each other's sisters. (Of course, since aborigines use classificatory kinship terminology, any woman born into a man's local group might be classed as his "sister.") After two groups have exchanged sisters for several generations, men from one group actually are marrying their cousins from the other group. A man marries his father's sister's daughter or his mother's brother's daughter, and these might be precisely the same person. Such cousins are called cross cousins, that is, children of siblings of the opposite sex (mother's brother's daughter and father's sister's son) to distinguish them from parallel cousins, who are children of siblings of the same sex (father's brother's daughter and mother's sister's son). Among the aborigines, where descent is reckoned patrilineally, parallel cousins would be members of the same patrilineal group. Because of the incest taboo which prohibits members of the same patrilineal, patrilocal group from marrying, marriage among parallel cousins is forbidden. The system just described is known as the Kariera System, after the aboriginal tribe of that name which furnishes the best known example of its practice.

The Kariera System can also be viewed as involving two large unilineal descent groups, or clans, whose members are divided into various local groups. Each local group is a smaller unilineal descent group, or *lineage*. Let us label the two clans A and B. The lineages composing each clan are A_1, A_2, A_3, A_4, and B_1, B_2, B_3, B_4, B_5. All the males of clan A remain in place, whereas all the females of clan A ("sisters" of the A men) are given to males of clan B as wives. Similarly, the female B's are given to the male A's as wives, while the clan B males stay in place. Any clan A male can take his wife from any one of the several B's (B_1, B_2, B_3, B_4, or B_5), and any clan B male can take his wife from any one of the several A's. A set of such marriage exchanges might, then, take the form shown in the diagram.[1] So long as these exchanges of women continue, and so long as no A men marry A women or B men marry B women, a man will always marry a woman who is his cross cousin, or of the same kinship type as his cross cousin. His female parallel cousins are members of his own clan and are, therefore, unavailable.

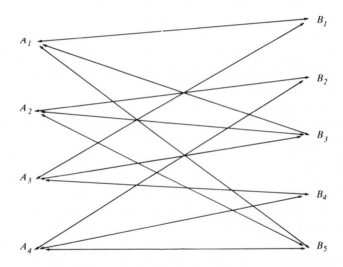

Any number of mind-bending elaborations on this system can be found among the aborigines. As these systems become more complicated, more and more distinctions are recognized, with the result that the category of kinsman whom one can or cannot marry becomes more and more clearly defined. The essential point, however, is that all of these systems subordinate the sentiments of the individual to the kinship rules of the group. Individual freedom is small, and choice is dictated by particularistic fiat.

The local group is, as we have noted, composed of persons related to one another patrilineally, so the ordinary aborigine belongs to and lives in one group with his father, his father's father, his sons, and his sons' sons. Since aborigines deny the male's physiological contribution to procreation, they cite a nongenealogical reason for a person's local group membership. They believe that a person's spirit exists in a given locale long before the person—or even the person's father—is born. Should the father happen to be in that locale, and should he dream that the person's spirit enters his wife's womb, she will conceive and the person will be born—the spirit is incarnated as a child. The child is then bound to the locale where the dream occurred, for it is in that locale that the child's spirit pre-existed, and since the dream usually occurs in the territory of the father's local group—the territory where he spends his time—it usually happens that the child is bound to the same territory as his father.

The aborigines believe, too, that a person must return before death to the place where his spirit preexisted. Should he die in a different place, his spirit would become lost and, wandering in anger and despair, might inflict pain on the living. The aborigine, there-fore, tries to remain near the place where his spirit preexisted. Obviously this hampers his spatial mobility. Contrast this to the Christian belief in Heaven. Heaven is located above the earth, not on any particular earthly spot. Accordingly, the Christian's soul can enter Heaven no matter where he is when he dies, and his spatial mobility is not limited by his belief—a situation that works to encourage the spread of modern, Christian patterns, as opposed to the primitive, aboriginal ones.

The aborigine is also affiliated with a nonlocal descent group. This group is matrilineal. One is allied to such a matrilineal group through one's bond to one's mother, mother's mother, and other kin traced through one's mother. Since women move out of the patrilocal groups into which they were born in order to live with their husbands (who stay fixed to the patrilocal groups into which they were born), it is likely that persons related through a common matrilineal bond will live in different places. Thus, the matrilineal clan is not localized. Although matrilineal kinsmen may be scattered, they consider themselves spiritually connected; the bond that unites them is symbolized by their totem.

Totemism and totemic cults

Members of an aboriginal group profess kinship not simply to one another, but also to one or more animal or vegetable species—the kangaroo or emu, or the lowly witchety grub—known as the group's totem. A patrilineal or matrilineal group's totem is called its flesh or meat, as well as its guardian, friend, or kinsman. When an aborigine states that the woolly-butt tree, his totem, is his uncle, he refuses to draw the modern distinction between men and nature; he counts the tree in the same class as a human. An aborigine should not kill, injure, or eat his group's totem, and since all who share the same totem share the same flesh, they must not intermarry. Union of the same flesh is incest.

Although both patrilocal groups and matrilineal groups among the aborigines have totems, it is in the patrilocal groups, where the totemic bond is reinforced by co-residence based on the notion of preexisting spirits, that totemic cult life is most intense. Each local group maintains a cult "lodge," composed of the fully initiated male members of the group. This "lodge" serves to preserve the group's portion of the tribal totemic myth, to celebrate its rituals, to guard its sacred totemic sites, and to perform rites that will encourage fecundity in the group's totemic species.

Located along paths that cross the territory of each local group are special sites where mythical heroes accomplished the feats celebrated in tribal mythology. As birds and animals, humans bearing animal and bird names, or animals and birds who talk like humans, these mythical figures are totems as well as heroes. Members of the local cult lodges adorn themselves with painted designs denoting attributes of their totem-hero; and in order to instill his image in the minds of the younger men, they ritually dramatize his adventures.

Not only do ceremonies performed at sites sanctified by the totem-heroes seek to stimulate the totem species to multiply, but they are also meant to assure that nature will sustain her proper order. Certain natural phenomena are associated with each totem—with the crow, lightning, thunder, rain, clouds, hail, and winter; with the cockatoo, the moon and stars. Each group must order its own part of the cosmos by performing ceremonies so that the entire universe will maintain harmony.

A totemic system thus forms a classification scheme in which each entity has its place. The cosmos is conceived as a set of categories each of which is composed of a particular cluster of animals, plants, and celestial bodies, all linked to a particular group and its territory. Should new elements appear, they can simply be inserted into one of these categories. When European sailors came to Australia, they were categorized along with other totems as belonging to a particular totemic cluster. The appearance of new elements does not require rearrangement of the scheme; it is loose enough already so that anything new can be incorporated into it. Looseness is in fact one feature distinguishing the totemic scheme from scientific theory—unlike scientific theory, the totemic scheme cannot be refuted by the appearance of new evidence. The totemic scheme is also distinct from a theology. No group "owns" the whole scheme, and no group regards its part as monopolizing truth. The concept of religious conversion therefore makes little sense to the aborigine. In the totemic view, it makes more sense for all groups to cooperate —through ceremony and rite—in a joint effort to order the cosmos.

The Dreaming and the secret life [2]

Totemism cannot be understood without some comprehension of a remarkable concept, which the aborigines call "The Dreaming."

The Dreaming is a sacred, heroic time of long ago, when man and nature came to be as they are today. But neither time nor history in the Western sense is implied by The Dreaming. The aborigines possess no word for time as an abstract idea, and The Dreaming does not denote a golden age located in some definite past epoch. One cannot fix The Dreaming in time and history—instead, "It was, and is, everywhen." [3]

Just as an aborigine's dreams by night affect his life by day, as when a father's dream causes a child's birth, so does The Dreaming mix with the aborigine's life. Indeed, dreaming—in our sense of the word—is important during aboriginal rites, for in these dreams the natives imagine themselves to be heroes of The Dreaming. Thus they merge within their own personalities the Dream-time and the here-and-now.

The Dreaming is a cosmogony—an account of the creation of the universe—and it is also a cosmology—a theory of how what was created became an orderly system. Great marvels are revealed and portrayed in accounts of The Dreaming: how fire and water were stolen and recaptured; how men erred and now their descendants must die for it; how certain customs and taboos were instituted; how tribes and clans were divided up; how marriage, exogamy, and sister exchange came to be. The aborigines believe that as life was created in The Dream-time, so it must exist today and through eternity. The Dreaming still exists, life still conforms to the eternal mold, life is therefore a "one possibility thing." [4]

Unlike the Christian's Kingdom of God and Kingdom of Man, The Dreaming and life are considered one. The Dreaming is no celestial realm that floats above life; it is like a fluid that seeps into life. Nor are heroes of The Dreaming, such as Biame and Darumlum, gods separated from the daily world by their superhuman powers and positions. They are simply heroes—manlike, not godlike, bound by bonds of kinship to the tribes and local groups which perpetuate them by rites and myths of The Dreaming.

Perceiving no clear distinction between the ideal world of The Dreaming and the actual world of real life, the aborigine feels no need for saints or illuminati to mediate between the ideal and the actual. Nor is there a need for prophets, an Isaiah or an Amos, to castigate men when they deviate from the ideal. For when ideal and actual are one, there can be no deviation. In the absence of a separate ideal world against which to compare, judge, and censure the actual world, there can be no mood of criticism, pessimism, dynamism, no craving for reform. The Dreaming has happened, and everyday life *is* The Dreaming. The mold for life is set.

In the West, much creative energy pours into the formulation of ideal worlds—theologies, ideologies, theories. But the aborigines, undistracted by ideal philosophical orders, concentrate on the living social order. Instead of abstract theories, the aborigines produce systems of social permutation and combination, with highly complex rules to decree who shall marry whom. These impressive products of the savage intellect inspired Claude Lévi-Strauss to write:

> . . . few civilizations seem to equal the Australians in their taste for erudition and speculation and what sometimes looks like intellectual dandyism, odd as this expression may appear when it is applied to people with so rudimentary a level of material life. But lest there be any mistake about it: these shaggy and corpulent savages whose physical resemblance to adipose bureaucrats or veterans of the Empire makes their nudity yet more incongruous . . . were [intellectual] snobs. . . .[5]

Within their complex systems of kinship the aborigines have arranged facets of nature which, to modern man, are independent of the social order and have no place in it. It would be as if we were to believe that the chordates are mystically linked to the upper classes of society, the arthropods to the middle classes, and the coelenterates to the lower; or that Protestants could be identified with worms, snails, and clams, Catholics with reptiles, fish, and mammals, and the Jews with birds, spiders, and squids. Obviously, the zoological schemes of the West bear no direct connection to social divisions as they do in an aboriginal totemic zoology—no species is the kin or the property of any social group. Similarly, there is a great difference in the concept of time. For the West, time is an abstraction, detached from any group or social phase, yet a framework in which all groups and social phases can be classified. For the aborigine time is generational and social—a staircase proceeding through a genealogical family tree.

In sum, the aborigines illustrate clearly the primitive fusion of ideal and actual, of cosmic and social, and because of this fusion there can be no saints, no prophets, no God, and no Heaven. Nor is there a secular equivalent of Heaven, a Great Society, or a socialist utopia, for the ideal is the actual and the cosmic is the social. Surely it is no accident that through study of the aborigines, Emile Durkheim was led to conclude that religion and society are one.

Although the aborigines have fused the sacred and the secular to a great extent, they have not done so completely. While The Dreaming permeates all life, it is most concentrated in the "secret life"—and the secret life, in turn, focuses on the initiation of youth into manhood.

Now and again, at special times, a group separates itself from the world of hunting and gathering and goes in search of the secret life. It makes a camp, where the women remain, while the men proceed to a remote and concealed site. There, in touch with the heroes and ancestors of The Dreaming, the men remain for hours, days, weeks, even months, singing and performing rites that are considered potent not only in their effects on the surroundings but on the participants as well. Indeed, the youths who share in these rites display profound changes of personality. Missionaries lament that even those who were raised in the missions are so altered by tribal initiation that they abandon the church entirely. They are lost from Christianity to the secret life which leads toward The Dreaming.

During the course of the rites a youth passes through several phases. In one region (the Broome-Sunday Island district) the youth must complete eight phases, few of which he regards as unalloyed pleasure. He begins as Leminem; then, at the end of the week, when several of his teeth have been knocked out, he is known as Lainyar. A few days later he is circumcised and becomes Palil. With this he is made privy to a few tribal secrets. Later he is taken through an important blood ceremony. He is now Djainanga and is fit to receive deeper revelations. Some weeks or months later, when his blood is drunk by elders from a vein opened in his arm, he is Gambel. And still later, when a bird wing is inserted in his head band, he is Rungor. With the placing of a pearl-shell pendant around his neck, he becomes Bungin. Finally, when he is admitted to the ranks of married men, he is ceremonially painted and becomes known as Mambangan. He is now a man and he comprehends some of the mysteries of The Dreaming.

All aborigine initiation rites proceed from a point when the novice is removed from camp, the women screaming and pretending to resist his abduction, on through the period of bodily operations to a time of seclusion, and finally into a stage when the secrets are revealed. During the latter period the neophyte learns the myths of The Dreaming heroes and is taught of their holiness. He is shown sacred objects such as the bull-roarer—a large wooden cylinder which, when swung by a cord, produces a roar frightening to the uninitiated: the "voice" of the sky-heroes and the totemic ancestors. Such consecrated objects, kept in secret storehouses and handled only with the permission of the elders, live close to the Dream-time. By touching and caressing them, the newly initiated youth is automatically transported back into the time of The Dreaming. He becomes part of the hallowed life of the heroes. In some tribes he is given his own object to bind him to his own alter ego or "secret sharer," in Joseph Conrad's sense—a Dream-period hero with whom the youth spends much time in the venerated storehouse. A new name, possibly that of the secret sharer, is bestowed on the youth, a name so revered and so private that it is never uttered except as a whisper in the sacred area. "It is indeed a password into the eternal, unseen world of ancestral and totemic heroes." [6]

Another rite weaving the here-and-now into the eternal Dreaming is the increase rite, meant to insure that the totemic species will multiply. Myths of The Dreaming tell how a hero created ceremonies to cause some species to multiply. Perhaps the hero left behind him, as a storehouse for the life and spirit of the species, a stone. Thus a spiritual power can be released even today by a rite performed near that stone, a sacrament of The Dreaming. At the site of the stone one commands: "Let there be plenty of kangaroos, here and there," or one takes powdered stone from the sacred place, mixes it with blood, and deposits it wherever he wants, or expects, the multiplication to occur. By such incantations and acts, the natives intend to excite a transfer of spiritual power from the stone to the land. The kangaroo spirits or images, imprisoned in the stone, are thereby set free and come forth incarnated as live animals.

Not control of nature by magic but cooperation with nature is the intent of the increase rites. They guide, direct, and inspire nature at just those seasons when an increase of the species is most propitious. Ritual actors do not see themselves as the operative cause of an increase in species; instead it is through the rite that they express their wish for it to happen and provide the animating force of the species with an opportunity to take flesh. Such a conception reflects a close mesh between seen and unseen; man's role is to unleash the unseen, The Dreaming, in his own space and his own time, here and now.

This presentation of aboriginal existence has perhaps exaggerated the dominance of kinship and the unity of cosmic and social, but it is precisely these features that contrast most strikingly with modern ones, and our concern is with such contrasts. One final contrast, implied all along, can be summarized in the notion expressed by Lévi-Strauss, that aboriginal society is "cold" and modern society is "hot." [7] Aboriginal mythology ignores change, while modern "mythology" is eager—perhaps overeager—to recognize change. Among the aborigines, men die and children are born, patterns of settlement alter, modes of food-getting shift; but such changes in

life are perceived as constancy because life is The Dreaming and
The Dreaming is constant. Life is perceived as static—"cold." According to modern Western concepts of history, on the other hand,
life is in flux; we greet even a hint of change in politics, business,
or society as "news." Life is perceived as active—"hot." But to
say that aboriginal life is perceived as cold, modern life perceived
as hot, is not to say that aboriginal life is changeless. However,
the aborigine's "cold" mythology probably makes him less ready
than the modern man to exploit change when it does occur.

SOUTHEAST ASIAN HILL TRIBES

Although most of the traits peculiar to primitive society are exemplified by the Australian aborigines, some are more vividly displayed by—or have been more carefully studied in—other primitive
societies. Certain facets of marriage, incest taboos, and cosmology
are better illustrated by numerous Southeast Asian hill tribes.

In this case the designation *primitive* is applied to societies technologically further advanced than the hunting-and-gathering aborigines. The hill tribes practice a form of agriculture known as
"slash and burn"; that is, unlike the aborigines, the hill tribes are
food-producing, rather than food-gathering. Aboriginal increase
rites might be regarded as an attempt at food-producing, but it is
plain that the hill tribes' techniques of slashing, burning, and planting are more efficient. Not only technologically but also socially
the hill tribes' patterning is more complex than that of the aborigines. The hill tribes distinguish clearly between aristocrats and commoners, and they have chiefs.

Circulating connubium

In chapter 2 we discussed the Trobriand *kula* ring, where goods of
one kind (necklaces) were exchanged for goods of another kind

(bracelets), the necklaces moving in one direction around the circle, the bracelets in the opposite direction. The hill tribes also engage in a circular system of exchange, but besides goods they exchange women. This system is called *circulating connubium*. It can be depicted, if somewhat simplistically, in the following way.*

Imagine three unilineal descent groups (which in actuality may be localized subdivisions of clans, but which we shall call simply clans), labeled *A, B,* and *C.* The clan *A* males remain where they are (the clan is patrilocal), and the females marry out of the clan's village to males of clan *B.* Since *B* males remain in their own locale, the *A* females must move in with them at marriage. Then, females born into clan *B* marry males from clan *C,* who of course remain where they are to receive them. Finally, females from clan *C* marry males from clan *A,* and the circle of movement through *A, B,* and *C* is completed. In practice there are often more than three clans (or subclans), but there cannot be fewer. Circulating connubium is thus more complex than the sister exchange of the aborigines, which involves only two groups.

Counterbalancing the movement of women in one direction is a movement of goods in both directions. Whenever a clan receives a wife it acknowledges its "inferiority" to the wife-giving clan by presenting goods and services to that clan. The wife-receiving clan may pay a bride-price of meats or chickens, knives or guns, rice beer, and gongs. In return for these "masculine" goods, it receives "feminine" goods such as cloth, a loom, brass plates, and baskets—gifts that accompany the bride to her new home.

---

* This analysis follows that of Rodney Needham, *Structure and Sentiment,* pp. 74–100. Although Needham's analysis has been harshly criticized (see Marvin Harris, *The Rise of Anthropological Theory,* pp. 506–512, for a summary of and references to the major critiques), its problems do not seriously affect the schematic picture we present here. The thrust of most criticism has been to show that numerous Purum marriages do not follow the circulating connubium pattern. It remains true, however, that circulating connubium is a highly valued ideal pattern for the Purum and that significant ceremonies, symbols, and important members of the society do conform to this pattern.

The hill tribes coin words to distinguish wife-giving clans and wife-receiving clans from one's own clan. Thus, among the Purum, an "old Kuki" tribe of Manipur living on the eastern border of India, the clan from which one's own clan receives wives is known as *pu,* whereas the clan to which wives are given is known as *tu.* Among the Kachin of Burma,[8] the equivalent of *pu* is *mayu,* and that of *tu* is *dama.* (The Kachin also recognize another set of groups, the *lawulahta*—kinsmen who are potentially but not presently either *mayu* or *dama.*)

How does one distinguish his *pu* from his *tu?* The rule of thumb is that a man should take his bride from the group to which his mother belongs. That group is his *pu.* A man's daughter should be given as a bride to the same group that took his sister as a bride. That group is his *tu.* A clan's alliance to its *pu* or *tu* persists for several generations, and in time it works out that a man's wife is always his mother's brother's daughter or a woman classified in the same category as his mother's brother's daughter. Because a man is thus required to wed a woman fitting the category of cross cousin on his mother's side, and is forbidden to wed his cross cousin on his father's side, the marriage system found among the hill tribes (as well as in other regions, such as Siberia or Bolivia) is called *matrilateral cross-cousin marriage.* In such a system, to marry one's patrilateral cross cousin would be to take a wife from a clan to which one's clan is obligated to give wives—to reverse the direction of circulation of women and goods—a taboo action regarded as sorcery or incest.

Why matrilateral cross-cousin marriage is encouraged and patrilateral cross-cousin marriage is forbidden has excited much ingenious analysis,[9] but the point we wish to emphasize is that matrilateral cross-cousin marriage, like aboriginal sister exchange, illustrates the importance of kinship in primitive society. Again, it is kinship that prescribes whom one should marry. Kinship controls marriage just as it controls so many other aspects of primitive life.

Incest taboo

Prescriptions of whom one should marry in a system of circulating connubium are balanced by proscriptions on whom one should not marry. One proscription is the incest taboo. The incest taboo among the hill tribes forbids one to marry within one's local kinship group. One must go outside the group for a spouse, a requirement that is useful for hill tribe society. The Southeast Asian hills are sparsely populated, and with no central government to unite the scattered groups, far-flung alliances of kinship and marriage encouraged by the taboo against marrying within the local group are useful integrating bonds. The incest taboo helps integrate the scattered local groups into a more or less unified society.

The incest taboo has long been regarded as a distinctly human custom. If animals may be designated as *natural,* and if men may be called *cultured,* then the incest taboo may be defined as a cultural rule created by men to curtail their natural urges to copulate with anyone of the opposite sex whether he be kinsman or not—urges which animals do not curtail. The cultural basis of the incest taboo is not always recognized by modern men; more often it is seen in a biological or genetic light as a way to avoid inbreeding and thus to minimize the incidence of feeble-minded children. Of course this particular interpretation cannot account for the hill tribes taboo against marriage to one's patrilateral cross cousin. After all, the rule does not prohibit marriage to one's matrilateral cross cousin, and this is as much a form of biological inbreeding as is the other. Folklore often recognizes the cultural basis of the incest taboo. In a Moroccan story a man turns into a monkey because he has had incestuous relations with his sister and has indulged in other anticultural activities such as copulating during the Muslim fast month, urinating in milk, and wiping himself with bread after defecating.[10] Here folk wisdom emphasizes that incest taboo is a trait of cultured humans rather than of natural animals.

The taboo on incest within the immediate family is one of the few known cultural universals. There is no society that allows fathers to mate with daughters, mothers with sons, or brothers with sisters unless, being of royalty, they enjoy the perquisites of a nearly god-like status. But in addition to the universal taboo on incest within the immediate family, there often exists in primitive societies (but rarely in modern societies) an incest taboo that extends far beyond the immediate family to distant cousins, as in the hill tribes' taboo on patrilateral cross-cousin marriage.

Perhaps the universal taboo on incest within the immediate family and the primitive taboo on incest among distant kin serve different functions. The wider taboo aids the integration of primitive societies such as the Purum, but the narrower taboo, found in modern as well as in primitive society, serves a nurturing function rather than a political function. If fathers openly lusted after their daughters or mothers after their sons, they would be distracted from the nurturing duties of parenthood. The incest taboo prevents such distraction, and thus helps the modern family to fulfill practically the only function it still retains: raising its children.

Not only is the incest taboo more extensive in primitive society than in modern society, primitives and moderns also differ in their attitudes toward it. First, primitives appear more preoccupied with incest if we judge from their mythology. Primitive mythology is permeated by the incest motif; in modern literature it is rare. Second, primitives seem to view incest in a more institutional fashion; among moderns it is viewed more psychologically. A theme common in primitive mythology is the founding of a tribe by a brother and a sister who married each other. When modern literature treats the topic of incest, it dwells more on sexual and emotional attraction and less on such institutional outcomes as the establishment of a family or society. In *The Sound and the Fury,* although brother and sister are attracted to each other, they never marry. Faulkner's concern was not with institutional consequences of incestuous feelings, but with the feelings themselves.

The contrast between these two treatments of incest may also reflect general differences between primitive and modern societies. In modern society, incest is part of the Freudian oedipus complex; involving intimate, unconscious emotions that flourish within the privacy of the nuclear household, it is ordinarily expressed only in fiction or confessed to the psychiatrist. In primitive society, incest is of public concern—it is a crime that threatens the integration of society itself. The emotions that surround it are codified into myths, known to all, that commemorate the founding of the society. Like other institutions, the patterns of incest and incest taboo reflect the minor role that kinship plays in modern society, by contrast with its major role in primitive society.

Cosmology

Incest, marriage, and religion are for the hill tribes a single complex. Consider the case of the Purum. Among the Purum, when a man wishes to arrange a marriage between his son and a maiden whose clan occupies the appropriate *pu* status, he takes a gift of rice beer to the girl's father. At the wedding he again gives the *pu* father rice beer along with meat. In both instances the *tu* man's gift to the *pu* father symbolizes the latter's superiority of status; by his actions toward *pu, tu* recapitulates the veneration expected of an inferior mortal to the superior spirits. Should *pu* accept the beer and meat— thus acknowledging the inferiority of *tu*—he gives *tu* his daughter as a bride, together with her feminine goods. Thus, the superior group receives masculine goods (beer and meat) and gives feminine goods to the inferior group.

This exchange is only one of many that symbolize the contrast between *pu* and *tu* categories. Other categories holding similar contrastive significance are the following: [11]

tu is associated with	*pu* is associated with
wife-taker	wife-giver
inferior	superior
mortals	gods
below	above
female	male
earth	sky
west	east
left	right
back	front
death	life
even	odd
profane	sacred
forest (jungle)	village
famine	prosperity

From this list emerges an image of the Purum conception of the cosmos. *Pu* is associated with one section of the cosmos, *tu* with another, and together they represent the total cosmos. Therefore, if *pu* and *tu* properly order their relations to each other, the cosmos will be ordered; and if the *pu/tu* alliance is sustained for generations, it will come to represent the enduring alliance of the two halves of the cosmos. Obviously in such a society incest is serious. When a man obtains a wife from his *tu* instead of from his *pu*, he does not merely commit a sexual transgression or violate a social institution. His crime, as Needham [12] puts it, is an "onslaught on the entire complex of identically ordered relationships which are the society, and on the symbolic classifications which are its ideological life." Incest not only mixes inappropriate mates and groups, but it also mixes cosmic compartments—all of the elements in the *pu* category are jostled into the *tu* category, the *tu* elements into the *pu* category. In the primitive pattern, the cosmic and the social are interlocked.

THE NDEMBU OF RHODESIA: A PRIMITIVE DRAMA

The previous discussion may give the erroneous impression that primitive society is a seamless fabric of socioreligious bonds, woven so tightly as to resist tearing. Under strain the social fabric of primitive society can become frayed. One source of such strain is the aberrant personality. Indeed, this type of person is a more direct threat to the primitive community than to the modern community. Modern society has specialists and specialized agencies either to "cure" or to conceal deviants: doctors and hospitals, policemen and jails. The primitive community must cope with the deviant directly and collectively.

Kamahasanyi's neurosis

Kamahasanyi was a male inhabitant of a Ndembu village in Northern Rhodesia, a member of a society in which descent is reckoned matrilineally, but residence is virilocal. Upon marrying, the Ndembu man is expected to leave his father's village, where he was raised, and to move with his wife to the village where his matrilineal kinsmen, including his mother's brother, reside. According to the anthropologist Victor Turner,[13] Kamahasanyi did not live up to this expectation. He could not bring himself to emigrate from his father's village until several years after his father's death when Kamahasanyi had already reached the age of forty and had been married several times. Because Kamahasanyi continued to live with his father's kin and did not move to join his mother's kin, he was stigmatized as a man who could not face responsibility. With the Ndembu, as with many matrilineal societies, it is among his matrilineal kin that a man acts like a man. It is here that he assumes adult rank and duties in matters of ritual, trade, and law; but among his father's kinsmen, a man is without status and function. Irritated by Kamahasanyi's presence, his father's kinsmen eventually insisted that he leave.

In addition to Kamahasanyi's problems with his patri-kin, he was personally a bit odd. While Kamahasanyi's father had been recognized as a man of great force and authority, Kamahasanyi was considered effeminate. He plaited his hair in a feminine style known as *lumba,* and spent his time gossiping in kitchens. Although he had married four times, he had failed to beget children. For his fourth wife, he had chosen a domineering woman upon whom he was dependent. Indeed, when through ineptitude he had fallen into debt, Maria had rescued him by selling cassava. Not only was Maria domineering, but she was also Kamahasanyi's cousin on his mother's side, so that when Kamahasanyi finally came to live with his mother's kin, he had returned to Maria's kin as well, to the village where she had been reared.

In this village lurked trouble for the unfortunate Kamahasanyi. Prior to her marriage, Maria had taken as a lover a man named Jackson, and upon her return to her natal village the affair was resumed. Liaisons are not uncommon among the Ndembu, but this one was conducted openly. When he encountered Maria's mother, Ndono, Jackson would rush away—as if Ndono were his mother-in-law. The Ndembu practice mother-in-law avoidance, so in this manner Jackson insinuated that Maria was his wife. To Kamahasanyi the insult was brazen and galling.

Probably as a result of his troubles, Kamahasanyi began to suffer from impotence, heart palpitations, and mild paranoia. Even if people were not actually maligning him covertly, Kamahasanyi imagined they were. Finally he withdrew to his hut, and the curer Ihembi, master of the Ihamba cult, was summoned.

The cure

Ihembi, a resident of the area, was aware of the conflicts and hostilities that afflicted Kamahasanyi—indeed, that afflicted all his kinsmen. Ihembi believed that to cure Kamahasanyi he must in effect cure the entire community, and to do so he prescribed seven ceremonies.

Ihembi elected to hold one of them at the site where Kamahasanyi had once dreamt that, out of anger with Kamahasanyi for quarreling with his father's kin, his father's spirit had bitten him. The spirit was obviously the immediate source of Kamahasanyi's pain, and Ihembi decided to begin at the source.

In diagnosing Kamahasanyi's illness, Ihembi suggested two causes —the faithless Maria and her mother, Ndono. Both were witches, Ihembi intimated. They yearned to "kill Kamahasanyi for his meat," and to obtain Jackson for husband and son-in-law, respectively. To dispose of Kamahasanyi they had magically sent little men who beat Kamahasanyi with hoe handles. This was one cause of Kamahasanyi's pain.

Not only the ill-wishes of Maria and Ndono caused Kamahasanyi's suffering, said Ihembi, but also those of his neighbors and kinsmen. The dream of the biting spirit was a product of all of them and, for this reason, curing the bad feelings would also cure the biting spirit and insure its departure. Ihembi's ceremony was designed to dramatize both happenings.

The ceremony proceeded fitfully. Horn cups through which the biting spirit was to leave were affixed to Kamahasanyi's body, and there ensued a phase of drumming and singing, with Maria, Ndono, Jackson, and all the villagers participating. This continued until Kamahasanyi fell into a fit of trembling. When a horn shook loose, Ihembi would order the drums to stop. After inspecting the horn and discovering that the spirit had not yet emerged, Ihembi would offer an explanation which included an account of Kamahasanyi's troubles and an invitation to the villagers to step forward and confess their own malice. Ihembi would then reaffix the horn cup, the drumming and singing would recommence, and soon Kamahasanyi would resume trembling. Thus the sequence was repeated again and again, until as the night wore on the group began to feel a unanimous craving for the spirit to emerge.

Finally, at Ihembi's command, Maria herself took action. She entered the bush and returned with leaves from the *mudyi* tree, which because of its milklike secretions is an Ndembu symbol of motherhood, matrilineality, and womanhood. Turner reports that Maria then chewed the *mudyi* leaves and spat the juice on her husband's temples, feet, and hands—the centers of his thought and action—to "give him strength." By these gifts of spittle she re-affirmed her wifely obligations to Kamahasanyi and the good will she bore him, at the same time denying the alleged witchery.

It was now Kamahasanyi's turn. He complained bitterly that his matrilineal kinsmen were remiss in their duties to him and had not helped to ease his suffering—he had had to send for the curer himself. But now, since telling of his grudge, he felt all would be well. His hard thoughts no longer blocked the cure.

With that, Kamahasanyi began quivering violently. The cup on his temple fell off, dropping what appeared to be a small chunk of flesh. The congregation felt certain, Turner writes, that the hidden animosities of kinsmen and neighbors were being drawn out of the patient. Ihembi, who had been sitting quietly, now fitted a long horn over the little finger of his right hand, pointing it at another cup attached to the patient. As Turner recounts:

> The whole congregation rose to their feet as one man, and Ihembi fastened on the twitching Kamahasanyi, who fell on his side, writhing convulsively. Kamahasanyi cried out and sobbed when Ihembi removed the blood-dripping horn in a large skin-purse. Mundoyi and Kachilewa [two men who assisted Ihembi in the ceremony] threw large quantities of medicine over the patient. Ihembi rushed to the small cala-bash (containing medicine and blood from previous cuppings) and threw the cupping horn now concealed by the purse into it. He then spat powdered white clay on the really ugly bulge on Kamahasanyi's neck where the horn had been, "to cool and purify it." Kachilewa now held his hand poised over the leaf-concealed calabash while all of us waited intently. He removed the leaves and dredged with his hand in the bloody mixture. After awhile he shook his head and said "Mwosi"

("nothing in here"). We were all disappointed. But Ihembi with a gentle smile took over. He plunged his fingers into the gruesome fluid and when he brought them up I saw a flash of white. Then he rushed with what was in his fingers out of the avid circle of on-lookers. From the edge of the village, he beckoned to the elders and to me . . . we went one by one to Ihembi. It was indeed a human tooth, we had to say. It was no bush-pig's tooth, nor a monkey's. Jubilantly we told the women, who all trilled with joy.[14]

Turner goes on to say that, with the ceremony completed, and the spirit's tooth extracted, people who had been cool toward each other now beamed and warmly shook hands. Even hours later, "a mood of quiet satisfaction still seemed to emanate from the villagers."

A year later Turner revisited the village to find Kamahasanyi well and Maria still his wife. Jackson had left for employment in town, and Kamahasanyi had worked himself into the community. In fact, by persuading his younger brother and sister to join him in living with their maternal kinsmen, he had extended his personal entourage and had gained considerable stature. Kamahasanyi was snaring game and also in other ways acting like a responsible adult male.

Implications

The difference between tensions found in primitive society and those common to modern or early-modern society is revealed by comparing Ihembi's psychotherapy (for in effect this is what it was) with the psychotherapy of Sigmund Freud. Freudian psychotherapy was evolved to cope with the tensions peculiar to modern and early-modern life: to cure in*tra*psychic tensions—tensions between id, ego, and superego. Ndembu therapy is designed to heal in*ter*psychic tensions—tensions between members of a community. By treating the community neurosis, Ihembi was also treating Kamahasanyi's.

Nor is Ndembu therapy quite like the group therapy that has been developed since Freud. Group therapy is not aimed at healing the tensions of the group; it is simply a means of relieving tensions suffered by individuals within the group. Group therapy sessions encourage these individuals to talk about their problems, thus to gain insight into them; but once the therapy is concluded and the job of curing its individual members is done, the group disbands—its members might never see each other again. Individuals in the Ndembu community group, on the other hand, may expect to live together for years. Harmonizing the relationships between individuals is necessarily as much an aim of Ndembu therapy as is the cure of their personal neuroses.

Freudian therapy and group therapy strive to prepare the patient to perform various roles successfully in groups away from the hospital or couch. But among the Ndembu the therapy group and the group in which the patient will play his life roles are the same. The contrast simply reflects once again the fact that in modern society units are more specialized. Hospital and clinic are separate from firm, family, and church, whereas in Ndembu society, the patient's therapy group is his kinship group, his economic group, and his religious group. The merging of groups, however, can also heighten the impact of intragroup conflicts on the individual psyche, for the better as well as for the worse. If Kamahasanyi's group could so strongly disturb his psyche, it could also cure it. Ihembi's therapeutic drama worked wonders, despite its brevity, while Freudian psychotherapy, to achieve the same result, takes years.

Curative power, such as that displayed by Ihembi, flows not only from the merging of a group, but also from the group's strength of faith. By manipulating symbols and beliefs that were already deeply ingrained in the Ndembu community life, Ihembi was actually exploiting a preestablished faith in the drama's curative efficacy. Modern psychiatrists cannot rely upon such popular faith in their curative techniques; laymen are not reared from birth to believe in a religion called "psychiatry" that underlies all facets of community life. Once more it becomes evident that in primitive society units are not specialized—religion, therapy, and community life are undifferentiated.

OVERVIEW

In primitive society, life is carried on in groups that are relatively unspecialized, with emphasis on kinship groups. Among the Ndembu, for instance, it is the matrilineal kinship group within which a man seeks political stature, debates legal issues, grows food, worships, falls ill, and becomes cured. Similarly, among the aborigines and the hill tribes a man lives largely within the confines of his patrilocal, patrilineal group. By contrast, in modern society a man typically divides his time, efforts, and concerns among several specialized groups such as family, factory, church, and hospital.

Primitive society is more particularistic than modern society; that is, primitive society places greater emphasis than does modern society on kinship status. The primitive man's kinship status determines to a great extent whom he marries, which totem he venerates, what manners he displays, and what political stature he achieves. Although the modern man's kinship status does have some effect on his life, he is much freer than the primitive man in his choice of mate, job, and religion.

Anthropologists have debated at length the issue of whether marriage or kinship bonds are more important in primitive society. Generally, anthropologists who did their research in Africa (*e.g.,* Fortes and Gluckman) consider kinship bonds more important, while those whose interests lie in Southeast Asia (*e.g.,* Leach and Lévi-Strauss) consider marriage bonds more important. From a wider viewpoint one could state that kinship bonds are more important in primitive societies and marriage bonds are more important in modern societies. Kinship controls marriage in primitive society since the aborigine or hill tribesman must choose his mate from a group that is kin to his own group in a specific way. Romantic love, which strongly influences the choice of a mate in modern society, is less influential than kinship rules in determining whom the primitive marries.

In unspecialized units such as primitive kinship groups, social relationships tend toward functional diffuseness—each relationship tends to be multidimensional. The primitive man is a kinsman, neighbor, co-worker, co-worshiper, and many other things simultaneously to *each member* of his local group, while the modern man's social relations tend to be one-dimensional: he plays but a single role to each member of his society. Therefore, disruption of the typical modern social relationship is less serious to the society and the individuals involved than is disruption of the typical primitive social relationship. If the modern man is merely a customer to his newspaper boy, the boy's forgetting to leave the paper one morning is hardly likely to provoke emotional damage or community uproar. Yet disruption of a single primitive relationship may have just these effects, and more serious ones as well. Defaulting on a primitive relationship not only can produce emotional disturbance and community disorder, but it can also play havoc with the entire universe—since individual, community, and universe are intimately connected in primitive culture. For this reason, primitives create rituals that are designed both to resolve psychic and social conflicts and to repair the associated cosmic disruptions. Rituals of this type, which Max Gluckman [15] has labeled "rituals of social relations," require the participants to play the same ritual roles vis-à-vis one another within the rite as they play in daily life. (Kamahasanyi and Maria related to each other as man and wife inside the rite *and* outside it.) Ritualizing these relations, thus giving them order, will through a mystical, suprasensory process transfer the same order to society, nature, and the cosmos.

Rituals of social relations tend to emerge wherever the members of a group interrelate diffusely. Diffuse, multidimensional enclaves even within modern society can inspire such rites; thus, communal hippy groups celebrate rites calculated to unleash "flower power," a force believed mystically to alter the universe. Most modern men depend not on rituals of social relations, however, but on specialized societal agencies such as courts to rectify disputes within their commonly one-dimensional relationships. Courts are expected to uphold contracts, but not to bring into line the natural and the supernatural, and if one wants further proof of the spread of functional specificity among moderns, he need only note that kinship, diffuse in primitive society, is in modern society a specialty of domestic relations courts.

Little has been said about primitive economics, but it is clear that none of the primitive societies discussed earlier depends strongly on a generalized medium of exchange, such as modern money, or on specialized economic systems, such as modern markets. Like so many aspects of primitive life, the exchange of goods and services is carried out in the context of kinship and ritual. The exchange of women, goods, and ritual services among the hill people of Southeast Asia is typical and illustrates that the media used by primitives are restricted rather than generalized. Male goods can be exchanged only for women and female goods.

Nor is any of these groups highly centralized or bureaucratized. The aborigines have no chief. The Ndembu and the hill tribes do, but their chiefs usually control only a small domain, perhaps a village or two, and they sanction their rule on the basis of kinship. As a relevant contrast, in archaic society there are kings and bureaucracies that rule through other fiat—by popular will, recognized authority, or force.

The primitive society has no king, nor does it have a kingly class that is distinct from, and not kin to, a commoner class. Primitive society is a one-class society in which all the members are kinsmen. Yet among primitives is found an interesting example of a borderline two-class system, the Kachin of Burma. As incisively analyzed by Leach,[16] Kachin society is composed of two types of groups: democratic (*gumlao*) and autocratic (*gumsa*). The Kachin democratic group fits the description of primitive one-class society: all persons within the group hold equal social status and place great emphasis on their kinship bonds to one another. In the Kachin autocratic group, however, nobles are clearly distinguished from commoners. According to Leach, these autocratic groups have borrowed a model of what we would call archaic two-class society from their valley-dwelling, king-ruled neighbors, the Buddhist Shan. Unfortunately, the hill-dwelling Kachin possess primitive features (a slash and burn agriculture, circulating connubium, a religion based on animism and on feasts of merit) that do not support this archaic pattern. Therefore, Kachin groups which set themselves up as autocracies are constantly breaking down and assuming the one-class democratic form. Yet with the autocratic ideal before them, the democratic groups constantly strive to be autocratic. Kachin society continuously oscillates between the two patterns, and the Kachin have never achieved a stable and enduring kingdom or anything close to it. We would say that the Kachin are moving toward the boundary between primitive and archaic, but have not yet managed to cross it.

Since primitive society is a one-class society and there are, therefore, no classes to move between, there is obviously less social mobility than in a multiclass society. Furthermore, since primitive society is not highly centralized, another type of mobility is impossible: mobility from periphery to center. There is no capital city to which the rustic from the provinces can move, one village is much like another, and so a primitive who changes villages does not radically change his life style—the sort of change implied by the notion of social mobility.* Although the mobility of the primitive individual is restricted, the primitive community is often highly mobile geographically. Many primitives relish a nomadic life. The Australian aborigines move about within a given territory, hunting game and gathering plants, and the Southeast Asian hill tribes move about slashing, burning, and planting. Primitive communities can

---

* Primitives today can change their life style by moving to modern settlements, towns, and cities, but this is not mobility *within* primitive society.

wander easily because they travel light. Their tools are easy to transport, as are their ceremonial objects. A primitive bullroarer is much lighter than an archaic temple.

Again, it should be emphasized that the spiritual and mundane aspects of primitive life merge into one complex. The Dreaming is "everywhen," as much a part of the here and now as of the distant past, and religion permeates everything. Incest threatens the cosmic order. Rituals to mend the social fabric are thought also to redress disturbances in nature and supernature. Cosmic figures, such as the heroes of The Dreaming, are not gods—they are too involved in the world to stand above and control it. Nor are they worshipped as gods. Men identify with them in rites of the secret life when "everywhen" becomes now, and men in their dreams become these heroes.

In primitive society, just as the cosmic is welded to the social, so the religious institution is part of the overall social organization. There is no church clearly distinct in location, function, and membership from other groups. The basic religious group among the aborigines is the patrilocal group, which is also the basic economic, political, residential, and kinship group. Among the Ndembu or Kachin, kinship groups form the basic religious groups as well. Primitives hew to no doctrine separating church and family.

How great is a primitive society's capacity for change? This is a difficult question to answer, partly because no anthropologist can live for several lifetimes in a primitive society—an opportunity that would allow direct observation of primitive history. Moreover, the problem of measuring the rate and the capacity for change is an immense one. Even so, if one were to plot on a graph the rate of technological change at various periods in human history, one would find that during the modern era technology has changed at an overwhelmingly higher rate than during periods prior to 7000 B.C.[17] Since all societies were primitive prior to 7000 B.C., one can say that the rate of technological change in a world largely populated by modern societies is greater than that in a world populated by primitive societies. Because sociocultural changes accompany technological change, one could generalize further and say that the rate of sociocultural change in a world largely populated by modern societies is greater than that in a world populated by primitive societies. We conclude, therefore, that primitive societies left to themselves—in a world without modern societies—change slowly. This implies that primitive societies do not contain within themselves a strong impetus to change.

Various "brakes" on change can be discovered in primitive religion. Since primitive religions are "cold," primitive peoples, instead of eagerly seizing as new each opportunity that the world presents, classify the new as simply another manifestation of the old. Similarly, since primitive religion pervades all spheres of life, every sphere is rendered sacred, hence difficult to change—for to change the sacred is to throw the whole of existence into turmoil.

But these arguments simply point to a conservative bias in primitive patterning, a bias that should not be exaggerated since upon contacting modern men some primitive societies have changed radically and quickly. What is at issue here is whether primitive societies have an *internal* impetus to change—whether, if left alone, they would spontaneously initiate changes. Here we return to the formulation proposed earlier. The primitive's ideal order is blended with his social order; hence the primitive possesses no transcendent, distinct, differentiated ideal order against which to compare and criticize his present social order. A major internal impetus for reform and change is therefore lacking.

TOPICS FOR DISCUSSION

Two approaches for applying the study of primitive society to the study of modern society can be distinguished: the Durkheimian, which is followed by most French and British social anthropologists, and the Weberian (after Max Weber), which is followed by this book. Durkheimians emphasize the similarities between primitive and modern patterns. They often attribute to modern rites, symbols, or customs, dynamics and functions that apparently underlie primitive rites, symbols, or customs. Weberians, on the other hand, emphasize the differences between primitive and modern patterns. They attempt to define the dimensions according to which modern patterns have evolved beyond the primitive patterns. Both of these approaches can illuminate our understanding of modern man, or of man in general, though their perspectives are different. The student might profitably consider the advantages and disadvantages of each of the two approaches.

Our discussion of Kamahasanyi's neurosis is derived from the intensive studies of Ndembu life by Victor Turner. Turner has pioneered in the analysis of what he calls "social drama," and his accounts of primitive life often differ strikingly from those of traditional social anthropologists. Social drama commonly focuses on the events in the life of a particular individual and abstracts a narrative of events with climax and resolution. By contrast, traditional social anthropology, exemplified by our treatment of the aborigines, seeks to delineate broad sociocultural patterns as expressed in the lives of many individuals and in group life. These two modes of abstraction, one emphasizing a narrative of events, the other emphasizing sociocultural patterns, could usefully be compared.

In his provocative analysis of Southeast Asian hill tribes, Leach has posed yet another methodological problem with respect to primitive society. Among the hill tribes, a group's cultural (*e.g.,* language) boundaries are rarely the same as its social (interactional) boundaries. This observation raises some important questions about the relationships between cultural systems and social systems and precisely how we are to determine a society's boundaries.

THE AUSTRALIAN ABORIGINE

The Australian Aborigines (paperback, 1966) by A. P. Elkin. A comprehensive, authoritative, and readable survey by one of the leading scholars on the Australian aborigines.

The Tiwi of North Australia (paperback, 1960) by C. W. M. Hart and Arnold R. Piling. A short book on a somewhat deviant aboriginal tribe. Suitable for the beginning student, and to elaborate and vary the picture presented in this text.

Black Civilization (1964) by W. Lloyd Warner. A classic study of the Murngin tribe. Too detailed for the average beginner, but excellent in its careful delineation of a single group.

"The Dreaming" (1965) by W. E. H. Stanner. A beautiful and profound portrait of aboriginal thought and religion.

Totemism (paperback, 1963) by Claude Lévi-Strauss. An analysis providing much insight into totemism in aboriginal thought and society.

The Savage Mind (1966) by Claude Lévi-Strauss. Provocative, if speculative, analysis of aboriginal thought and society.

The Elementary Forms of the Religious Life (originally, 1912; paperback, 1965) by Emile Durkheim. The classic analysis of aboriginal religion; still well worth reading for its theoretical as well as empirical insight.

SOUTHEAST ASIAN HILL TRIBES

The Elementary Structures of Kinship (1969) by Claude Lévi-Strauss. Classic analysis of circulating connubium, particularly among Southeast Asian hill tribes.

Structure and Sentiment (1962) by Rodney Needham. Deals with the theory of circulating connubium and matrilateral cross-cousin marriage.

"The Structural Implications of Matrilateral Cross-Cousin Marriage" (1966) by Edmund Leach. Seminal analysis of marriage patterns, including that of circulating connubium in Southeast Asia and elsewhere.

Political Systems of Highland Burma (paperback, 1965) by Edmund Leach.

The Structure of Chin Society (paperback, 1963) by F. K. Lehman.

The Economics of the Central Chin Tribes (1943) by H. N. C. Stevenson.

The Social Organization and Customary Law of the Toba-Batak of Northern Sumatra (1964) by J. C. Vergouwen.

THE NDEMBU

Schism and Continuity in an African Society (1957) by Victor Turner.

The Forest of Symbols: Aspects of Ndembu Ritual (1967) by Victor Turner.

The Drums of Affliction: A Study of Religious Processes Among the Ndembu of Zambia (1968) by Victor Turner.

PRIMITIVE RELIGION IN AFRICAN AND AMERICAN TRIBES

Nuer Religion (1956) by E. E. Evans-Pritchard. Classic treatment.

Divinity and Experience: The Religion of the Dinka (1961) by Godfrey Lienhardt. Outstanding.

*African Worlds: Studies in the Cosmological Ideas and Social Values
of African Peoples* (paperback, 1954) edited by Daryll Forde.
Introduction to Zuni Ceremonialism (1932) by Ruth Bunzel. An
American contribution to the study of religion.
Ceremonial Patterns in the Greater Southwest (1948) by Ruth M.
Underhill. Outside the British social-anthropological tradition.

PRIMITIVE RELIGION—GENERAL WORKS *

Religion in Primitive Society (1961) by Edward Norbeck.
Primitive Classification (paperback, 1963) by Emile Durkheim and
Marcel Mauss.
Religion Among the Primitives (paperback, 1964) by William J.
Goode.
"Myth in Primitive Psychology" in *Magic, Science and Religion and
Other Essays* (paperback, 1954) by Bronislaw Malinowski.
"Les Rites de Passage" in *Essays on the Ritual of Social Relations*
(1962) edited by Max Gluckman.
Purity and Danger: An Analysis of Concepts of Pollution and Taboo
(1966) by Mary Douglas.
"Colour Classification in Ndembu Ritual: A Problem in Primitive
Classification" and "Betwixt and Between: The Liminal Period in
Rites de Passage" in *The Forest of Symbols: Aspects of Ndembu
Ritual* (1967) by Victor Turner.
"Religion as a Cultural System" by Clifford Geertz in *Anthropological
Approaches to the Study of Religion* (1966) edited by Michael
Banton.
Religion: An Anthropological View (1966) by Anthony F. C. Wallace.
Sacrifice: Its Nature and Function (1964) by Henri Hubert and
Marcel Mauss.
The Birth of the Gods: The Origin of Primitive Belief (paperback,
1960) by Guy E. Swanson.
Reader in Comparative Religion (1965) edited by William A. Lessa
and Evon Z. Vogt. Includes mainstream articles and an extensive
bibliography.

* For readings on primitive kinship, see references listed after chapter 2.

MODERN RELIGION

The Religious Factor: A Sociological Study of Religion's Impact on Politics, Economics and Family Life (paperback, 1961) by Gerhard Lenski.
Protestant, Catholic, Jew (paperback, 1955) by Will Herberg.
The Secular City (paperback, 1965) by Harvey Cox.

These works treat modern religious patterns and provide a useful contrast to primitive patterns.

FILMS

Primitive People. Depicts the life of the Australian aborigines.
Djalambu. Depicts a mourning ceremony of the aboriginal Emu clan.
The Great Unfenced. Portrays the desert environment of the aborigines.
Tjuringa: The Story of Stone Age Man. Portrays aboriginal ritual and the quest after food.
Walkabout: A Journey with the Aborigines.

Archaic society and culture

THE SWAZI

The Swazi are a Bantu-speaking people living in Swaziland, a country about the size of Hawaii, surrounded on three sides by the Union of South Africa and on the fourth by Portuguese Angola. In the early 1940's when research on the Swazi was completed,[1] they numbered about 184,750. At that time Swaziland was a British colony, ruled by King Sobhuza II. Today, still under the rule of King Sobhuza II, Swaziland is prospering (Swazi exports almost tripled during the period 1965–1968). On September 6, 1968, Swaziland obtained independence.

Swaziland's scenery, climate, and soil vary widely—ranging from the high veld of the West, broken, wild, and often veiled in mist and drizzle, to the warmer and drier middle veld and lowlands of thick bush, squat thorn trees, and short, sparse grass. In these regions the Swazi plant grain, tend cattle, and hunt game, thus exhibiting a form of food-getting more advanced than that of the Australian aborigines. The tempo of these endeavors is set by the rhythm of the seasons as they change from hot to cold, from rainy to dry. On these cycles depend the ripening of crops, the conditions of the herds, and the availability of game. Partly because the Swazi's life is so closely bound to the seasonal cycles, the cycles carry a ritual significance for them. The great Incwala, a ceremony held at the height of summer when the first crops have ripened, is one example.

Swazi kingship and society

Swazi commoners live in homesteads that are scattered about the countryside and are occupied not just by the immediate family, but often by additional kinsmen, such as brothers of the homestead head and their families. The eldest male acts as the head, or patriarch. More than seven people reside in the homestead of the average Swazi commoner, while more than twenty may live with a chief or prince. Although the polygynous homestead—in which each of a man's several wives lives with her own children in a separate hut—is considered ideal, in practice the average Swazi can rarely afford more than one wife. (The rich, powerful aristocrat, however, may have several wives.) Aside from the extra huts for the additional wives, every homestead includes a "great hut," decorated with the skulls of animals sacrificed to patrilineal ancestors. The great hut is under the charge of a woman called the patriarch's "mother," who may actually be his first wife. No ordinary wife may enter this hut—only the mother.

The Swazi king lives in a homestead in many respects similar to that of the commoner. The king's homestead, however, includes many nonkinsmen and is much larger than the commoner's—in fact, it might be better defined as a village. In 1934 King Sobhuza II had 265 persons living in his capital homestead, Lobamba. The king's village, like the commoner's homestead, is built around a great hut, but the king's great hut is really a compound of huts called the Great Abode, an exceedingly sacred area. The Swazi maintain that if an inappropriate person, such as one who has recently had contact with menstrual blood or participated in sexual relations, should enter the Great Abode, he would bring madness on himself and disaster to the land.

The queen mother, a central figure in Swazi society equal in importance to the king himself, resides in a village apart from that of the adult king. As a child the king lives in his mother's village, but upon reaching manhood he moves away to establish his own village, the nation's capital. The king's village serves as the nation's administrative and military headquarters; the queen mother's village serves as the ceremonial center and the home of the national ritual objects.

The king's capital village, the queen mother's village, and the villages occupied by the king's wives are all major sites of national activity. Here courtiers compete for royal favors, leading legal cases are discussed, festivities are celebrated, and large labor forces are organized. The sophistication and excitement of court life is highly coveted by the ordinary Swazi, who speak of the deeper wisdom, the finer polish of those who mature in the villages of the "great," rather than in the common households "away from the people."

The territory of Swaziland is divided into principalities and districts ruled by the princely relatives of the king, by royal governors, and by hereditary chiefs. All of these officials are either the king's direct appointees or have had their authority ratified by him. The districts over which they rule range in size from about four square miles to more than twenty, and vary in population from 100 to 2,000 persons. Since the boundaries of these districts are established partly by traditional hereditary rights and partly by national decisions of the king, they are often vaguely defined and remain so until a dispute occurs, which is settled by the king or by one of his governmental deputies. The Swazi appear to be more concerned about the precision of land boundaries than are the Australian aborigines. To Swazi agriculturalists, who own fields and pastures, boundaries mean more than they do to the nomadic aboriginal hunter-gatherers. And because Swazi territory is alienable—it can be bought and sold—the opportunity for title disputes is greater. A centralized ruler and a bureaucracy are empowered to resolve such disputes and to set precise boundaries. The aborigines, lacking such agents, could not delimit precise boundaries even if they wished to do so.

By decree of national ideology, the ownership of all national territory is vested in the king, not in local groups or in citizen landowners. The king allots land to his people through his noble magnanimity. To the Swazi mind, he is not selling land but "serving" it; in analogous fashion, certain foods are never sold, but are served to strangers and hungry neighbors. In practice, however, the king finds upon acceding to the throne that his kingdom is already divided into districts and, within these, into plots of land to which individual Swazi have staked hereditary claim. The king, therefore, simply ratifies a preestablished arrangement. If a commoner believes he has been treated unfairly or evicted unjustly by a local leader, or if he cannot obtain land equal to his needs, he may appeal to the king or the queen mother. The king has the power to depose a leader or to dictate a leader's heir, and in this way he can control malfeasance on the local level.

Each Swazi clan is fragmented into numerous segments scattered among the various districts. Since any local settlement is likely to include homesteads belonging to several clans, therefore, a dispute among such homesteads cannot be settled by any single clan's authorities. To resolve their disputes, the homesteads must consult "cold people," district authorities who govern all homesteads in their districts and who are not necessarily kin to any. Clan authority, then, has given way to governmental authority.

This situation did not always exist among the Swazi. At one time Swazi society comprised a number of small, localized clans of approximately equal status and power. Through a gradual process of assimilation and conquest, one clan, the Dlamini, became the royal clan and assumed rulership over the entire nation. Hence, at least since the reign of King Mbandzeni in the late nineteenth century, Swazi society has been a pyramidal hierarchy of clans and lineages, with the Dlamini clan at the apex. Many common clans no longer maintain their own territorial identity, but distinguish themselves from other clans solely by their contributions to the royal Dlamini clan. The Matsebula and Motsa clans, for example, contribute specialists in ritual to certain royal ceremonies, and the Hlophe clan furnishes tutors for princes. Myths which in the past glorified individual clans have been supplanted by national sagas. Thus, Swazi society has become increasingly centralized—a society in which clans have surrendered their local territorial sovereignties and have become arms of the central government and king.

The breakdown of Swazi clan organization was further encouraged by the emergence of age-graded warrior regiments. Formerly, men of all ages fought together for their own clan against rival clans. Now, each Swazi male owes military service directly to the head of the Dlamini clan, the king, and each man is classified into an age-graded regiment. Every five or seven years the king forms a new regiment. All males falling into the age range established for that regiment leave their homesteads and take up group residence in all-male barracks composed of huts quartering four to six men each. The men are organized into squads (*siceme*) consisting of eight to twenty men who drill and dance together ceremonially. Several squads make up a platoon, which is often commanded by a son of the king or of a district chief. Platoons are combined into local regiments, which in turn are combined into the entire age-class regiment.

Each regiment follows its own leader, flourishes its own emblem, shouts its own cry, and forms a conspicuous unit on national occasions when age mates from scattered districts gather together in a single enclosure in the royal capital to take part in national ceremonies. Living together, eating together, smoking hemp together, age mates develop a strong camaraderie. At the same time, the age-grading system serves to detach father from son, older brother from younger brother, and to substitute for these familial loyalties a new loyalty—to age group. Furthermore, since loyalty to the age group means loyalty to the regiment, it means also loyalty to the supreme commander of all regiments, the king. In fact, certain regiments are stationed in the royal capital to serve the king, much as marine units attend the White House. Any man of the proper age class can join these elite regiments, and no father, guardian, or district chief can prohibit a man from "working for the king, father of the nation." A father is eager, as a rule, to have at least one son remain several years in the capital to be educated as an elite soldier. These young men aspire to deeds of bravery for the regiment and the king, and in the days of active warfare, death on the battlefield was the one death that no kinsman could mourn since it was for the sake of the nation.

Since the Swazi reckon descent patrilineally, the king inherits his position from his father. Only the son of a king may become king, but since a king has many wives and thus many sons, an heir must frequently be chosen. Wars of accession are averted by ranking the king's wives and thus eliminating at least some of the children from contention for kingship. Usually the king's heir is the eldest son of the king's highest ranking wife, and since the royal Dlamini clan is permitted to marry within itself (although the king and his wife may not have kinship ties closer than a common great-grandfather), the heir is considered to have "the blood of kingship" from both maternal and paternal sides.

Because it is the king's mother who by her rank confers royal status on the king, she is a figure of prestige and influence. Called "Lady Elephant," she sustains a delicate balance of power between herself and her son, the king "Lion." It is believed that conflict between the king and the queen mother will menace the entire nation with civil war, drought, or flood. Harmony between king and queen is essential, and to the Swazi it is more likely to exist between mother and son than between husband and wife.

The king relies heavily on his closest royal kinsmen, especially his half brothers and his uncles. Not only are these senior princes consulted on all important issues of state, they are also appointed by the king as governors of vacant district posts, insuring the loyalty both of kinsmen and of district residents. The royal kinsmen, with other councillors drawn from less noble clans, act also as the king's teachers and as his critics. They may be summoned to help determine the heirship of a noble line, to arbitrate a property dispute, or to name a successor after the king's death.

Even more closely identified with the king than his kinsmen, however, are two men who are not kin, called the *tinsila*. Although they represent common stock, they undergo a ritual transference of blood, elevating them to a mental and physical status that in many ways connects them more intimately to the king than any status sanctioned by kinship. The rite turns the *tinsila* into ritual doubles of the king. The Swazi believe that if sorcery or evil is directed at the king, it will be deflected onto his doubles; it is therefore considered advantageous if these ritual alter egos are sickly, for by these symptoms it is apparent that they are doing their job well. Besides being interceptors of evil, the *tinsila* mediate disputes and, above all, endeavor to keep peace among the people. To aid in this task, they have administrative authority equal to that of the highest prince.

Other nonkinsmen who also assist the king are the *tindvuna,* or councillors of the royal villages. These too are drawn from commoner clans, and are selected by the king in consultation with his advisers. The *tindvuna* try legal cases, render judgments, and advise the king on the mood of the people. They are also accorded powers and privileges equivalent to those of the royal kinsmen themselves, and they may actually be conferred membership in the royal clan. If they are granted membership in the royal clan, they will be permitted to eat from the dishes used by the royal princes, will be forbidden to marry a close relative of the king (symbolically that would be incest), and upon death may expect to be buried with royal ritual. But no matter how great their talents or how numerous their responsibilities, these councillors still lack royal blood, hence they are never eligible for the kingship itself.

Kingship in Swaziland is, in part, the reign of the royal clan, which is extended throughout the nation through bonds of blood and marriage. As the Swazi say, "A wise king recognizes the value of kinship." Yet by comparison with primitive societies, many of the most significant bonds that unite the Swazi nation are not those of kinship but those of loyalty to the concept of Swazi kingship and to the king as the embodiment of that concept. The age-graded regiments and the services of the ritual doubles and the royal councillors contribute to this pattern. A third institution, that of vassalage (*kukhonta*), makes a further contribution. Chiefs offer homage to the king, commoners to their local chief, youths without property to some wealthy homestead headman. In each case the underling begs of his superior the right to be his "boy" or "dog." Especially at the lower levels of society, this system of *kukhonta* establishes between nonkinsmen a quasi-kinship bond. Thus, a vassal who has been assisted by his superior in obtaining a wife may establish his family in the superior's household, rather than in the household of one of his own kinsmen. It is a great honor to be

sought as a lord by a would-be vassal. By helping the poor or unfortunate, the lord demonstrates his generosity and his nobility.

Notions of status and hierarchy pervade Swazi society. Although
chiefs and leaders are trained to "feel with" their subjects, no
subject dares to stand upright in the presence of a chief, instead,
he "shuffles forward with bended knee and utters exaggerated
praise." [2] Even more exalted than chiefs are the king and the queen
mother, in relation to whom all other Swazi are ranked. The king is
"The Lion," "The Sun," "The Bull of the Nation," "The Milky
Way"; the queen mother is "The Lady Elephant," "The Earth,"
"The Beautiful," "Mother of the Country"; the highest officials, by
contrast, are "tiny stars" or "little ant heaps"; and the average man
is a "dog," a "stick," a "nothing."

Despite these bold metaphors distinguishing the lowest from the
highest, differences in Swazi rank are not correlated with wide
variations in wealth or standard of living. Swazi technology, although more developed than that of the aborigines, is still crude.
It cannot support, for any length of time, those who do not directly
contribute to the basic needs of survival, such as food and shelter.
Even royalty works—queens toil in the fields, princes erect their
own houses—but, it is true, they do not work as hard as commoners. Some older princes "allow their nails to grow into long
talons to show that they need not exert themselves." [3]

As in many other African societies, cattle are the key symbol of
wealth and power in Swaziland. Men devote considerable energy
to building up great herds of cattle—for ritual purposes more than
for nourishment. Cattle symbolism is common throughout Swazi
culture. For example, in the days of intertribal wars, a strategic
military formation required the army to advance in a semicircle,
which represented the curved horns of a bull; also the king is considered the bull of the nation. For reasons of ritual as much as of
survival, the king and the aristocrats maintain large herds of cattle,
and are able to do so because, having many wives, they can produce many daughters—prime currency to exchange for cattle.

The line separating royalty and commoners is obviously more

sharply defined for the archaic Swazi than it is for the primitive Kachin. The Kachin tend to distinguish the elite from the lowly on the basis of birth, but their overall social system is so unstable that this tendency has never become crystallized into a kingdom. Kachin aristocratic (*gumsa*) groups always break down into democratic (*gumlao*) groups. It is not known whether this ever took place among the Swazi, but clearly the shift from a one-class to a two-class society is accompanied by strain. Some of this strain is reflected in Swazi royal ritual.

Swazi kingship and ritual

The Swazi king is the symbolic focal point of the nation—the man who is "more than man," who is the "father" and also the "son" of the people. Because king and nation are so closely identified in Swazi thought, the king's health and strength are equated with the health and strength of his subjects, and further with the fertility of nature. The king's illness brings dread, his death disaster. Therefore, one role of ritual is to protect the monarch, and thereby the nation, from such threats.

Since the king, in a very real sense, is "akin to" the nation, as he matures the nation matures, and each stage of his and the nation's maturation is marked by a national rite. When the king attains full manhood, the nation provides him with his first two wives, ritual queens traditionally chosen from two special clans. The first is his "right-hand queen," Matsebula; the second his "left-hand queen," Motsa. Matsebula, called also "a man, a ruler," accompanies the king to the royal harem. Here, in a ritual hut, her blood is mixed with the king's; and, to symbolize his manhood, the king spits medicines of fertility through holes cut in the walls. Henceforth, the right-hand queen is regarded as part of the king and is addressed as "mother." A few weeks later the king marries the left-hand queen, Motsa, in a similar ritual. Only after the king has married his two ritual queens may other wives or concubines enter his harem.

So removed must the king be kept from death for fear that the nation will be contaminated that he may not partake in more than a few days of mourning for anyone; as the Swazi say, "When the king is in blackness, the whole nation is without strength." Understandably, the death of the king himself represents a grave threat to his people, and thus the event is kept secret until a successor has been ritually installed. Only the queen mother, the governors of the royal villages, the *tinsila,* specialists in the royal death ritual, and two intimate attendants are aware of it. Day and night the king's body is guarded with reverence and ceremony. Though the people may suspect the truth, they dare not speak their thoughts lest they be accused of "wishing to kill the country." Secretly, in the dark of night, the king's body is moved to the ritual hut in the harem where he celebrated his marriage to the first ritual queen, Matsebula. Only after his heir is announced does burial take place. The Swazi believe that at this point the king's spirit joins the other royal ancestors in an afterlife that is hierarchically constructed in the same way as the world he leaves behind. The dead king is mourned for three years, with sacrifices offered in his name as well as in the name of the nation. The dead king becomes the link between the living nation and the dead royalty, and by these ceremonies the bond is strengthened between the nation and its entire ancestry.

The central ceremony of kingship is the annual Incwala ceremony, the "heavy play of all the people." The leading actor of the Incwala is the king. When the king is still young, the ceremonies are kept simple, but as the king and his capital mature, the ceremonies increase in complexity and potency. When the king reaches the age of twenty-one, the first full Incwala is held; and when he is in his prime, the Incwala—now fully formed, rich and elaborate in symbolism and nuance—is also at its peak. Since the last five kings have died in their prime (by sorcery, the Swazi believe, for no death is from a natural cause), the Incwala ceremony has not recently been allowed to decline in richness as the king declines in vigor.

Special national priests are in charge of the Incwala ceremonies; one group is known as the *bemanti* ("people of the water"), the other as the *belwandle* ("people of the sea"). The *bemanti* fetch river water and the *belwandle* fetch sea water to strengthen the king. They participate in no other ceremonies, but duty in the Incwala alone is enough to confer national stature; the head priest of each group ranks as a leading chief. Although the head priests are not members of the Dlamini royal clan, they are among the most prominent citizens of Swaziland. When one of them dies he is buried with the full honors of a Dlamini prince.

Joining the main participants—the king, the priests, the *tinsila,* and the royal regiments—the rank and file of the Swazi nation come in local contingents, each led by a chief or his deputy. Although not all the Swazi take part in the Incwala, practically every male Swazi does so at least once in his life.

Before the official ceremony begins, a black ox—which plays a key role in the Incwala—is stolen from the herd of a loyal subject who is not of the royal clan. The anger and pride felt by the owner when he discovers the theft is thought to "help the medicine" of the Incwala.

Also before the ceremony begins, the water priests (the *bemanti* and the *belwandle*) gather in the cattle enclosure of the capital, ready to undertake their exodus to the river and the sea. While an official "praiser" shouts praises of the great journey to come, the priests squat to inhale snuff provided by the queen mother. They then set off on their mission, quietly and in single file. Once they have left the capital, the priests' posture of humility changes to one of arrogance. They pillage the countryside, drink beer, and levy fines on the citizenry, as they move toward their destinations. They return with the sacred waters—still pillaging, strutting, and drinking as they go—and wait at a royal village near the capital until they are summoned to bring their water "medicines" (serving ritual rather than health purposes) for use in the first part of the Incwala, the little Incwala.

On the opening day of the little Incwala, messengers summon to the capital the water priests, who bear the sacred strengthening

waters. The honor of opening the Incwala falls to the regiment
from the village of the king's grandmother. Members of this regiment between the ages of fifty and sixty-five clothe themselves in
leopard skin loincloths and black plumes and sing the first of the
sacred songs:

> Uye uye oyeha—you hate the child king mu u u oyeha,
> you hate the child king (repeated).
> I would depart with my Father (the King),
> I fear we would be recalled.
> mm m u oyeha—they put him on the stone:
> mm m u oyeha he—sleeps with his sister:
> mm m u u u he—sleeps with Lozithupa (Princess):
> uye uye oyeha—you hate the child king.[4]

The song celebrates the people's hatred of the king and recognizes
the royal clan's right to marry incestuously. During the song, the
men and women of the capital and the members of the regiment
of the king's grandmother's village whoop and dance into the cattle
enclosure. After a time a second chant is started, the men shaking
sticks and the women holding wands quivering in rhythm:

> shi shi ishi—you hate him
> ishi ishi ishi—mother, the enemies are the people. . . .[5]

Other chants follow, while the king is treated with the priests' medicines. As the sun sets, the king enters the sacred enclosure. The
dancers vary the pattern of their dance—imitating the shape of the
moon as it goes through its phases—and again and again the people
sing the *simemo,* a litany for all the important occasions of the
king's life, such as his first marriage and his burial:

> Jjiya oh o o King, alas for your fate
>   (refrain)
> Jjiya oh o o King, they reject thee
> Jjiya oh o o King, they hate thee.[6]

Abruptly the song ends. A priest in the enclosure with the king cries
"Out, foreigners!" and non-Swazi and all those of the royal Dlamini

clan, including women made pregnant by men of the Dlamini clan, must leave. When the king is surrounded by only his most loyal (unrelated) supporters and subjects, the priest shouts, "Eh! Eh! He stabs it with both horns. Our bull!" In this way are the people informed that the king, by spitting the medicine, has "broken" the old year to prepare for the new. The people shout, "He stabs it!" The king has produced what all desired; as the medicines strengthened him, so has he strengthened the earth. He has nudged the sun out of its "hut" to begin its journey through a new year. The day's climax has been reached, a concluding anthem in praise of the king is sung, and as the regiments and women disperse, the king enters his harem for sleep.

At dawn the people awake, once more to hurl insults at their ruler: "Come, Lion, awake, the sun is leaving you!" The *simemo* is sung, the king again spits to the east and to the west, and again everyone rejoices and shouts, "He has bitten the passing year!" The warriors "work for the kingship" by weeding the queen mother's garden, and in return the queen mother provides beer. There is feasting. The people then return to their houses until the moon is full. The little Incwala is over—in a few days will come the great Incwala.

Each day of the great Incwala bears the name of its main event. The first day, devoted to fetching the "sacred tree," a species of acacia, is called *lusekwane*. Just as in medieval legend only "knights without stain" might set forth in quest of the grail, so only pure Swazi youths may fetch the sacred tree. Early in the morning they are enjoined, "Go out! With all powers! At once!" "As you say," they respond, and, flourishing sticks, they rush into the cattle enclosure. There, joined by the king, they dance for hours under the midsummer sun, then depart on a journey of twenty-two miles —practically without food—to the sacred tree. Reaching the tree as the moon rises, they hack down branches with knives or spears, journey to a resting place where they tarry briefly, and then return with their branches to the capital at dawn.

As the sun rises on the second day of the great Incwala, the king,

fetched from his harem, meets the returned pilgrims and leads them
into the sacred enclosure. Lustily singing about how their branches
will comfort the king, the youths drop them in a heap and begin
another dance, again in the blazing sun. The youths, who have gone
virtually without food or sleep for thirty-six hours, are then dismissed and permitted to rest.

The third day is the day of "leaves" and of the bull. The sacred
enclosure is covered with foliage, with an aperture left open at one
end. Through this the "bull" (actually the ox stolen earlier from a
commoner, but now made potent by the medicines) rushes toward
the naked and ceremonially purified youths. When one of them
manages to take hold of the madly charging beast, the rest, singing
vigorously, pummel the animal until it is near death. The ox is killed
by the *belwandle,* and pieces of it are then cut off to serve as medicine for the king.

Another black ox is driven into the enclosure. The king straddles
it, naked, while his hands are bathed in a foamy, medicated water
meant to confer potency. The *simemo* ritual is enacted again, then
the men go to the river to wash while the water priests prepare for
the next day's climactic ceremonies.

On this day, called the "great day," the people are awake, singing
and dancing for the king, before dawn. He emerges from his sanc-
tuary clad only in a white ivory penis cap. His potent nudity evokes
weeping from his subjects, and the queen mother says, "It is pain
to see him a king. My child goes alone through the people." The
king spits some "medicine" (unstrained beer, in this instance)
through the holes of the hut in which he was wed to his first ritual
queen (a place deemed mystically bound to the national well-
being). A councillor cries, "Eh! Eh! He stabs it!" By this act of
spitting, it is believed that the king's strength and potency will
penetrate "right through and awake his people." At this stage the
king is strong enough to "bite" (*i.e.,* eat) the most potent of the
new season's crops, and after this the people spend the morning
performing their own "first fruits" ritual. The midday and early
afternoon are devoted to a display of finery by the people; then,

late in the afternoon, the Incwala enters a new phase. The king reenters, with his royal regiment and the royal clan surging behind him, and a new song is sung:

> We shall leave them with their country,
> Whose travellers are like distant thunder,
> Do you hear, Dlambula, do you hear?

The women sing:

> Do you hear?
> Let us go, let us go.

According to Kuper:

> The words and the tune are wild and sad like the sea "when the sea is angry and the birds of the sea are tossed on the waves." The royal women move backwards and forwards in small, desperate groups uttering their cry. Many weep. The men's feet stamp the ground vigorously and slowly, the black plumes wave and flutter, the princes come closer, driving the king in their midst. Nearer and nearer they bring him to his sanctuary. The crowd grows frenzied, the singing louder, the bodies sway and press against the sides of the enclosure, and the king is forced within. The priests follow; the princes draw back a little; an old man in full Incwala finery jigulates in the doorway, spurring on the dancers, keeping them from seeing what is happening to their king.[7]

Some of the Swazi claim that the king's royal relatives are symbolically urging the king to join them and to migrate away from nonkinsmen strangers, whom king and kinsmen have befriended and ruled, but whom they still distrust. Kuper feels, however, that the explanation offered by other informants is more accurate:

> The Malangeni [royal group] show their hatred of the king. They denounce him and force him from their midst.[8]

This seems to be confirmed by what follows. As the song again changes, the royal princes attempt to lure the king from his hut, inviting him by song to come forth:

There emerges a figure weird as the monster of legends. He is *Silo,* a nameless creature. On his head is a cap of black plumes that cover his face and blow about his shoulders, and underneath the feathers is glimpsed a head-band of a lion's skin. His body is covered in bright green grass and evergreen shoots that trail on the ground. In his left hand he holds a shield smeared with fat of the sacred herd, the *mfukwane.* His right hand is empty and as it moves it gleams with the lines of dark medicine. . . .

In this powerful costume the king appears reluctant to re- turn to the nation. He executes a crazy, elusive dance with knees flexed and swaying body. The movements are an in- tuitive response to the rhythm and situation, a dance that no ordinary man knows and that the king was never taught . . . his eyes shine through the feathers as he tosses his head, his face is dark with black medicine, dripping down his legs and arms are black streaks—he is terrifying, and as the knife-edged grass [of his costume] cuts into his skin he tosses his body furiously in pain and rage.[9]

Warriors who had earlier helped capture the "bull" appear with large black shields like those used in ancient warfare. They dance and sing, the king approaches, retreats, approaches, and retreats again, all the time holding a long black wand. Finally, the king appears with empty hands—the signal for aliens and royalty to leave. When he next appears he is bearing a vivid green gourd, a sacred calabash he has kept in his possession since the Incwala of the previous year. It is the *Luselwa Lwembo*—the wild gourd from Embo, the region from which the Dlamini clan first emigrated to Swaziland. Amidst the wild stamping of feet, frantic hissing, and the excited thumping of shields, the king throws the gourd onto the shield of one of the warriors, which is held horizontal. The king is then led away, his bizarre costume, except for the medicine painted on his body, is removed, and he enters the hut of the right-hand queen for the night.

During the fifth day, the king remains unapproachable because he is "painted in blackness." Only his two ritual wives are believed strong enough to withstand the demonic power possessing him at this time. The people, too, are in seclusion and in a taboo state—with sexual intercourse, late sleeping, merrymaking, and other pleasures suspended. Finally, on the sixth day, the king, the queen mother, and the entire nation are reinvigorated and are prepared to face the coming year. The sixth day, and the Incwala itself, end in feasting and revelry.

Considerable attention has been devoted to the Incwala, not only because it is important for the Swazi, but also because it illuminates an archaic concept of kingship. As Kuper [10] points out, the words of the Incwala songs may surprise the European, who is accustomed "to hear royalty blatantly extolled, the virtues of the nation magnified, and the country glorified" at national celebrations. The Incwala songs do not extoll the Swazi king; instead, they express hatred and rejection. The king is reviled and insulted more than he is glorified and eulogized. Despite this ritual display of hostility, Kuper believes the total effect of the Incwala is to strengthen the institution of Swazi kingship, and with it, the entire Swazi nation.

This line of reasoning has been developed most fully by the British anthropologist Max Gluckman,[11] who terms such ceremonies as the Incwala "rituals of rebellion." The Incwala allows Swazi citizens to display openly their ambivalent feelings toward the king's authority, which Gluckman feels ultimately strengthens the kingship. "Ritual rebellion" is in effect a catharsis, a purge of emotional grievances, and a way to avert political rebellion. Indeed, it is a substitute for rebellion, but it is also more than that. Gluckman maintains that the Incwala helps to remind the Swazi that their kingship is so solidly entrenched in their society that ritual rebellion can occur without endangering the kingship. Such ritual rebellion could not occur in the historic kingdoms of Europe, because if they did occur the basic form of government would be questioned or even undermined. Ritual rebellion can only exist, therefore, in traditional, or archaic, societies where kingship is firmly and unquestionably ingrained—societies in which kingship and society are one.

The American anthropologist Thomas Beidelman [12] challenges Gluckman's view. Beidelman feels that the *simemo* and the other activities of Incwala that vilify the king are not primarily expressions of hostility or ambivalence. Rather, they are delicate ritual devices that serve to separate the king symbolically from the various groups making overlapping, and potentially conflicting, claims upon him. Thus, certain phases of the Incwala separate the king from his own royal kinsmen, those who might seduce him from his national obligations; by freeing him from factional demands, the Incwala strengthens the king for the burdens of kingship and national priesthood.

Beidelman observes that in the first portion of the Incwala, the king's magical potency is gradually heightened until he is able to influence the supernatural forces that animate the world. At the climax of the ceremony, when the king appears as an otherworldly monster apparently transcending normal society by means of the strength and disorder of the demonic forces coalesced within him, these forces are set loose. When the king emerges naked except for his penis cap, the queen mother moans that it is a pain to see her child go "alone through the people," the ritual queens say, "We pity him," and the others agree that "the work of the king is indeed heavy." Beidelman suggests that the Swazi, through this ritual, recognize the king's "lonely, denuded status outside any single social category" [13] which enables him to gather within himself the extraordinary forces of the cosmos. When the king hurls the sacred gourd onto a warrior's shield, Beidelman terms the act a symbol of the king's return to the nation and to the world of men. He places his dangerous and unruly power back within the confines of the social order. The last phase of the Incwala, therefore, is a gradual deintensification of the potent, dangerous forces that had accumulated around the king during the first phase.

Although Beidelman's analysis of the distinctive and rich meanings of Incwala symbolism may be more subtle than Gluckman's, the two analyses are not mutually exclusive. Since rituals are highly condensed symbolic acts with meanings at *many* levels, the Incwala could serve simultaneously as emotional catharsis and as symbolic intensification-deintensification.

As Beidelman's analysis suggests, the Incwala could also be viewed as illuminating the theme of social evolution. When the Swazi first entered the region known as Swaziland, the institutions of clan and kinship affected their society in a manner similar, perhaps, to the way in which these institutions affected the Southeast Asian hill tribes. Somehow—precisely how is not known—the Swazi were able to add a new dimension of complexity to their society by transforming themselves into a nation based on a set of loyalties superseding those owed to kinship. However, because kinship bonds still remained strong and important, strains developed not only among the people, but also within the king's psychological makeup. The king had to find a way to balance his loyalties to royal kinsmen evenly against those to nonkinsmen, that is, to his nation. Since the populace is not easily persuaded of the king's impartiality, the Incwala serves to segregate the opposing loyalties, and, by excluding the royal clansmen from the ceremony at climactic points, it helps to reaffirm the king's fundamental commitment to his nation, above and beyond his clan. Perhaps, in this way, the Incwala both relieves popular suspicion and displays to the nation the king's unique power of transcending clan loyalties in a way commoners cannot. In this manner, king, kingship, and nation are all buttressed.

ANCIENT EGYPT AND MESOPOTAMIA [14]

Religiously endowed kingship is central to archaic society. The most elaborately developed god-king complex in history is found in ancient Egypt.

Although ancient Egypt exemplified during the course of her history several societal types, an archaic society existed from roughly 2700 to 1465 B.C.—the era designated as the Old Kingdom and the Middle Kingdom (which includes the Intermediate Period). During this span of time came the development and consolidation of the elaborate notion of divine kingship—a belief and a way of life that deeply penetrated Egyptian culture.

Archaeologists working in the area near the Nile have been able to trace the gradual transition (which took place over thousands of years) of a society with a social pattern based on hunting and gathering to one with a more settled style of life based on farming along the banks of the Nile. In the early phases of this transition, Egyptian society was isolated from neighboring societies and so developed more or less in its own way. Some evidence indicates, however, that just prior to the establishment of the first Egyptian dynasty, Mesopotamian culture did provide impetus for Egypt's development by introducing the cylinder seal, the building material of sun-dried bricks, and the idea of writing (the hieroglyphs, which came later, were the Egyptians' own invention). In spite of these early Mesopotamian influences, Egyptian society developed a socio-cultural style that differed radically from Mesopotamia's and from those of other neighboring societies.

Scholars generally agree that Egypt's unusually favorable geographical features contributed greatly to the development of her particular sociocultural patterns, characterized in part by a distinctive societal unity. Two features were especially important: first, Egypt's relative isolation from her neighbors by the mountains to the south, the massive deserts to the east and west, and the Mediterranean Sea to the north; second, the existence of the Nile River. The land of Egypt, for all practical purposes, was the area adjacent to the Nile. The Nile's seasonal inundation, which supplied life-giving fertility to this area, encouraged all who lived there to stay there. In addition, the Nile provided a channel of unifying communication.

Although some of Egypt's geographical features encouraged national unity, others encouraged regional divisions. Upper Egypt (the southern part of the country) was a narrow trough, a valley four to twenty miles wide, lying between the river and the cliffs that directed the river's course. The cliffs of Upper Egypt were never out of sight, effectively isolating the valley residents up to the point where the Nile's upper (southern) reaches disappeared into the equatorial wilderness. Lower (or northern) Egypt was, by contrast, a vast riverine delta, offering wide arable expanses and more contact with civilizations of the Mediterranean and the Near East. The attitudes and behavior of the people living in the North were thus more commercial and cosmopolitan than those of the people living in the South; and out of these differences between Upper and Lower Egypt crystallized differences of dialect and temperament that endured throughout ancient Egyptian history.

Egypt's earliest societies, of the hunting-gathering type, could support only small populations. With the emergence of agriculture, however, population increased and, with it, social complexity. Over many centuries and in many regions, petty princedoms presumably arose, but none was able to dominate and endure. The birth of Egyptian greatness came with the union of Upper and Lower Egypt under a single leader. This probably occurred in the third millennium B.C., with the founding of the first Egyptian dynastic rule.

Divine kingship in Egypt

The rulers of predynastic princedoms might have claimed divine qualities, but the full and popularly accepted merging of ruler and divinity into one being did not come until the time of Egypt's unification under the first pharaoh. Indeed, divine kingship was probably essential to the act of Egypt's unification, for if the gods existed above all regions of the land, the king who could identify himself successfully with the gods became liberated from any one region. The regions of Upper and Lower Egypt merged under the protection of a single divine ruler, a unity symbolized in several ways. Although there were two crowns, the White Crown of Upper Egypt and the Red Crown of Lower Egypt, they were united in the pharaoh's rather ungainly Double Crown. The pharaoh also proclaimed himself "The Two Ladies," signifying a combination of the two goddesses who stood respectively for Upper and Lower Egypt. As his pharaohdom was consolidated, the pharaoh's divinity was proclaimed ever more elaborately. By the fifth dynasty he was identified as the son of Re, the sun god, and often the Supreme God; or as son of Hathor, the mother goddess; or as Horus, the falcon god. Upon his death the pharaoh became Osiris, god of the dead and father of Horus—in the minds of his subjects he was transformed into his own father.

Although national divinity overarched the entire land, different locales became centers for the worship of different deities, each vying with the other to enthrone its own god prominently in the national pantheon. Thoth, scribe of the gods during the early dynastic period, was proclaimed creator of the world by his supporters in the city of Hermapolis. Heliopolis was, during the same era, a center for the worship of the sun god Ra-Atum, whose supporters proclaimed him creator of the world. The city of Memphis, which became the royal seat of the Old Kingdom, was a center for the worship of Ptah, who was regarded as an ancestor of Ra-Atum. It is not surprising that the political success of a god's supporters could affect the god's rank in the pantheon. Thus, when a dynasty ruling in the Middle Kingdom shifted its royal seat to the city of Thebes and patronized the obscure Amon—the hidden god of air and atmosphere—Amon soon rose to prominence as Amon-Ra, becoming identified with the sun god himself.

Partly because the Egyptians habitually ascribed to several gods the attributes of one and to one the attributes of several, the Egyptian pantheon became extremely complex and tangled. The Egyptians tolerated as reasonable what appear to us paradoxical and contradictory claims about the character of a god. Thus, in life the pharaoh was Horus, son of Osiris, but upon dying the pharaoh became Osiris himself, an expression of one incest theme latent in the Egyptian divine-royal mythos.

Incest played a role in the actual conduct of Egyptian kingship. Although the pharaoh had wives and concubines in his harem, as did the Swazi king, and although these wives and concubines could be expected to bear him children, the heir to his throne would be the child who possessed the purest royal blood. To guarantee an offspring of the required purity, the pharaoh would ritually mate with a close female relative—a sister, a half sister, or a close cousin. He drew religious sanction for this act from myths that described similar matings between the gods, for example, Osiris and his sister, Isis. Although incest was prohibited among nonroyalty, its practice by royalty served an important administrative function. Just as the pharaoh freed himself from the risk of close territorial or kinship interests by identifying with overarching national deities, so he freed himself through incest from obligations to in-laws, obligations that would have been inevitable had he produced his successor by mating with a nonroyal wife. Incest made the pharaoh self-sufficient and omnipotent. Furthermore, the royal line, by perpetuating itself through incest, displayed divine traits and thus reinforced its own claim to being of divine origin.

To the Egyptian, pharaoh and society were the same. His vocabulary lacked any word for "government," "state," or "nation" as institutions or sociopolitical systems. Society and state were simply extensions of the pharaoh's divine personality. During the early period of dynastic consolidation, the pharaoh was involved personally in all key decisions of government, but in time the kingdom became too complex for him to supervise directly. His duties then became more those of ritual—to insure the proper ordering of the gods, the seasons, and the world—and the task of day-to-day administration fell instead to a complex bureaucracy. Since government derived from divinity, temples and priests played as great a part in the bureaucratic system as offices and officials; but in spite of the kingdom's bureaucratization, its officials remained simply extensions of the pharaoh's person, ranked in importance by their proximity to the divine ruler. This concept is reflected in the Old Kingdom custom of placing the tombs of officials near the pharaoh's tomb, apparently so that the officials might follow the pharaoh easily into the next world and there continue as his "arms."

Vast cities of temples and palaces, irrigation projects, mines, soaring pyramids to serve as the eternal home of the pharaoh, the 365-day calendar, which was evolved from years of observing the Nile floods, were all accomplishments of the early Egyptian bureaucracy and were made possible in part by the willingness of the people to accept the pharaoh's divinity. Work for the pharaoh was considered a religious as well as a civic duty and that notion, aided by the sting of the lash, allowed the bureaucracy to mobilize a huge labor force—a significant advance in terms of efficiency and yield over the primitive headman's reliance on his kinsmen or affines.

Many of the most impressive architectural feats of ancient Egypt, such as the building of the giant pyramids, were achieved during the Old Kingdom period. Perhaps the transformation of Egypt from a primitive to an archaic system, fostered by the creation of divine kingship, stimulated a sudden vitality. The unification of Egypt brought peace, which in turn brought economic and welfare assurances in the form of the reclamation of swampland, the construction of irrigation works and storehouses for surplus grain, and the development of new medical techniques. As a result, perhaps, of these and other advances, the rate of population growth increased, prompting a rise in labor manpower and a consequent surge in public construction. In fact, one could speculate that any shift from a primitive to an archaic societal pattern will encourage a population increase, hence a rise in cultural achievement.

The pharaoh as god-king became the link between society and divinity. In some respects, the bond between the social and the cosmic found in archaic Egyptian society is like the fusing of these same orders in the aboriginal Dreaming. But for the Egyptian, the cosmos was far more objective and systematized than for the aborigine. Gods of the Egyptian pantheon were more clearly identified and arranged and more carefully distinguished from ordinary men than the aboriginal heroes of The Dreaming. By their ability to record the cosmology in writing, the Egyptian priests could achieve more precision, systematization, and permanence of characterization than the aboriginal laymen, who can only recount their myths orally from memory. The setting down of thoughts in writing also tends to abstract them, to objectify them, and to make them more distant from the writer. The systematized cosmology of the Egyptians, objectified beyond the self and the flux of daily life, tended to appear above self and life and in control of them. The Egyptians saw the cosmos and cosmology as an eternal, constant order directing the fluid movement of daily existence (again in contrast to views held by the aborigines, who perceive daily existence as fixed and static).

This eternal, constant order, called *Ma'at,* is described by Wilson as

> the cosmic force of harmony, order, stability, and security, coming down from the first creation as the organizing quality of created phenomena and re-affirmed at the accession of each god-king of Egypt. In the temple scenes the pharaoh exhibited *ma'at* to the other gods every day, as the visible evidence that he was carrying out his divine function of rule on their behalf. Thus, there was something of the unchanging, eternal, and cosmic about *ma'at* . . . it was the order of created things . . . it was the just and proper relationship of cosmic phenomena, including the relationship of rulers to the ruled. . . . *Ma'at,* then, was a created and inherited rightness, which tradition built up into a concept of orderly stability, in order to confirm and consolidate the status quo, particularly the continuing rule of the pharaoh.[15]

According to Wilson, the Egyptian perceived transitory phenomena of life as expressions of the timeless and eternal order of *Ma'at.* For the Egyptian

> the phenomena and activities of his little world were asserted to be momentary flashes of the everlasting, rocklike order of the gods. So this little pharaoh who sat upon the throne of

Egypt was no transitory human but was the same "good god" that he had been from the Beginning and would be for all time. So the relationship of beings was not something which had to be worked out painfully in an evolution toward even better conditions but was magnificently free from change, experiment, or evolution, since it had been fully good from the Beginning and needed only to be reaffirmed in its unchanging rightness. Aspects of the divine kingship and of *ma'at* might be subject to temporary misfortune or challenge, but the generalities of these two concepts came to be fundamental in acceptance because they gave timid man freedom from doubt through the operation of the immutable.[16]

The pharaoh himself was both the personification and the ultimate interpreter of *Ma'at,* and its distinctive capacity to categorize the temporal as expressive of the eternal is exemplified in the succession of pharaohs. The death of a pharaoh and the enthronement of his successor implied, in a very real sense, the creation of a new world. The old Horus became Osiris and created a new Horus. Yet the new Horus and the old Horus were believed to be the same, one, eternal Horus. Change in the political order and the progression of historical events were classified as an expression of the immutable cosmic order: dynasties rose and fell, but Egyptians construed their world as without change.

The pyramid can be seen as a symbol of the rigidly hierarchical Egyptian society. At the pinnacle, the apex of cosmos and society, stood the pharaoh. Directly below him were his "servants," the elite—nobles, high officials, priests, and major landowners—who drew influence in proportion to their spiritual and political proximity and similarity to the pharaoh, fount of all power. At the base of the pyramid were the toiling peasants and artisans. Egyptian society was basically a two-class society, with a very sharp cleavage between the elite and the masses. While kinship and marriage bound noble to noble, peasant to peasant, and artisan to artisan, the bond between the elite and the masses was essentially forged not out of kinship and marriage, but out of worship and authority.

Mediating kingship in Mesopotamia

"Horizontal" Mesopotamia presents an interesting contrast to "vertical," or hierarchical, Egypt. If the structure of Egyptian society could be compared to a giant pyramid, the structure of Mesopotamian society can be compared to a series of small mounds, each fairly independent. There was no single, overriding figure, such as the pharaoh, to unify the cities; therefore they functioned as semi-autonomous city-states.

Extending from the central part of the Mediterranean Sea, through the islands, peninsulas, and coasts, eastward to the valleys of the Tigris and Euphrates rivers—the heartland of ancient Near Eastern society—Mesopotamia, unlike unified but isolated Egypt, was in constant contact with other cultures. With its vast open lands, Mesopotamia was vulnerable to unpredictable storms that would sweep across the open spaces and was, therefore, denied gentle, steady, and fructifying seasonal rhythms like those enriching the Nile valley. Partly as a result of these geographical features, Mesopotamia tended to be fragmented, factional, unstable, and dynamic.

To the Mesopotamian view, the lands owned by the city-states were really the property of the city-state's gods—hence, under the control of the temple priests and officials, the gods' human agents. Each city-state was a confederation of land-holding and labor-mobilizing temples. In each city only one god reigned supreme; the other gods were members of the supreme god's family or were considered his neighbors in the cosmic community. The citizens of each city were the people of that city's god, and the chief priest of the god's temple served as governor of the city-state. Not only did the priest-ruler superintend worship of the supreme god, but he also administered the city's irrigation system and negotiated with other cities in matters of diplomacy and trade. Unlike modern communities, in which separate functions are well defined, the Mesopotamian city-state was an independent religio-politico-economic community, in which it was difficult to separate one function from the others.

The elite of Mesopotamia normally inherited their positions, and as with Egypt and Swaziland, kinship was important in structuring Mesopotamian government. However, the bond between the elite and the masses was again not of kinship and marriage, but of politics and religion. The god of the city-state made known his wishes to the governor, who then gave orders and directives to the people. In carrying out the god's commands, in effect by worshipping him, the people insured the proper ordering of the portion of the cosmos identified with that god.[17] The city-state, then, was populated by worshippers of a particular deity, of a god who occupied a place among the other gods, who collectively represented the total cosmos and its association with all Mesopotamia. Among the foremost deities were the cosmic gods: Anu, god of the heavenly regions; Enlil, god of the atmosphere and of storms; Enki, god of earth; Utu or Shamash, god of the sun; Nannar or Sin, god of the moon; and Inanna or Ishtar, god of the morning star. To this pantheon of gods, with their influence over the total cosmos and society, the god of each of the city-states served as a bridge.

By an extension of this reasoning, the relations among the city-states were thought to reflect the relations among the gods of the various cities. The leaders of a city were expected to champion the position of their god in the intercity pantheon, thereby strengthening the city's position politically. The result of this rivalry was warfare. The goal was not to convert worshippers from one god to another, but to force the enemy to acknowledge that his god was inferior to one's own. To demonstrate how inferior, one city-state might conquer another city-state and then tear down its walls, wreck its irrigation works, and exact financial tribute. This pattern, which really involved putting one's deity above others in the spiritual order through distinctly unspiritual force, is reflected in the rise and fall of several empires—Sumerian, Babylonian, Assyrian—each dominated by a particular city worshipping a particular god. As a city became dominant, its scribes would see to it that the myths of the surrounding area were rewritten so as to celebrate and elevate the dominant city's god. Thus, feats attributed in Sumerian mythology to Enlil were ascribed by the later Babylonians to their own god, Marduk, who was superseded in turn by the god of the conquering Assyrians, Assur.[18]

Eventually, however, there emerged in Mesopotamia a form of kingship that proved successful in uniting the various city-states. Military men were appointed by the city's leaders to cope with occasional emergencies, but since the state of emergency persisted, the temporary generals evolved into permanent kings. Unlike the Egyptian pharaoh, who merged society with the cosmos, the Mesopotamian king mediated between society and the cosmos. God and man were more distinct than they were in Egypt, a difference in conception that gave rise to other differences as well.

Since the Egyptian pharaoh was a god, one needed only to talk with him to learn the wishes of the gods. In Mesopotamia, where the king was not a god, the gods' wishes were less easily communicated. Mesopotamians needed different channels. Thus, since the important gods were celestial, they turned to the heavens for signs of their gods' bidding, an orientation that both stimulated and exploited notable developments in astronomy—not as a science (as we know it) but as a technique for decoding the cosmic cipher. A way of speaking to the gods was also needed. The rite of sacrifice filled this need. By sacrificing animals to the gods, people curried the favor of the gods and made the gods receptive to the people's wishes. The gods, in turn, could communicate their commands to the king by dreams, omens, and portentous natural events, and the king would interpret these for the people. If the king had understood the gods properly, and if the people had properly obeyed the king, the gods rewarded the people with prosperity and happiness. Failure to comprehend or to implement the commands of the gods resulted in drought, famine, flood, and defeat in war. The king's authority depended, therefore, on his ability to mediate between the gods and the people in such a way as to achieve harmony and to fend off disaster.

Separation of the cosmos and society also promoted in Mesopotamia the development of law. In Egypt, law was the pharaoh's word, an expression of the eternal unity of the cosmos and the eternal verity of *Ma'at*. There was no law transcending the pharaoh's personal decree, nor could there be. In Mesopotamia, where gods transcended the king, their decrees necessarily transcended his own. The gods made the laws, and the king himself was bound by them; indeed, it was his duty to codify the gods' laws. Thus, there emerged a number of law codes, the most famous being the Code of Hammurabi (*ca.* 1700 B.C.), from which sprang the concept of the free citizen of city-state or empire, who was guaranteed the right to hold land and property, to enter into contracts of trade and marriage, and to obtain legal redress. The rights of the Egyptian, by contrast, were defined only by custom and the pharaoh: whether one was treated justly or unjustly depended on one's kinship connections or on one's influence in high places. Compared to Egyptian justice, Mesopotamian justice was universalistic. However, Mesopotamian law did not accord all men equal rights. It systematically allowed greater privilege to aristocrats than to commoners; it decreed harsher punishments for crimes committed by common men than for those committed by the elite. And, as might be expected, slaves were denied all rights. In general, however, the Mesopotamian citizen could expect to be treated according to a codified set of standards; he was less subject to whim, favoritism, or accidents of kinship.

Another consequence of the Mesopotamian legal system was the encouragement of trade. In Egypt, commerce was relatively undeveloped. Rudimentary money (a piece of metal that served as a measure of value) was employed, but most transactions involved barter. In Mesopotamia, not only was money common within the city-states, it was also negotiable among them. Traders ranged widely, spreading Mesopotamian currency through the Delta and the Persian Gulf, overland to Persia, Egypt, and the Mediterranean coast, possibly as far west as Crete and even into the Aegean Sea and Greece. Money transactions implied the notions of contract, an institution particularly well developed in Mesopotamian law, and of lending, which was done at interest. The man who inscribed the terms of a contract on clay tablets could depend on the law and the courts to validate and uphold the contract. To the Mesopotamian trader, this was a boon; supported by laws binding upon all citizens, he could negotiate confidently with all citizens, rather than merely with kinsmen, neighbors, or those to whom he had particularistic ties. He had greater freedom than the Egyptian; furthermore, since he could depend on the stability of codified law to define his rights and obligations, he could calculate his risks with greater certainty.

Although Egypt and Mesopotamia represent basically the same general type of society—the archaic—Mesopotamia advanced further toward modernization than did Egypt. There is another society, likewise a variant of the archaic, that should be noted— the lowland Southeast Asian society.

EARLY LOWLAND SOUTHEAST ASIAN STATES [19]

Early in the first millennium A.D., a number of empires, such as those of the ancient Khmer and Javanese, emerged in the lowland areas of mainland and archipelago Southeast Asia. These lowland Southeast Asian states illustrate the interrelationship of several factors in the emergence of archaic society. First, we observe the role of divine kingship, as in Egypt, and of the temple-dominated city-states, as in Mesopotamia. These Southeast Asian societies may also serve to illustrate how the transition from a primitive to an archaic pattern can be stimulated by contact with alien societies rather than primarily by indigenous processes as was the case among the Swazi, the Egyptians, and in Mesopotamia. And, finally, the lowland states illustrate the contribution of technological advance, such as irrigated agriculture, to the development of archaic society. This last point is best supported by contrasting the lowland Southeast Asian states with the Southeast Asian hill tribes discussed earlier.

On the mountain slopes they inhabit, the Southeast Asian highland tribes practice a slash and burn form of agriculture; that is, they cut down and burn trees to prepare the land for crops of dry rice, millet, or Job's tears. Irrigation is not required because these crops are watered sufficiently by the annual monsoonal rainfall. The fertility of the fields, however, is quickly exhausted, and the tribesmen are thus forced to relocate frequently. Every year or every few years, a community will clear new land, leaving the old to regain its fertility for reuse in perhaps a decade. Since each group must circulate among many fields, these mountain areas can be only sparsely settled. It is estimated that each family of five requires twenty-five acres of land per year, so that the maximum population density can be only 130 persons per square mile.

Quite different is life on the lowland plains. For two thousand years the lowland farmers have cultivated rice in irrigated fields; accordingly, lowland population densities are much greater than in the highlands. The same irrigated field can be used year after year, less land is needed per person, and the density of population ranks with the world's highest. In rural areas of central Java, for example, there are more than 1,000 persons per square mile.

These contrasts in agriculture and demography are correlated throughout Southeast Asia with differences in society and culture. The highland society of the mainland remains a patchwork of incredibly individualistic and fragmented tribes, with even close neighbors often unable to understand each other's languages. Many of the hill tribes were constantly at war prior to the *pax colonialis* imposed by British and French colonialists, yet despite their bellicosity, or perhaps because of it, they were never able to weld themselves into strong centralized states that could muster large armies to conquer lowland areas. As was discussed in chapter 3, the tribes were united only by systems of kinship and marriage, not by an overarching government; and as the analysis of the Kachin illustrates, attempts to centralize by creating kingdoms always failed. The lack of centralization was encouraged by the hill tribes' pattern of agriculture: slash and burn farming cannot support a large concentration of people in one spot, such as the capital city of a centralized empire.

The irrigated rice agriculture and high population density of lowland Southeast Asia have, by contrast, encouraged extensive political centralization in the form of cities, kingdoms, and empires. What is known of their prehistory suggests that the lowland dwellers moved gradually from a hunting and gathering mode of life toward a settled one based on irrigated agriculture, and that a major surge of population growth and political centralization possibly occurred about the time of Christ. Archaeological finds (such as large and elaborately decorated stone temples bearing records of the deeds of emperors, priests, and gods) made throughout the lowland plains indicate that during this period there emerged complex, archaic societies, perhaps not unlike those of Mesopotamia. These emerging civilizations were influenced by India, many hundreds of miles to the west. Lowland chiefs had "witnessed from afar the splendor of India," [20] and had adapted Indian myths and religion, alphabets and writing systems, stone techniques, and symbols of royalty in their own advance toward centralization and civilization.

Precisely how or why the contact between India and Southeast Asia came about is not clear. The lowlanders probably met Indian merchants and adopted some of the latter's patterns simply because it was politically advantageous to do so. For instance, the Indian concept of the god-king (*deva-raja*) allowed the Southeast Asian kings to be regarded as incarnations of such gods as Siva or Vishnu. With such exalted status, they were able to mobilize great armies and kingdoms. To the people a divine fragrance diffused from the god-king's body throughout the surrounding countryside, coating it with prosperity, happiness, and security. In return for these benefits, the people gave the god-king their loyalty, their crops, and their labors to build intricate irrigation networks, roads, hospitals, and magnificent temples such as Angkor Wat in Cambodia and Borobodur in Java.

The Indian-derived god-king institution of Southeast Asia resembles that of ancient Egypt, and the associated temple-cities are reminiscent of ancient Mesopotamia. Each temple-city dominated an agricultural hinterland and was ruled by a god-king, who was believed to be the incarnation of the god to whose worship that city's temples were devoted. As in Mesopotamia, each temple-city schemed and struggled to establish the ascendancy of its god over the gods of the rival cities; hence, the history of the early Southeast Asian empires is one of power shifts among cities and dynasties.

During its archaic phase, lowland Southeast Asia was a two-class society composed of a religio-political elite—including the god-king and his officials, priests, kinsmen, and in-laws—and a toiling peasant mass who supported the elite by worshipping and paying tribute to them. Although this archaic patterning was inspired by India, certain local differences were significant. For example, the priests who attended the temples were always subordinate to the divine king, a deviation from the Indian pattern, where the priest (*Brahman*) is deemed superior to the warrior or king (*Ksatriya*). Incorporated into Southeast Asian societies were the Indian notions of the god-king, of hierarchical society, and of the capital city as a core of temporal society and of the universe itself. Even without the stimulus of these Indian elements, archaic society and culture might have emerged in Southeast Asia, but because Indian patterns were available, the transition was facilitated.

OVERVIEW

A simple way to identify and distinguish between archaic and primitive societies would be to say that archaic society is based on kingship, primitive society on kinship. Moving from the Australian aborigines, the Ndembu, and the Southeast Asian hill tribes to the Swazi, Egyptians or Mesopotamians, and Southeast Asian states, we shift from one-class societies composed of kinsmen, all of whom are roughly equal in status, to two-class societies composed of commoners and an elite—kings, priests, and aristocrats—with the two classes bound by ties of authority and worship rather than kinship.

Primitive societies do make a distinction between leaders and followers, but never are these leaders set above the people so markedly as they are in archaic societies. As can be seen from the Kachin, when chiefs act like kings in a primitive society, their followers revolt and set up separate communities based on the *gumlao* (egalitarian) ideology.

One cannot assert that kinship and marriage bonds are unimportant in archaic society since elite (or nonelite) status is inherited. Among the Swazi, for example, the king is considered the "father" of his people; but in archaic society such terms are used metaphorically. No ordinary Swazi would claim the king as his genealogical father, or even as a kinsman; indeed, in archaic society customs frequently exist to insure that the king will not be related to the masses or even to other members of the elite. Thus, only the Swazi royal clan has the right to marry within itself; and in Egypt, only the pharaoh could marry his sister.

In archaic societies, the elite class—especially the king—is deemed superior in every field. The king is either divine (as in Egypt), or has special access to the gods (as in Mesopotamia), or is the cosmos itself (as in Swaziland). His political power and his wealth are also great. The elite, other than the king, function as priests, officials, and business managers. In sharp contrast to primitive society, the masses in archaic society are as disadvantaged religiously, politically, and economically as the elite are privileged. For example, among the aborigines all males are not only approximately equal politically and economically, but they also participate directly in ordering the universe through their identification with the heroic figures of The Dreaming. In other words, they are equal religiously, with each man functioning as a priest.

The social cleavage between the elite and the masses implies a degree of specialization in archaic societies exceeding that found in primitive societies. In primitive society there is some specialization of labor—for example, the role of the headmen among the Australian aborigines or of the curers among the Ndembu—but almost all men in a primitive society perform essentially the same tasks. In archaic society, the specialization of labor is dramatic and is based on the premise that some men are innately better qualified than others to pursue certain callings. The elite specialize in mediating between gods and men, or in similar functions; the masses, in manual labor.

It might be argued that archaic society is more universalistic than primitive society—that the archaic man's status is more strongly based on his deeds, the primitive's man's on his descent. It is true that kinship is a major factor in determining the archaic man's status, but if he did not perform effectively in that status, he could be removed from it. The ineffective pharaoh or king could be deposed in a palace coup; it would be harder to indict the aborigine if a rite failed to produce results. In primitive society, many persons or factors, often the entire community, can be blamed. In archaic society, however, one can point to the specialist. Thus, with the increase in specialization emerges the notion of individual responsibility, setting the stage for a new image of the person.

Consider, in this regard, Mesopotamian law. In Mesopotamia roles implied by the contractual-commercial relationship were separated by law from those implied by the kinship-personal relationship, suggesting that archaic man possessed some freedom to enter a contractual-commercial relationship without kinship-imposed restrictions. To some degree, a man from kinship group X could choose among commercial-contractual relations A, B, C . . . ; he need feel no obligation to deal only with a fellow X. Each member of group X could choose among a variety of trade contacts, and members of group X were likely to vary widely in the number and kind of their contacts. In the extreme approached by primitive society, by contrast, each member of kinship group Y could relate only to his fellow Y's, and therefore the members of group Y would vary hardly at all in the number and kind of their contacts. A member of archaic society, therefore, would be more likely to be regarded as a unique configuration of social roles—that is, as a *distinct self*—than a member of primitive society.

Although relationships in archaic society—such as those between masses and elite which involve mixed political, religious, and economic obligations—are diffuse by comparison with those in modern society, they are less diffuse in archaic society than they are in primitive society. Since archaic man spreads his desires and duties among nonkinsmen as well as kinsmen, he never experiences the primitive man's concentration of all facets of social life within a single extremely diffuse relationship, the kinship relationship.

Archaic societies are more centralized than primitive societies. In archaic societies populations are concentrated and coordinated into cities, kingdoms, nations, and empires; and with the increase of centralization, there inevitably emerges a high degree of bureaucratization. Because of centralization and bureaucratization, archaic kings achieved a control over the populace that allowed them to exploit the people as a labor force in the construction of gigantic projects such as the pyramids of Egypt and the temples of Southeast Asia. Primitive man excels in coping with his environment, archaic man surpasses him in exploiting it.

It was certainly not by chance that archaic societies such as Egypt, Mesopotamia, and early lowland Southeast Asia developed extensive irrigation works. In Southeast Asia, primitive and archaic societies can be neatly discriminated according to the presence or absence of irrigation. In the Near East and Far East, scholars such as Karl Wittfogel [21] have perceived similar correlations. Archaeologists have also observed connections between irrigation and archaic patterning in Meso-America and Peru.[22] What is not clear, however, is whether the irrigation systems had to be developed before archaic society and culture could flourish. The Meso-American, Peruvian, and Mesopotamian cases suggest not, since in these societies great irrigation systems seem to have emerged only after archaic society was well under way. Taking into account these findings as well as others (the Swazi, for example, have archaic patterns but no irrigation system), we can conclude that irrigation is not a necessary condition for the emergence of archaic society and culture; however, a society must develop some system of food production, as opposed to food-gathering, before it can advance to the archaic stage.

In archaic society, the cosmic and the social world are distinct and different; in primitive society, the cosmic and the social world are fused. Among the Australian aborigines, sacred order and social order are considered the same. Sacred figures are identified with ordinary men. And when men *become* their gods, the aborigines suffer little doubt about their gods' intentions; they need only ask their god-selves what they think or what they desire. Archaic gods, on the other hand, are separate and distinct from men. Men cannot identify with them easily. Yet the thoughts and desires of the gods must still be ascertained. The gods must also be dealt with, for they live in the midst of men—not in a heaven, as in historic religion, but in a forest, on a mountain, or as a god-king in a capital city.

How, then, does archaic man communicate with these gods who live with him and control him, yet who are so distant from him spiritually that he does not know their wishes? One important way is by sacrifice, an institution more prominent in archaic society than in primitive society. Sacrifice, especially in Mesopotamia, allowed gods to keep their distance from men. Since archaic men did not identify with their gods during sacrificial ritual any more than they did in daily life—and certainly never to the extent of the aborigine in his "secret life"—they were forced to interpose between themselves and the gods a sacrificial animal or plant, perhaps even a priest. If the mediating element successfully bridged the gap between men and the gods, men would know the gods' commands, and the gods in turn would learn men's needs. Sacrifice involved more uncertainty than did the aboriginal secret life. The archaic man could not control how the god would respond to his offering, whereas by fusing himself with the heroes of The Dreaming, the aborigine to some extent could. Thus, sacrifice was an agent and a reflection of the general increase in freedom that accompanied the shift from primitive to archaic society.

The archaic society's separation of cosmos and society is reflected in its division between classes. Archaic elite claim a special kinship to the cosmic, either by serving as intercessors between it and the people or by identifying themselves with it. Although the elite claim special sanctity, other elements of archaic existence are sacred as well. Not only is the state the object of worship and cult, so too are household and lineage, health and illness, life and death, crafts and agriculture. Since all life is sacred, any change in it might anger the gods; hence archaic life is warped in some measure toward conformity and conservatism.

A question appropriate to each evolutionary level would be: How much more likely to move in the direction of modernization is a society at the level under consideration than a society one level below it? In comparing archaic society with primitive society, one could suggest that because the separation between the cosmic and the social world in archaic society is greater, there is greater potential for change. Archaic man could imagine modeling the social world after the cosmic, for the two are clearly differentiated and defined. Primitive man would find such a process almost inconceivable, because for him the cosmic and the ordinary are fused. On the other hand, archaic society has its own inhibitant to change: when the king is god, it is difficult to revolt against him in the name of god.

TOPICS FOR DISCUSSION

In our discussion of the Swazi Incwala ritual we noted that Beidelman ("Swazi Royal Ritual") and Gluckman ("Rituals of Rebellion in Southeast Africa") offer alternative interpretations of the same event. This phenomenon is common in anthropology. Given the frequency of alternative interpretations, the student might consider the methodological question: Can alternative interpretations be allowed by a true science?

The student might also have observed that two types of data furnish a basis for the sociocultural portraits presented in this chapter and in the related readings: archaeological and ethnographic. The portraits of the ancient Egyptian, Mesopotamian, Southeast Asian, and North and Middle American civilizations were reconstructed mainly from artifacts discovered by archaeologists. The portrait of the contemporary Swazi kingdom was reconstructed from an ethnographer's observations of living people. An interesting exercise would be to compare the two methods of reconstruction.

THE SWAZI

An African Aristocracy: Rank Among the Swazi (1965) by Hilda
Kuper. The standard work on the Swazi.
The Swazi: A South African Kingdom (paperback, 1963) by Hilda
Kuper in the "Case Studies in Cultural Anthropology" paperback
series. An excellent summary, designed for the beginning student.
Bunyoro: An African Kingdom (paperback, 1960) by John Beattie.
Also in the "Case Studies" series. The Bunyoro can be usefully
compared with the Swazi.
"Rituals of Rebellion in Southeast Africa" (1963) by Max Gluckman.
An interpretation of Swazi ritual.
"Swazi Royal Ritual" (1966) by T. O. Beidelman. An alternative in-
terpretation of Swazi ritual.

EGYPT AND MESOPOTAMIA

The Culture of Ancient Egypt (paperback, 1956) by John A. Wilson.
An outstanding general account of Egyptian society and culture
suitable for beginning students.

Everyday Life in Ancient Egypt (paperback, 1967) by Jon E. M. White. A useful if elementary introduction.

Kingship and the Gods (1948) by Henri Frankfort. On Egypt and Mesopotamia.

Before Philosophy: The Intellectual Adventure of Ancient Man (paperback, 1967) by Henri Frankfort *et al.*

The Face of the Ancient Orient (paperback, 1962) by Sabatino Moscati.

The Greatness That Was Babylon (paperback, 1968) by H. W. F. Saggs.

Oriental Despotism (paperback, 1957) by Karl A. Wittfogel. Provides an interesting argument on the connection between technology and culture in the ancient Near East and elsewhere.

LOWLAND SOUTHEAST ASIAN STATES

Hill Farms and Padi Fields: Life in Mainland Southeast Asia (paperback, 1965) by Robbins Burling. A sound introductory treatment. See especially chapter 5.

The Making of Southeast Asia (1966) by George Coedès. A stimulating synthesis.

Angkor: An Introduction (1963) by George Coedès.

Conceptions of State and Kingship in Southeast Asia (1956) by Robert Heine-Geldern. A classic work. Still useful, although it does not refer exclusively to the archaic pattern.

Southeast Asia: Crossroad of Religions (1949) by Kenneth Landon.

NORTH AND SOUTH AMERICA

Mexico (paperback, 1962) by Michael D. Coe.

Ancient Mexico (paperback, 1959) by Frederick Peterson.

Peru Before the Incas (paperback, 1967) by Edward P. Lanning.

An Introduction to American Archaeology, I: North and Middle America (1966) by Gordon R. Willey.

These works treat aspects of the archaic pattern as it developed in North and South America.

FILMS

The Ancient Egyptian. A brief but visually rich film.
Ancient Mesopotamia. Attempts to reconstruct Mesopotamian society.

5

Historic society and culture

The cultural foundations for historic societies were laid down by the great historic religions: Buddhism, Christianity, and Islam. By conceiving a wide gulf between this world and the otherworld and then devaluing this world, historic religions made salvation the focal problem of life. Historic man's attempts to solve that problem drove him toward new social advances.

BUDDHISM AND THAILAND [1]

Speakers of Thai dialects are scattered throughout the contemporary states of Southeast Asia, but most Thai speakers live in Thailand. Bounded on the west by Burma, on the east by Laos and Cambodia, and to the south by Malaysia, Thailand covers an area of about 200,000 square miles. Most of its 26 million people cluster in the fertile valley of the Caw Phra Jaa River.

Thai history begins in the thirteenth century with a kingdom called Sukhothai, located in a northern province and composed of a number of semiautonomous city-states. The earliest inscriptions from Sukothai indicate that its inhabitants were followers of Theravada Buddhism, a religion they had adopted from their Mon and Burmese neighbors. While practicing Buddhism, the Thai continued to cling to animistic beliefs in spirits and magic and to follow certain Hindu rituals. As a result, Thai religion was an amalgam. Today, although this is still true, Buddhism dominates and is the state religion.

Thai Buddhism

Buddhism developed around 500 B.C. in India, and subsequently divided into two great schools that are still recognized today. The Northern school, commonly called Mahayana, spread from India into Tibet, China, Japan, and from China into Vietnam. The Southern school, called Theravada (or Hinayana) spread into Ceylon, Burma, Thailand, Laos, and Cambodia. Many scholars regard the Theravada tradition as being closer than the Mahayana to original Buddhism.

Although Christianity and Islam conceive of an otherworld infinitely more glorious than this world, Buddhism goes even further in devaluing this world. In its extreme philosophical position, Buddhism holds that the visible, physical world is sheer illusion. Only the otherworld, represented by religious symbolism, is real. Fundamental to this "real" world are the doctrines of *karma* (in Thai, *kaam*) and of multiple rebirths.

The doctrine of karma holds that every action is deserving of merit (*bun*) or demerit (*bab*). Every person is the product of the sum of his meritorious acts balanced against the sum of his unmeritorious ones, of his *bun* balanced against his *bab*. A kind of cosmic computer (not a god) keeps track of these sums automatically, so that each person at all times is treated by the cosmos in accordance with the amount of merit he has accumulated.

The doctrine of multiple rebirths holds that an individual's religious life extends through a series of several lifetimes. The individual is repeatedly reborn, and the status he occupies in each new life reflects the meritoriousness of his deeds in the life before; the more merit he accumulated in his last life, the better his status in this life. Ultimately, the Buddhist may even make so much merit that he is freed from the treadmill of birth and rebirth. Then he has attained Nirvana.

The creatures of the universe are, in Theravada Buddhism, ranked according to the amount of merit they have accumulated. At the top of the scale sit the gods (*thewada*), such as Siva and Indra, who live in the heavens. Below the gods stand men (*manut*). Below men crawl the animals (*sad*). At the bottom skulk the spirits (*phi*) and demons (*preet*). At each level there are subdivisions; thus at the level of men, monks are of exalted status. Thai Buddhists believe that deep and basic differences separate the various ranks, that all men are ranked relative to one another, and that no social relationship is between equals—in short that all existence is structured *hierarchically*.

Although Buddhism emerged from Hinduism and still retains many Hindu concepts, it has imbued these with distinctively Buddhist meanings. Generally Buddhism provides a more individualistic emphasis. In Hinduism the individual's moral status is irrevocably fixed by the status of the caste into which he is born. By faithfully obeying the commands and taboos, the *dharma* of one's caste, one may be born into a higher caste in the next life, but one has no hope of rising socially in this life. In Buddhism, however, a person's moral and social status is thought to depend more on his own actions and qualities than on the group into which he is born.

Buddhism also differs from Hinduism in its universalism. For the Hindu, it was as much a sacrilege to adhere to the rules of a caste other than one's own as it was to disobey the rules of one's own caste; but for the Buddhist, certain rules apply to every man, whatever his caste. All Buddhists are expected to follow the five precepts; to refrain from stealing, fornicating, killing, lying, and drinking alcohol. Pious laymen may on special occasions, such as the Buddhist Sabbath, undertake to obey three other precepts: to refrain from eating solids after noon, from indulging in entertainment and adornment, and from sitting or lying on a high or wide mattress filled with cotton. Furthermore, any man who is especially eager to accumulate merit may become a monk and assume the burden of following a total of 227 rules. The Buddhist who wishes to do so may follow any or all of these rules, whereas the Hindu may follow only the rules of his own caste.

The monk in Thai society

The Buddhist monk's shaved head, orange robe, and secluded temple quarters separate him from the layman, as do the 227 rules.

He may not marry or even receive objects from a woman's bare hand. Unlike the Christian monk, the Buddhist monk is not allowed to grow his own food because while plowing the land he might inadvertently take the life of some animal, and thus violate one of the rules. The monk earns the respect of all Thais by submitting to a life of restraint. By his discipline he demonstrates that he is morally superior.

To affirm the monk's superiority ritually, laymen sit at a lower level and address monks in honorific speech. In fact, in the Thai language the gulf between monks and ordinary men is constantly stressed, since speech to and about monks employs the modifier *ong,* meaning "mana-filled object" and used in regard to gods, king, and the Buddha, as well as monks. Ordinary people are referred to simply as *khon,* meaning "person."

Since the rules the monks follow do not allow them to work, the laity must support them. Each morning monks pass along the paths and roads, silently accepting the food offerings placed in their alms bowls by the laity. Westerners see this as an expression of the monk's dependence on the layman, but the Thai take the opposite view. By accepting the layman's offerings, the monk furnishes the former with an opportunity to accumulate merit. Although charity and generosity are always good, directing them toward a monk is particularly meritorious, for it demonstrates a willingness to part with worldly goods for the sake of the otherworld represented by the monk.

The monks are organized into the Sangha, Order of Buddhist Monks. The primary concern of the Sangha is to provide a secluded realm, a retreat in which the monk can follow the 227 rules. The Sangha also plays a missionary role, spreading Buddha's teachings so as to perpetuate the Buddhist order. In the past the temple schools of the monks provided the only education in Thailand—religious education, to be sure, but also schooling in reading, writing, healing, and crafts. The young men who composed the bulk of the student population (for women were allowed little contact with monks) often studied to prepare for bureaucratic careers. They needed not only literacy, but also indoctrination in Buddhist belief so that they might acquire moral qualities proper for careers in a Buddhist state.

Unlike the vows of the Christian monk, the Buddhist monastic vows are not binding for life. A monk can leave the order any time he desires. Ideally, every Thai male should spend a brief period as a monk, and as many as one man out of fifty does so during a typical year. The shortest time that a man may spend is one "lenten season," the three months during the rainy season when farm work is light. The ideal that all men should serve as monks reflects the Thai feeling that monks exemplify a virtue proper for all men—the capacity to maintain an impassive, retiring demeanor in the face of danger and the vicissitudes of life.

Monastic discipline epitomizes the basic Buddhist belief that one acquires merit by renouncing the world. Part of the monk's ordination rite is the renunciation of his kinsmen and friends. The young monk's parents also give him up, and by so doing they gain merit for themselves; this is particularly true of the mother, who is considered especially attached to her son. Some youths actually become monks in order that their mothers may gain merit, for women do not enjoy many merit-making opportunities.

The Sangha penetrates more deeply into Thai society than does the state, for the state administers no unit below the level of the district, whereas the Sangha enters directly into the life of the village. It must be kept in mind, too, that Buddhism, personified by the Sangha, is a more important object of moral commitments than the state. Indeed, the state draws much of its legitimacy from its relationship with the Buddhist Sangha.

Bureaucracy and the Thai king

Relationships between the Sangha and the state have always been intimate. In traditional belief, which held sway until the 1932 coup, the king was regarded as a Chakravartin, or Buddhist World Emperor. He ruled not only because of his power and status, but also because of his unique religious qualities. He was to a degree divine. In the coronation ceremony priests consecrated the king as a Hindu-Buddhist god; he was endowed with the same *ong,* or mana, as the monks.

The king acknowledged his subordination to the Buddhist order, and pledged to serve as protector and defender of the Buddhist faith. He was expected to hold monastic lands in trust, to supervise examinations for promotion within the Sangha, to wage war on neighboring nations who might threaten Buddhism, and to stage ostentatious and exemplary merit-making ceremonies. The king's fundamental duty was to insure that his kingdom was one in which Buddhism could flourish. He was to preserve harmony and peace, and also prosperity, so that the laity would have the material means to support the monks. If the people could thereby gain merit, the Buddhist order would eternally endure.

Because of his status as a Chakravartin, the king's life was hedged by numerous complex rules. An elaborate court etiquette prescribed in detail the king's daily schedule, and a corps of court Brahmans (priests) labored as astrologers to determine auspicious occasions. Moral codes such as the Dharmashastras, a Buddhist version of the Hindu Code of Manu, defined the general ethics of kingship. Occasionally in Thai history, a king attempted to claim more power than he was given under the rules designed to constrain him, but he was always thwarted. Thus, the eighteenth-century king known to the West as Taksin claimed to be the living Buddha. He was deposed as a madman and eventually executed.

Thai kingship and bureaucracy were patterned after the Hindu-Buddhist conception of the cosmos. The cosmos was conceived of as a set of concentric circles at the center of which was located Mount Meru, home of the gods. Similarly, the kingdom was conceived of as a set of concentric circles at the center of which was located the capital city, with an artificial mountain in its midst representing Mount Meru. The innermost circle of the capital was the treasury, under the control of the Department of the Center (Klang). The next circle was the Department of the Royal Palace (Wang), which administered the affairs of the court and palace. Surrounding this circle was the Department of the Capital (Myang), which took charge of affairs inside the capital but outside the palace. The outermost circle was the Department of Lands (Na, literally "rice fields"), which supervised the countryside and performed many of the duties that would today be expected of a department of agriculture and public works.

The activities of these departments were as much ritual as administrative. Thus, the Department of Lands not only maintained the irrigation works, but also supervised the annual rites that insured the order of the seasons and the prosperity of the nation. Even in modern Thailand, vestiges of this pattern remain, for the people still consider the performance of rites to insure national prosperity the responsibility of the government, and court priests still schedule the annual rituals.

Since Hindu-Buddhist theory placed the king at the center of the cosmos and nation, every Thai was assigned a status relative to the king. Even remote villagers were attached to one of the king's bureaucratic departments. Every lowly person was a "client" to some more prestigious "patron," who in turn was some still more exalted patron's client. Eventually such chains of patron-client relationships converged on the person of an official who headed a department; and ultimately, of course, all of these officials, with their attached chains, were clients to the supreme patron, the king.

In the fifteenth century, King Trailok promulgated the Law of Civil Hierarchy whereby every Thai was assigned a number indicating his rank in society—which is to say, in bureaucracy, since Thai society was composed of human chains converging on the royal departments. These ranks, called *sakthina* ("power of the fields") assigned the number 25 to an ordinary farmer, 50,000 to the brother of the king, 2,400 to an outstanding monk. Periodically, royal officials traveled around the countryside, registering the people, recording their allegiances to the royal departments, and assigning them their proper numbers. A royal department could mobilize its allied chains, even down to the level of peasants, for war or for several months of annual service.

The Thai pattern of interlocking and converging patron-client chains differs strikingly from the feudal pattern familiar to students of medieval European history. Feudal manors provided lords with localized bases of power from which they could oppose the king. But in Thailand there could be no independent landlords since the king owned all the land, and all power revolved around the capital and the king. Under the patron-client system, the closer an official was to the capital and king, the greater was his power. Regional officials could, of course, build a local following, but since they owed their position to the king, they rarely opposed him. Thai kings were more often overthrown by palace coups than by provincial revolts.

Who would succeed the king on his death was always unclear, for there were no definitive rules of succession. As a step toward narrowing the slate of eligible competitors, the Thai instituted a rule of declining descent whereby with the accession of a new king all of the old king's relatives became one degree less eligible for the kingship; after five generations, they dropped from the ranks of royalty altogether and became commoners. Another device was the appointment of a "second king," or Uparat, who would be strongly favored to succeed the king. Despite these arrangements, however, the throne was in effect available to anyone; a prince, an official, or even a commoner might succeed in usurping the throne by intrigue, assassination, or glorious military deeds. Whoever seized the throne automatically demonstrated the moral qualities necessary for rule.

Thai villagers

Approximately 85 percent of the Thai live in rural villages devoted to irrigated rice agriculture. Unlike the stereotyped "pastoral peasant," however, these villagers are strongly oriented toward the larger Thai society—the nation and its capital, Bangkok—and in this attitude they are encouraged by Buddhism.

By joining the monkhood, youths are freed from ties to local villages and embark on pilgrimages from temple to temple, thereby widening their experience and outlook. A related custom, *pai-thiaw* (literally, "going around"), calls for young men to leave their natal villages and wander around the nation seeking their fortunes. Many of these youths go to the cities, some never to return home. Many do return, of course, bearing a small stake with which to establish a household. The whole affair is regarded as fun and adventurous, like the German *Wanderung*.

The Thai willingness to abandon local ties and go out into the larger society is striking. Perhaps it reflects the Buddhist attitude that worldly commitments, such as commitments to locale, are to be eschewed in favor of higher callings. Of course, conditions other than the religious also encourage movement away from the villages. For example, since the establishment of a national school system in the nineteenth century, village youths have had an additional incentive to leave home. Temple education is no longer sufficient for a bureaucratic career, and advanced schooling is found in Bangkok.

Before summarizing the implications of the Thai case for an understanding of "historic" society, certain other examples should be considered—first India, then the Near East. "Archaic" India provides a useful contrast with Thailand by illustrating how historic ideas alone were insufficient to create historic society.

HINDUISM AND TRADITIONAL INDIA [2]

Considerable archaeological evidence reveals that a complex civilization existed in the Indus River Valley prior to 3000 B.C. Great cities such as Mohenjo-daro and Harappa were made possible by the channeling and the exploitation of the flood waters of the Indus. Enduring for a thousand years, the Indus civilization developed a system of public sanitation, various projects of urban planning, and a government on the order of that of the Mesopotamian city-states. Eventually the Indus civilization disappeared, perhaps in part because of gradual processes such as population pressure and deforestation, but largely because of sudden and cataclysmic forces. It may have been conquered and destroyed by fierce invaders, the Aryans.

The nomadic Aryans began to penetrate India around 1500 B.C. They introduced a new language, Sanskrit, and a new religion centered on the Vedic gods. They imposed their Indo-European culture, along with their authority, on the Dravidian peoples whom they encountered upon their arrival.

The Aryan conquerors were said to be lighter in color than the Dravidian natives. Whether this indicates a racial difference between the two groups or simply reflects a cosmology that attributed light colors to the ruling class is unclear. In any case, Vedic religion divided society into three groups called *varnas* ("colors"), which were distinguished according to vocational specialty: the Brahmans were the priestly caste, the Ksatriya were the warriors and nobles, and the Vaicyas were the landowners and merchants. Membership was reckoned patrilineally, and intermarriage was taboo. These three *varnas* comprised the "twice-born," those who were synbolically reborn through initiation rites, hence were religiously privileged. Below them were the Sudras, tillers of the soil and servants of the twice-born. Eventually, the Sudras divided into two groups, the untouchables and the touchables. The untouchables performed such ritually polluting tasks as butchering cattle, and even a glimpse of an untouchable's shadow was sufficient to pollute a member of the twice-born.

The ranking of the *varnas* was based in part on the degree of ritual purity versus pollution. The Brahmans were the purest. A Brahman's willingness to perform ritual for a group determined that group's purity (Brahmans were unwilling to perform any rituals for the untouchables). Since Brahmans did not pollute, they often served as cooks; food prepared by them was pure. Indeed, because of their purity alone, the Brahmans—who lacked great wealth and power—were ranked as the top caste. Purity was sufficient to sustain the Brahmans' high position even though they never constituted an organized religious elite, as did Buddhist monks or Christian priests.

Although some of the Brahmans worked (*e.g.,* as cooks), their primary occupation lay in the priesthood, and their primary achievement was a speculative philosophy that rendered their ceremonies metaphysically meaningful. From such speculation emerged the Hindu concepts of *karma* and of transmigration. The cycle of births and rebirths was regarded as a mere surface manifestation of the deeper reality called Atman. The visible world was simply illusion, and the goal of religion was to escape from the *karmic* cycle and to merge with the eternal Atman.

Although Hinduism rejected the visible world in favor of a deeper reality, Hindu philosophy, because of the doctrine of *varnas* and castes, had the ultimate effect of bestowing sanctity on the visible world. Unlike Buddhism, which decreed that salvation could be attained by any man, Hinduism stated that a man's moral stature was set at birth according to the caste into which he was born; only the twice-born were qualified to seek salvation. Furthermore, each Hindu was enjoined to obey the *dharma* of the caste into which he was born—not to strive or rebel, for that might result in his rebirth as a lower creature, even an animal. Hinduism thus had the effect of sacralizing and conserving the established order.

India, then, was not a very universalistic society. Hinduism encouraged a marked inequality and separation of groups, and this has rendered India difficult to centralize. It is striking that in precolonial India, only one Hindu empire, the Gupta dynasty of the fourth century B.C., was of any size or duration. Fragmentation made India vulnerable to foreign conquest, such as the Muslim invasion resulting in the Mogul Empire, and, finally, the colonization by Great Britain.

ISLAM AND THE ISLAMIC EMPIRES [3]

In the sixth century A.D. the Arabian peninsula was a no-man's-land wedged between two contending empires, the Byzantine and the Persian. It boasted important trading towns, such as Mecca, but no large-scale governments, other than the puppet states serving the great empires as buffers and outposts. Its inhabitants were largely wild and nomadic tribesmen who belonged to patrilineal descent groups that were not united under a central authority. Much conflict existed among the various tribes, subtribes, and lineages; blood feuds were common. The fragmentation into diverse tribes, subtribes, and lineages was reflected in the native religion, which was a potpourri of practices associated with the diverse groups and places.[4]

Through Islam, these scattered units were welded into a single entity, "God's elect." Under Islam the united Arabs were inspired to spread Allah's kingdom throughout the world, creating the great Islamic empires that held sway from Spain to Southeast Asia, from the sixth century to the twentieth. Although the message of Muhammad, Allah's prophet, was initially directed at the fragmented Arab society, Allah was deemed Lord of all creation, his message true for all men. Hence, the Muslims were driven to missionize, expand, and centralize.

Muhammad viewed himself as the end of a long line of prophets that began with Abraham and continued through Jesus. As the final vehicle of God's revelation, Muhammad professed to clarify what earlier prophets had obscured. The notion of a line of prophets parallels a linear notion of history in general. Like the Christian, the Muslim conceives of history not as a cyclical process of births and rebirths, but as a continuous line extending from the Creation through various revelations, prophesies, and errors to a final Judgment Day. Not only the history of mankind, but the history of each man is viewed linearly. Each man lives a life that proceeds from birth to death, with no instant repeated. Each man is given only one life in which to accept or reject the message of Allah. The wrong choice means infinite suffering in hell, the right choice offers infinite joy in a heaven of sensuous delights. Life, therefore, is a tense struggle to assure one's salvation before it is too late. There is no second chance. Without doubt, this view of time and history intensified the urgency with which the early Muslims pursued and spread their faith.

The Qur'an (often written "Koran") codified Muslim ethics and law. Although this codification did not produce a complete legal system, it was an advance over the earlier Arabic practice of simply listing past legal decisions to guide future ones. Arabic tradition, however, heavily influenced the substance of Muslim ethics and law. Thus, Muslim laws of inheritance favor the "naturally superior" male. Polygyny is allowed, though the limit is set at four legal wives (plus an unlimited number of slave concubines). Divorce is easy for a man. A husband, without being required to state his reason, can simply say three times to his wife, "I divorce you," and the deed is done. On the other hand, certain attitudes of Islam improved the position of women. For example, Muhammad's wish to include women in the spiritual life of the community was contrary to Arabic tradition.

Muhammad set forth a system of rituals which the faithful are compelled to enact. The believer must state his uncompromising acceptance of Allah as the one true God and of Muhammad as Allah's true and final prophet. He must pray five times per day while facing Mecca, fast during the holy month of Ramadan, abstain from intoxicants and the flesh of swine, give to the poor by paying a tax, and make the pilgrimage to the holy city, Mecca. What is striking is how little communion between believer and Allah is offered by these rituals. Even the five daily prayers are less a personal communion with God than a ritual display of commitment to God. Although in later Muslim history, Sufi mysticism gained popularity, orthodox Islam regarded Allah as distant and remote, not to be reached by prayer or meditation.

Islam inspired egalitarianism. Muhammad attacked the foundations of the old Arabic order by preaching that Allah scorned noble ancestry and that all believers were equal. Muslims regarded class distinctions as of little religious significance (by contrast to the Hindus with their caste system). It should not be concluded, however, that Islam achieved a fully egalitarian community. In fact, after Muhammad's death, the trend toward equality was reversed; a new and religiously legitimate basis for social distinction emerged with the notion that a descendant of the prophet was "more equal" than other Muslims.

Islam spurred urbanization. Wherever the Muslim conquerors went, they founded cities. In cities, all the conditions of proper Islamic social and ritual life—a market, a public bath, and a central mosque—could best be instituted. Furthermore, a city, Mecca, was the symbolic focus of Islam. Toward this urban shrine the believer had to turn daily in prayer, and to it he had to make his pilgrimage. Certainly these rituals, serving as foci of the daily life and the total lifetime of the believer, helped inculcate urban-oriented attitudes.

Islam encouraged the commercialism for which Muslims in some countries are famed. Regarding the Islamic view of business, von Grunebaum writes:

> Only the ascetic, the mystic, the scholar, and the public official are exempt from the duty of earning their bread by the work of their hands or commerce. From their conduct of business the character of the people will be known and their religion and piety be tested. The good merchant will conceive of his trade as a social obligation, for with the cessation of trade the community would perish.[5]

Particularly for Muslim merchants, sometimes as far from Mecca as India or Southeast Asia, the cost of the pilgrimage itself must have stimulated the desire for profit and the pursuit of commerce. The medieval Islamic community was political and social as well as religious. It was a theocracy, a commonwealth that Allah controlled, but that his deputy, Muhammad, administered. The community's political and religious boundaries were the same. The ruler and all citizens were believers. The People of the Book, *i.e.,* Christians and Jews, were allowed to live within the community as *dhimmi,* persons protected by a special treaty; they were not, however, regarded as citizens equal to the Muslim believers and were accorded only safety of person and property. For pagans and idolaters, there was, in theory, only the choice between conversion and death.

To Arab tribesmen, warfare had served to establish ranks, to avenge slights, to gain booty; but Islam gave warfare new purpose. Allah was an awesome, transcendent, and uncompromising figure. By comparison to Him, the devout were regarded as sinful and inadequate. They could not compel His forgiveness, they could only worship and obey, and in a heedless moment they might nullify a lifetime of piety, dooming themselves to eternal suffering. Yet if the faithful were persuaded of their own puniness and sinfulness in the eyes of Allah, how much more flawed did they consider the infidels and idolaters who flouted His rule. The inner guilt and desperation of the faithful was projected outward toward the wretched infidels. These should be compelled to convert, or die. The world was divided into two domains, *dar al Islam,* the region of God's elect, and *dar al harb,* the region of war. There being no neutral ground, the Muslim was obliged to combat the infidel. The pressure to conquer, and if possible to convert, never ceased, with holy war (*jihad*) bringing religious merit. Through warfare, Allah's dominion was extended and his faith expanded, all with incredible speed.

The spread of Islam generated dilemmas such as the practical one that conquest was often too fast to allow conversion of the conquered, the result being a political state without a religious base. But a more fundamental problem was rooted in theology. Islam assumed that all of life should conform to the divine, and that since there was only one God, there could be only one acceptable way of life. Yet with the spread of Islam into new areas, new situations arose that were not treated by the orthodox and immutable doctrines. What should the believer do in situations not covered by the Qur'an? This dilemma encouraged a tendency toward formalism and legalism. "Customs" (*sunna*) and "sayings" (*hadit*) were collected to fill gaps left by the Qur'an. No central board of experts was empowered to distinguish heresy from orthodoxy and decree which sayings should be included and which omitted. Islamic tradition thus became an infinitely expandable collection of items, with diverse schools focused on the various subcollections. Which school was heretical, which orthodox, depended largely on which boasted the greatest power and following.

An associated problem centered on leadership. During the life of Muhammad, he was the unquestioned political and religious leader of the Muslim community, the *umma*. Upon his death, however, there arose two schools of thought regarding succession. The Sunnis championed as leader the *caliph*, one empowered by the community to serve as its defender and ruler, but religiously the equal of all other believers. The Shiites, on the other hand, thought that the community's leader should be an *imam*, a religious teacher who possessed unusual spiritual powers. The Shiites believed in a special line of prophets endowed by God with a divine spark; the *imam* would inherit this spark from Muhammad. What is of interest is not so much the particular disputes between the Sunnis and the Shiites or other schools, but the effects of these disputes on Muslim society. The conflicts obviously hampered unification of the *umma* (community), rendering unattainable Muhammad's vision of a politically united Muslim world.

Unification of the *umma* was also blocked by the awesomeness of Allah and the formalism of Muslim ritual. The failure of the ritual to provide personal communion with God apparently left an emotional gap that the believer was tempted to fill by mysticism or by animistic practices derived from folk traditions. Certainly it is more true of Islam than of Christianity, especially Protestant Christianity, that belief in magic and spirits is retained even by the pious. An encouragement to such belief is that formalistic Islamic ritual requires primarily *outward* expression of faith, perhaps leaving intact inner attitudes flowing from traditional religions.

To summarize, Islam encouraged primitive Arab society to advance to the historic level. It undercut particularistic and diffuse social relationships, such as those of kinship, and it inspired an aggressive centralization resulting in empires far exceeding in size and power any achieved by archaic society. The centralization was in part stimulated by Islam's transcendent God, in whose name the unworthy were energetically to be transformed. At the same time, divisive and formalistic qualities of Islam limited the development toward centralization and modernity.

OVERVIEW

The single outstanding characteristic of historic religions is their dualism. Archaic religions conceive of a wider gap between the cosmos and society than primitive religions, yet archaic man still believes in a single world inhabited by both gods and men. Historic man rejects such monism in favor of a dualism that conceives of a radical gap between the real world and the religiously-defined order, between this world and the otherworld.

Not only is the otherworld separate from this world, it is infinitely better. The Buddhists are most radical in this view, for they consider this world mere illusion. Both Muslims and medieval Christians * idealized life after death; the latter, especially, regarded this life as simply a dreary interlude before salvation. Nirvana,

* This overview will concern itself not only with Buddhist, Hindu, and Muslim religion, but also with historic Christianity, which will be discussed further in connection with Protestantism in chapter 6.

Heaven, or Paradise are infinitely preferable to anything this world has to offer.

Historic man, accordingly, was obsessed with the need to be saved, to achieve the eternal bliss of the afterlife. Among other things, the quest for salvation fostered universalism. In primitive religion, a man's fate depends on his kin status, in archaic religion, on his class status. In historic religion, on the other hand, it depends on his actions toward salvation. How much merit does he accumulate? Does he pray five times a day and make the pilgrimage to Mecca? Historic religion undercuts particularism by regarding even the humblest man as capable of salvation—through proper action.

Historic religion fosters a new sense of selfhood. In archaic society an individual atones for a particular error with a particular sacrifice, but in historic society man worships by begging forgiveness for a deep sinfulness within his total self. Whether through inheritance of some "original sin" or simply through deeds, the Christian, Buddhist, or Muslim comes to possess a sinful personality. Because it is the total personality that is sinful, sacrificial correction of one or a number of wrongdoings is insufficient. Salvation is attained only by commitment of the total self to the ultimate, to Allah, God, or Atman. This concept presupposes and encourages a sense of selfhood, a notion of personality as integrating and transcending discrete acts. It also poses a great risk for the total self, and a great opportunity: promises the total self possible participation in the ultimate, yet threatens it with the danger of hell-fire, perpetual rebirth, or other horrible alternatives to salvation.

Here a difference between the Buddhist and the Muslim or Christian is worthy of note. The Muslim and the Christian conceive of each individual as having only a single life in which to work out his salvation; hence, each individual is under great pressure. The Buddhist, on the other hand, expects to be reborn again and again; hence, if he fails to achieve salvation in this life, he may try again in the next.

Despite this difference, all historic religions, Buddhism included, proclaim that much is at stake for the individual. Facing the choice between damnation and salvation of the total self, he has much to gain if he is saved, much to lose if he is not. It is logical for him to devote all his time to the search for salvation, and it is appropriate for the Buddhist and Christian monks to withdraw from life in order to devote themselves to worship. Islam has no monks, but instead conceives of the entire *umma* as a pure body withdrawn from the sinful world in order to seek salvation.

The existence of a monkhood institutes a new social pattern. Archaic society is two-class, with a religio-political elite separated from the common people. Historic society is a three-class society, with the elite dividing into religious and political groups that are separated from each other and from the masses.* The religious elite, for example, the monkhood, claim a monopoly on the channels to salvation. The political elite, the kings and ministers, are more strictly political and no longer claim to control the religious elite. This situation is clearly illustrated in Thailand, where Sangha and government, though intimately related, are separate. The relationship between the medieval Christian church and the state was similar. The Muslim theocracy does not so clearly separate the religious and political leadership in theory, but in practice considerable separation does occur.

The division between political and religious elite in historic society furnished new potential for confrontation. Whether conflict was between Buddhist monk and king, Muslim teacher and *caliph,* or Christian Pope and emperor, the new assumption was that politics could be confronted by religious standards that transcended

---

* It could be argued that historic society tends toward a four-class arrangement, with a differentiation among the masses that parallels that among the elite. With increased urbanism, the urban masses became more clearly distinct from the rural, and not uncommonly the rural folk were regarded as second-class citizens religiously by comparison with the more devout urbanites. Thus, there were religious and secular elite and religious and secular masses making up the four classes. We believe that in historic societies the division within the masses is less distinct and universal than within the elite, hence we refer to historic society as composed of three classes, but we have no strong preference for the three-class as against the four-class designation.

the political, that religious commitment could justify political rebellion and reform. Now one *could* oppose the king in the name of God. At the same time, political interests could oppose religious ones, as in Henry VIII's bout with the church.

Aside from particular issues dividing religious and political interests, one general difference is important. In historic society religion tends to be more universalistic than government. Buddhism, Christianity, and Islam made entry into the religious elite open theoretically to all men, whereas entry into the political elite continued to depend on inherited status. This situation might have served to sustain the status quo, since the lowly, who were excluded from the high circles of politics, could compensate by religious achievement. On the other hand, the religious universalism provided a vision of a condition beyond political particularism, and stimulated a drive to change the political in the direction of that vision. The challenge to hereditary Arab aristocracy mounted by Muhammad's equalitarianism provides an example.

In historic society, culture and learning also underwent great changes stimulated by religion. Christians and Muslims achieved significant advances in medicine, engineering, mathematics, and science. Buddhists, on the other hand, turned their speculations inward and discovered some of the secrets of psychology. All of the historic religions encouraged literacy by their emphasis on scripture and sacred language. Vast libraries of revealed truth were recorded in Pali or Sanskrit for Buddhists, in Latin for Christians, and in Arabic for Muslims.

One consequence of these sacred languages, all of which, because of their sacredness, were set apart from daily speech, may have been to symbolize and accentuate the separate and transcendental character of the sacred or the otherworldly, thereby reinforcing the dualism of historic religion. Historic religion achieved a cultural unity that was more extensive than any political unity achieved by historic society. A comparison of the Catholic community with the Holy Roman Empire, of the Muslim community with any Muslim empire, of the Buddhist community with any

Asian empire, is sufficient to show that historic political empires were neither so broad nor so permanent as were historic religious communities. Historic empires were, however, more extensive than archaic empires.

The case of India, which we have treated as an example of archaic society, is instructive for the understanding of historic society. Hinduism, which contained many historic ideas, emerged in India. From Hinduism came Buddhism, clearly a historic religion. India was not, however, receptive to Buddhism, and Buddhism was thrust out. Nor did the historic ideas of Hinduism spread widely in India. They were restricted to the Brahmans. The Hindu ideas that did spread, such as *dharma,* served to reinforce an archaic and particularistic caste structure. Thus, the mere presence of historic ideas was not enough to alter a well-established archaic social pattern.

A similar situation is apparent in China. Despite the vast expanse of the classic Chinese empire and its remarkably universalistic bureaucracy and philosophy, we consider it archaic because it was organized around a kinship unit, the patrilineal clan. Yet historic religions and ideas existed in China. For a time Mahayana Buddhism was potent there, but through persecution and other means Confucians, who supported the patrilineal pattern, managed to isolate Buddhism from the majority of the people, and China remained essentially archaic until this century. Perhaps China, like India, had advanced so far in archaic organization that historic ideas did not promise enough further progress to encourage the incorporation of these historic ideas into the structure of society. Today, both China and India confront not historic but modern or early-modern ideas, and many of the archaic patterns that withstood the historic onslaught are now dissolving.

This brief discussion of China and India is not meant to minimize the power of religion to provoke social change. The spread of historic society could never have occurred without the spread of historic religions and ideas. Nevertheless, the cases of China and India suggest that the mere introduction of new religions or new ideas is no guarantee that social change will occur.

TOPIC FOR DISCUSSION

This chapter has focused on the major dimensions of historic society as they have emerged through the spread of historic religions. Historic religions have been perpetuated, elaborated, and spread by a literate urban elite. Peasant society is a topic usefully introduced in connection with historic society, for the urban-centered "great traditions" are commonly balanced by the rural-centered "little traditions" of the peasant masses who make up the bulk of the population of historic societies. Anthropologists have placed considerable emphasis on the study of peasantry, but study from an evolutionary point of view indicates that in all historic societies peasants are continually changing in the direction of the more modern patterns displayed by the religious traditions and national culture centered in the major cities. Accordingly, it seems that if an anthropologist wishes to understand the direction in which society is moving, he should place less emphasis on the peasantry and more on the "great traditions" emanating from the cities. Yet the question remains worth exploring: In what ways does the study of peasant life contribute to an understanding of historic societies?

BURMA, THAILAND, AND BUDDHISM

Hill Farms and Padi Fields: Life in Mainland Southeast Asia (paperback, 1965) by Robbins Burling. For contrast read chapter 7 on the Thai and chapter 6 on the Burmese.

The Golden Road to Modernity (1965) by Manning Nash. An excellent comparison of two Burmese villages.

Burmese Supernaturalism (paperback, 1967) edited by Melford E. Spiro. An illuminating analysis of Burmese religion.

Anthropological Studies in Theravada Buddhism (1966) edited by Manning Nash. A collection of essays.

Ancient Siamese Government and Administration (1965) by H. G. Quatritch Wales. On ancient Thai society.

HINDUISM

The Religion of India (paperback, 1958) by Max Weber. A basic source.

Philosophies of India (1956) by Heinrich Zimmer. Discusses philosophical and religious aspects of Hinduism.

Societies: Evolutionary and Comparative Perspectives (paperback, 1966) by Talcott Parsons. Chapter 5 provides a useful synthesis.

ISLAM

Medieval Islam (1961) by Gustave E. von Grunebaum. A basic source.

History of the Islamic Peoples (paperback, 1960) by Carl Brockelmann. A good discussion of early Arab history.

Mohammedanism: An Historical Survey (paperback, 1962) by H. A. R. Gibb. An excellent and readable historical account.

The Social Structure of Islam (paperback, 1962) by Reuben Levy. A basic sociological source.

Islam Observed: Religious Development in Morocco and Indonesia (1968) by Clifford Geertz. A vivid comparison of Islam in the Near East and Southeast Asia.

CHINA

The Religion of China (paperback, 1951) by Max Weber. A basic work, complex and detailed.

Chinese Civilization (paperback, 1958) by Marcel Granet.

Under the Ancestor's Shadow (paperback, 1948), by Francis L. K. Hsu.

Peasant Life in China: A Field Study of Country Life in the Yangtze Valley (1946) by Fei Hsiao-t'ung.

The Family Revolution in Modern China (paperback, 1968) by Marion J. Levy, Jr.

PEASANT SOCIETY

Peasants (paperback, 1966) by Eric Wolf. General treatment.

The Primitive World and Its Transformations (paperback, 1953) by Robert Redfield. A classic statement.

Peasant Society: A Reader (paperback, 1967) edited by J. M. Potter, M. N. Diaz, and G. M. Foster. Contains useful articles and extensive bibliography of classic monographs on peasant life in various parts of the world.

FILMS

Apu Trilogy by Satyajit Ray. Includes *Pather Panchalli, Aparajito,* and *The World of Apu.* Available in 16 mm.

North Indian Village. A more orthodox ethnographic film, depicting a village and various social institutions of India.

Journey to Mecca. Shows pilgrims from Turkestan, India, Yugoslavia, and as far away as Malaya and the Philippines making the pilgrimage to Mecca.

Moulay Idriss. Depicts the holy week during which pilgrims converge on Mecca.

6

Early-modern society
and culture

To illustrate a particular level of sociocultural evolution, each previous chapter chose several societies from among the many primitive, archaic, and historic ones that exist or have existed in world history. Since the primitive era, the trend of history has been toward larger and larger societies. Finally, in the early-modern era, all societies are merging into a single system, the world society, which, strictly speaking, should constitute our illustrative case for this chapter. Rather than make the entire world the subject of our analysis, however, we shall follow the less ambitious approach of treating the origin of this early-modern pattern. The region of origin is Europe, and our focus will be on European history. In order to sketch something of the diffusion of the early-modern pattern to non-European areas of the world, we shall analyze Japan as an example of a highly successful latecomer to modernization and Indonesia as an example of a problematical new nation.

The question of the origin and spread of the early-modern pattern will be treated from the theoretical perspective known as the Protestant Ethic Thesis and commonly identified with the German social theorist Max Weber. In spite of the controversial character of Weber's views, his theories are comparative and evolutionary, hence can contribute much to social and cultural anthropology. Furthermore, Weber's Protestant Ethic Thesis provides a general framework for a discussion of the interplay of cultural, social, and psychological forces of evolution.

THE RISE OF HISTORIC CHRISTIANITY

Christianity emerged from Judaism. The Jews regarded themselves as the "chosen people" of a transcendent and monotheistic God, Jehovah (or Yahwe), with whom they had established a covenant; in return for obeying the commandments of Jehovah and worshipping Him above all gods, the Jewish people would be exalted above all others. Ancient Judaism was thus more archaic and less universalistic than Christianity in that the Jewish God was the God of the Jewish people, whereas the Christian God was concerned with all men, regardless of their nationality.

In broadening its appeal and widening its mission to include all men, Christianity eliminated certain practices that were conspicuously tied to the society of its origin (for example, the Jewish customary laws concerning circumcision and food taboos) and that were distasteful to some peoples of the Greek and Roman world. It is not certain whether Christian proselytizing was given its force and power through the universalization of Christian custom or the distinctive theological message of Christian preaching—that the millennium was imminent and the need for conversion was great. Whatever the reason, Christianity succeeded in spreading throughout the Roman Empire.

At first, Christianity was greeted with hostility by the Roman elite because it threatened the archaic religions that sanctified imperial power. However, the conversion of Emperor Constantine in the early part of the fourth century gave Christians a favored place in the official religious complex. Christian bishops proved willing to cooperate with a Christian emperor, considering him chosen by God for his high office. The alliance between Christianity and the imperial establishment reached its logical conclusion at the end of the fourth century when Emperor Theodosius proclaimed Christianity the state religion and prohibited all rival faiths.* Christianity thus became the exclusive official religion of the Roman Empire, and thereby of the entire "civilized" Western world.

Once Christianity was firmly established, its influence extended even beyond the limits of the Roman Empire by the successful conversion of the foreign and primitive barbarian hordes that swept through Rome on expeditions of sacking and looting. Christianity

---

* This alliance was the forerunner of the "divine right" of kings—an institution that became established in the West at a later date—and was very different from the archaic "divine kingship" in that the king himself was not considered a god, but was legitimized by God and church.

introduced universalistic ideas that undermined the barbarians' tribal organization and encouraged them to establish feudal king- doms, such as those of the Goths, the Visigoths, and the Franks.

CHRISTIAN IMAGERY AND MEDIEVAL SOCIETY

Like the other historic religions, Christianity saw a radical gap between the divine order and the social order in which men lived— a view that contrasted with those of archaic religions of the day. Thus, the archaic Greeks localized their pantheon on Mount Olym- pus, but the Heaven of the Christians was above the world of men and was not associated with any earthly spot; the Greek could see his Olympian Mountain of the Gods in a way no Christian could see his Heaven.

Besides creating a chasm between the divine and the everyday, Christianity placed infinite value on the divine, little value on the everyday—an attitude, once again, that contrasted with those of archaic religions of the day. Thus, in archaic Judaism the question of life after death was secondary to the task of preparing for the messiah so that the Jews, as God's chosen people, would collectively enjoy exalted status in the world. In Christianity, by contrast, the primary question was that of the individual's salvation, that he might enjoy a life after death. Because salvation was so important for the Christian, the Christian ideal was withdrawal from this world, as in monastic life, in order to concentrate on gaining salva- tion in the otherworld; if one could not withdraw from this world, it was good to emulate Saint Paul and "be in the world, but not of it."

As Christianity spread through the Roman Empire and beyond, and the expected millennium that was to create God's Kingdom on earth did not materialize, symbolic and social hierarchies were built to connect this world and Heaven. The gap between Heaven and

Hell was bridged by such intermediate stations as purgatory and Limbo. Heaven itself was hierarchical, with God at the pinnacle, then ranked orders of angels, a pantheon of saints (some of whom were probably ancient pagan heroes and spirits incorporated into the Christian hierarchy after their worshippers were converted), and the souls of the departed faithful. The sacraments and rituals of the church and the church's hierarchy of bishops, priests, monks, and nuns furnished additional steps to God.

These symbolic and social hierarchies were philosophically grounded in the notion of a Great Chain of Being. The cosmos was imagined as a hierarchy of positions stretching from God down to the most insignificant creature. Each creature had its place on this continuum, each formed one link in the Great Chain. Each was expected to submit to God's plan, stay in its place, and thereby contribute to the harmony and order of the universe. Save for withdrawal into a monastery or convent, movement from one's inherited place was a flaunting of God's will.

Particularly in Western Europe, the church was able to establish a more stable and inclusive social system than was achieved by any secular empire. The acceptance of the Pope's position as the Bishop of Rome, the successor of Saint Peter, and the undisputed leader of the Western church provided a single locus of authority.* Unification of the church hierarchy was also aided by the adoption of Latin as a common language for all men of learning and all churchmen. Lacking these unifying forces, the secular society was fragmented into numerous kingdoms and diverse languages and dialects.

Nevertheless, medieval society displayed a uniform feudal pattern, partly because most medieval men were Christian. Preoccupied with

---

* These remarks apply more to the Western portions of the Roman Empire than to the Eastern portions. In the West, the church achieved considerable unity under the Pope, although the political hierarchy was unstable. In the East, the reverse was true: no single authority dominated the Greek-speaking church, since authority resided in the council of bishops and each bishop was nominally the equal of the others. Nevertheless, the political hierarchy was united under the Byzantine emperor residing in Constantinople.

Christian teachings that promised to save their souls, medieval men were taught to think in feudal terms. The Great Chain of Being implied a hierarchy of positions fixed by birth—in other words, a feudal hierarchy. The medieval conception of society as a vast organism, created and animated by God, carried similar feudal implications. Secular society was the body politic, and the church was the visible body of Christ. Like a body, society was composed of members interdependent, but not interchangeable. In a body, a foot could not replace a hand; in society, one member could not perform another's special task. This Organic Analogy, like the Great Chain of Being, taught that every man should stay in his place.

The Organic Analogy carried a monarchical bias since it implied that society, like the body, should have a single head to which all other members were unalterably subordinate. Furthermore, the Organic Analogy discouraged change. The healthy body was harmonious and regular in its functions, and any radical modification of its normal shape was a sign of deformity and disease. Treatment was aimed at restoring the status quo. Innovation, like a tumor, was best excised as soon as possible so that the body could return to its former condition.

History, viewed in terms of the Organic Analogy, was cyclical, paralleling the body's cycle of birth, maturation, and death. Christian notions of Genesis and Judgment Day may have favored a view of history as a line, stretching from a beginning to an end of the world, but the Organic Analogy encouraged medieval Christians to view history as recurrent cycles of rise and decline. Biblical tales as well as the history of classical civilizations such as Greece and Rome could readily be understood from this viewpoint, for the societies of antiquity had risen, matured, declined, and disappeared.

The family was another image dominant in medieval thought. God, the Father, superintended the deeds of men, his children. The church was the Holy Mother, the priest was father to his flock, monks and nuns were brothers and sisters. Just as religion drew its imagery from the family, so the family gained sanctity from religion. The family was an integral part of nature established by God, but even more significantly, the family was sanctified by the sacrament of Matrimony, instituted by Christ, which proclaimed family bonds indissoluble. Children were believed to be granted to parents by God, and the authority of parents was strengthened by God's explicit command. The parent-child relationship was one of tender authority and innocent submission, solidly rooted in the natural and sacred orders.

The medieval family was not the nuclear family of modern society. Family relations extended lineally back through time and laterally out into space to include both ancestral and local bonds, so that each family was part of a ramified kinship network. Based on the hierarchical parent-child relationship, this extended family network became a model for all society; the relationships of subject to king, vassal to lord, and apprentice to master were imbued with the hierarchical and authoritarian aura of the parent-child bond. Like the family, the quasi-familial feudal hierarchy was sanctioned by the church.

In sum, Christianity lent religious sanctity to feudal society. Feudal institutions of inherited status, hierarchy, and degrees of privilege drew meaning and force from the Christian concepts of the Great Chain of Being, the Organic Analogy, and the sacred family. These concepts endowed medieval society with a rigidity of shape and style that persisted for centuries, until the concepts were challenged and radically changed by the Protestant Reformation.

CALVINIST IMAGERY AND NEW SOCIAL FORMS *

The feudal pattern, in spite of its common core, varied from region to region, and so did the Protestant Reformation. But everywhere

---

* Our analysis of medieval imagery and of the changes in it wrought by Calvinism leans heavily on Michael Walzer, *The Revolution of the Saints,* especially chapter 5. Medieval imagery did not disappear with the rise of modern society, as our discussion may seem to suggest, but it did cease to guide the total field of social behavior, becoming instead restricted to certain limited contexts.

the Reformation was accompanied by the decline or collapse of the medieval hierarchical structure, a breakdown especially pronounced with the Calvinistic branches of Protestantism, which we, following Weber and others, take as prototypic of early-modern religion.

The Calvinists, like most Protestants, retained the medieval Christian notion of a radical gap between God and man, but they rejected outright the hierarchical structure that had served as a ladder to God and repudiated the very idea that such mediation between God and man could exist. The result was a yawning gap between man and God. Calvinism transcendentalized God, made him more distant, more omnipotent, and totally inscrutable. In the absence of mediating devices, confrontation between this God and puny man could be terrifying.

As God became a more distant and elevated monopolist of good, man became a more lonely and despicable vessel of evil. Satan, the embodiment of evil, was frighteningly close at hand, enticing men to follow their naturally evil inclinations. The Calvinist was forced, therefore, to guard continuously against natural impulses by exercising a rigid self-discipline. Paradoxically, although Calvinists had repudiated the monastic style of life, the Calvinist came to live as ascetically as the monk, but in the world instead of in seclusion.

By sweeping away the mediating hierarchical structure and transcendentalizing God, the Calvinists undermined the concept of the Great Chain of Being. If God monopolized power, man and nature could not share that power; instead of a continuum of power between man and God, there was a gulf. From God's lofty vantage point, all men were weak. Authority, power, and inequality among men were meaningless in the eyes of God; therefore the social order lost its sanctity, indeed it ceased to be an *order*. The world was a playground for sin and evil, and man was inherently wicked, hence the natural state of society was chaos. Only the implacable will of God and the unceasing struggle of His servants could impose a minimal order on the unheeding world.

Rejecting the medieval church's distinction between monks and laity, the Calvinist substituted the distinction between the elect,

who were predestined by God for salvation, and the damned—
the vast majority of men, in the Calvinist view—who were predestined for eternal perdition. The elect were the chosen few
who would carry out God's plans, just as the monks had been
God's special servants. But unlike the monks, the elect would do
God's will in the wide world and would dress and live like ordinary
men. No one knew for sure who the elect were: they were not set
apart by appearance, nor were they exclusively the highborn, for
God did not regard a man's social rank. To Him a man's service-
ability counted more than his status.

A crucial task for the Calvinist was ascertaining precisely what
God called him to do. His inherited status was not a reliable sign,
and he recognized no religiously superior priests who could provide
authoritative advice. One recourse open to him was to seek direct
revelation from God; another recourse was the Bible. Although the
Calvinists had rejected the ceremonies and rituals of the church,
they retained the Holy Scriptures, the literal, revealed truth of God.
Since the Bible was for the Calvinist the sole remaining visible and
codified statement of God's word, it assumed for him an over-
powering importance. In order that every man might be able to
read God's word, the Calvinists rejected the Latin Bible in favor
of Bibles written in the vernacular, and they encouraged literacy
and education.

From the Bible, the Calvinists derived the notion of a covenant
between God and man. In return for worshipping and obeying
Jehovah, declared the Bible, the Jews became the chosen people.
This account accorded with the Calvinist notion of a covenant between God and the elect. The covenant was like a contract, although
it was hardly between equal parties, and Calvinists could not coerce
God to keep his agreements, as the ancient Jews had tried to do.
God was seen as the creditor of all mankind, but only His elect,
His saints, were, by His grace, enabled through their obedience
partially to repay man's debt. "The covenant was a way of activat-
ing men, not of controlling God." [1]

The Calvinist covenant was not between God and a group, as

in the case of Jehovah and the Jews, but rather between God and each individual. God in His grace sought an individual who was predestined for salvation, and by His grace allowed him to enter a covenant with Him. The individual then became a saint and an instrument of God's purpose. Since the saint could if necessary transcend social constraints to carry out God's will and plan, the concepts of covenant and calling gave religious sanctity to individual striving and accomplishment.

Calvinism also sanctified the devout voluntary group that stood apart from the traditional social order—the sect. The sect, like the saint, was God's instrument within the wicked world. A sect was led only by God and the Bible. Even the minister merely taught the Scriptures, which could be read by all. Membership in the sect was voluntary, dependent on the individual's active consent.

The voluntarism and individualism of Calvinism clashed with medieval images of polity. Calvinists found the image "ship of state" more congenial than the old one of "body politic." The leader of the state should, like the ship's captain, hold his post because of skill rather than inherited status; if the captain proved unskillful, the crew could legitimately mutiny. It is no accident that where Calvinism found deep roots, the rule of kings and nobles was undercut or overthrown. The political murder, as opposed to assassination, of Charles I by the Puritans is only the most glaring example of Calvinist politics.

The Organic Analogy of medieval times inspired a cyclical view of history—history followed no plan, moved in no direction. Calvinism, on the other hand, viewed history as guided by God's purpose. God employed ordinary mortals as instruments of that purpose, even when they were unaware of it; and the rise, decline, and fall of societies were according to God's plan, even when mere mortals could not comprehend it. The image of a ship of state reflected the Calvinist sense of purpose: society, steered by a captain, is on a voyage.

Family imagery was not repudiated by the Calvinists, but it was modified to fit the Calvinist world view. Calvinism rejected the medieval Christian idea that the authority of parents was rooted in the natural order, which was sanctified by God. For the Calvin-ist, the natural order was wicked. Parental authority was, therefore, not "natural," but was derived specifically from God's command-ments as stated in the Scriptures. The individual who accepted the calling of parenthood was obligated to mold his children into God-fearing Christians, a task that demanded careful guidance as well as constant evaluation of the child's achievements and godliness. Parental concern was thus focused inward, toward the child and immediate family, rather than outward, toward extended kin. Cal-vinistic notions of parenthood encouraged the nucleation of kinship.

Calvinist rejection of the medieval sacraments also affected family organization. The medieval sacrament of matrimony sanc-tioned enduring and irrevocable bonds between husband and wife and, by extension, between other kinsmen as well. Calvinists, how-ever, viewed marriage as a civil contract between two consenting parties, rather than as a sacramental bond. And if marriage was simply a legal contract, it did not irrevocably bind extended kins-men who did not directly consent to the marriage. The contractual view of marriage thus further encouraged the nucleation of kinship and the breakdown of extended kinship networks.

In sum, Calvinism postulated an order in the universe different from that envisioned by historic Christianity. This altered vision was expressed not only in such specific doctrines as predestination, the majesty of God, and unmediated salvation, but also in Calvinist imagery. Images could be more potent than doctrines in that they were not explicitly religious, hence might attract those who opposed particular Calvinist doctrines. Such persons might discover that the new images rendered their lives more meaningful than did the old Catholic images. Of course, many Calvinist images were neither new nor exclusively Calvinist. The Reformation leaders themselves claimed to return to a pristine and primitive Christianity that the church had debased and corrupted, and they chose images to sym-bolize the ancient order. But these images were incorporated into configurations fit for a world drastically different from the world of antiquity within which early Christianity had existed. This new world was feudal-historic, and Calvinism bore its stamp even as it sought to destroy it. Thus, Calvinism assimilated the Catholic notion of monkhood, conceiving of all men as voluntary ascetics in the service of God: "every man a monk and the whole world a monastery."

Calvinist notions did not always have immediate impact, like sledgehammers loudly smashing medieval structures. Yet the long reach of Calvinist patterning is apparent even today. Feudal systems have been replaced by early-modern systems. These make themselves felt not so much in class hierarchies as in competing and contending factions, such as political parties, labor unions, business firms, religious denominations, professional associations, and academic organizations, each of which is joined voluntarily. America, the "nation of joiners," is perhaps the most notable example of such a society. Precisely how Calvinism contributed to the emergence of early-modern society is an exceedingly complicated question, but it is clear that Calvinism supported the concept of the voluntary group. The Calvinist congregation was a model voluntary group in that each member joined of his own free will, in effect signing a contract that obligated him to assume certain responsibilities in return for the advantages of membership. The religiously sanctioned model of the voluntary group doubtless helped inspire voluntary and contractual modes of organization that could replace the declining feudal system.

The social fragmentation that is encouraged by the proliferation of voluntary groups is countered in early-modern society by the clustering of the groups into giant organizations—political, educational, scientific, economic, religious, medical. Whereas in medieval society only the church could stand against the state, in early-modern society any of these giant organizations can do so. Naturally, they can also team with the state to form such entities as the "military-industrial complex."

Early-modern society is in constant flux, partly because of its competing interest groups and partly because the idea of social reform became a guiding value of early-modern society, built into its ideologies, laws, constitutions, and governments. This pattern was at least partly inspired by Calvinism. Calvinism departed from the traditions of historic religion by emphasizing that *because* the Kingdom of God was radically better than the Kingdom of Man, man should incessantly reform the latter in the image of the former. The world was wicked, not sacred, and therefore any reform of it could only glorify God; certainly it would not violate His will, as the historic Catholic believed. Quite the contrary—the Calvinist felt guilty when he was not feverishly engaged in reform, an attitude that pervades America to this day.

The Western industrial society, with its Calvinist origins, is the prime example of the early-modern type—a society characterized by self-reforming political-legal institutions, voluntary associations, mass literacy, nuclear families, contractual relations. The classic theory of the Calvinist origins of early-modern Western society was advanced by Max Weber in his voluminous *Religion-Soziologie;* and although we have already anticipated many of Weber's points, we will summarize his argument and discuss some criticisms of it.

THE PROTESTANT ETHIC THESIS [2]

Weber agreed with Marx that capitalism was a unique phenomenon, which was nonexistent before the advent of the modern world. By "capitalism," Weber meant a bureaucratically organized, rational, ascetic system for the pursuit of profit. Capitalism is bureaucratically organized in that it is carried on within a complex organization of firms, factories, and associated governmental, legal, and social agencies, all of which are oriented toward economic profit. It is rational in that it is systematic and methodical rather than sporadic and adventurous. It is ascetic in that its profits are regarded as a measure of the success of the enterprise and a means for its perpetuation rather than as a reward to be hedonistically enjoyed.

Weber took great pains to show that bureaucratically organized, rational, ascetic capitalism did not flow from human nature. Far from being common to all men, it was unique to men in early-modern society. From where, if not human nature, did this "unnatural" development derive? And how did it survive once it appeared? Weber observed that the capitalist threatened the traditional order with his rationally exploitative procedures that made "tallow out of cattle and money out of men." [3] The early capitalist was, therefore, frequently persecuted and ostracized in pre-modern Europe. Weber believed that some extraordinarily powerful force was required to keep the early capitalist functioning and, more important, to transform the values of traditional Europe into those vehemently capitalistic ones that have inspired the gigantic capitalistic complexes dominating the West today. Weber concluded that this force was Calvinism.

Calvinism called men to work in the world as a devotional program to glorify God. Life was a God-assigned task that required continuous and methodical striving. Wasting time was the deadliest of sins, for it distracted men from that task. Hard, continuous physical and mental labor glorified God and purified the soul, while "idleness is the Devil's workshop." Regular work was the most desirable, irregular or casual work was, at best, a necessary evil. No sport was justified except when it increased work capacity and moral purity. Theater, idle talk, sex, or self-adornment were sinful. Sober utility ranked far above beauty, since the beautiful object was contemplated for itself rather than employed as a means toward God's purpose. A Faustian or Renaissance yearning to do and be everything was condemned in favor of specialized and disciplined work, which was necessary in order that one's special task be completed.

Why should men assume such a burdensome calling? For Weber, the answer lay in Calvinist theology. God had predestined that some men be saved and others be eternally damned. Neither ritual, nor faith, nor good works could change God's decision. No one but God knew whether a man was to be saved or damned. Desperately clutching at clues to God's will, Calvinists eventually accepted an individual's work and achievement in an earthly calling as a sign of his chances for salvation. The individual was therefore driven to work and achieve in a disciplined and ascetic style in order to prove that he was one of the elect who would be saved. No other method—neither magic, ceremony, priest, sacrament, nor special group—could either bring about or signify salvation.

Medieval Christianity did not force each believer to organize his life according to a systematic plan. Indeed, the sacramental system permitted a man to live for the moment—to sin when he felt like it, repent when the mood demanded, then sin again, knowing that the sacrament would provide forgiveness. Ethically, the ordinary medieval Christian could live "from hand to mouth." [4] But the Calvinist, who had rejected the sacraments, yet feared damnation, felt compelled to gear his entire life systematically toward achieving inner conviction of his salvation. Weber argued that this plan-ahead attitude was useful for operating in a bureaucratically organized, rational, ascetic capitalist system. Thus, Calvinism inadvertently taught attitudes and values useful for capitalism.

Weber's argument is more complex than this presentation of it might make it seem. It entwines numerous lines of thought, some of which he elaborated more than others. For example, he emphasized the debt of Calvinism to Judaism; Judaism also taught belief in a transcendent God who called men to carry out His commands on earth. Weber treated Calvinism and capitalism as part of the broad trend away from traditionalism and reliance on kinship ties that had been gaining momentum in the West since the time of the Roman Empire.[5] Obviously, Weber did not claim that Calvinism was the only stimulus to the rise of capitalism. Nor did he ignore the role of economic factors; after all, he was an economic historian. But Weber's argument was in part directed against Karl Marx's interpretation of capitalism, which in Weber's view overemphasized economic factors. Weber believed that a complex configuration of cultural, social, and psychological, as well as economic factors had to be considered in order to comprehend the by no means inevitable rise of capitalism.

Weber followed two methods of argument, the comparative and the structural. Arguing structurally, Weber delineated the *Geist* ("spirit") of capitalism, the set of mental attitudes that guided it, and then went on to show that these attitudes were logically or "structurally" congruent with those encouraged by Calvinism. Since the points of agreement were so strong, it seemed that Calvinism and the spirit of capitalism must have sprung from a common condition or have mutually influenced each other. But Weber further claimed that Calvinism had influenced capitalism more than capitalism had influenced Calvinism. Through a study of Calvinist writings, Weber was able to show a transition from an early anti-capitalist theology to a later theology encouraging capitalism. Weber argued that the transition came about not as a response to socio-economic changes, but as a logical working out of theological dilemmas. Once the new Calvinism emerged, the stage was set for the generation of attitudes favorable to the rise of capitalism, which then began in earnest. This argument opposed the simplistic and popular one that Calvinism was simply an ideology created by already practicing capitalists to justify and excuse their material ambitions.

Weber studied and compared a wide range of actual situations to demonstrate that where the Protestant Ethic flourished, capitalism and the spirit of capitalism flourished as well, whereas the absence of the Protestant Ethic tended to be correlated with a limited development of capitalism. Focusing on the West, Weber made use of statistics showing that German Protestants, for example, tended to choose a technical, scientific, or business education, whereas German Catholics tended to choose a humanistic education. Weber suggested that Protestant education was oriented more toward capitalism than was Catholic education, and that this orientation was reflected in the relatively larger number of Protestants than Catholics who owned and managed capitalist enterprises in Germany. The accuracy of Weber's statistics has been questioned, but the criticisms are not fundamentally damaging to his argument. Extending his analysis beyond Europe, Weber compared the West to China and India. At certain points in Chinese and Indian history, Weber suggested, natural and social conditions favored the rise of capitalism even more, perhaps, than they had in the West, yet capitalism did not flourish in China and India. What was lacking, Weber believed, was a religious ethic like that of Calvinism.

In ancient China, for example, commerce and a bureaucratic merit examination system encouraged markedly greater social mobility than existed in the feudal West; and this relative mobility should have encouraged capitalism.* Also favorable to capitalism should have been China's peace and stability during long periods, as well as its remarkably centralized, rational, and universalistic bureaucracy. In spite of these favorable conditions, however, nothing remotely approaching Western capitalism emerged in China.

Weber maintained that Chinese religion was the culprit. Yet at first glance even Chinese religion would seem to favor capitalism. Confucianism, the core of Chinese religion, was worldly and rational. Displaying little concern with the otherworld, the Confucianist was primarily interested in the practical world of government and society. His demeanor was not intemperate or erratic, but disciplined and orderly, for Confucianism taught that orderly behavior insured an orderly universe. Why, then, did Confucianism not promote capitalism? Weber argued that Confucianism, precisely because of its worldliness, failed to inspire a drive toward changing the world. The Confucian gentleman, unlike the Calvinist reformer, did not envision a transcendent Kingdom of God in the image of which he must constantly remold the world. Therefore, the Con-

---

* Note, however, Levy's "Contrasting Factors in the Modernization of China and Japan," pages 169–170, which shows that the marked mobility in China did not necessarily encourage capitalism there. Because Chinese values ranked the landed gentleman-scholar-bureaucrat at the apex of society and the merchant at the bottom, merchants who acquired wealth used it to buy land and join the landed class. Thus, the very openness of the traditional Chinese class structure encouraged constant flight of the most able merchants out of the merchant class. Presumably, this inhibited China's capitalistic development.

fucianist was content to harmonize with the world as given—to accept its magic, its clans, its traditions. Confucianism encouraged conservatism rather than the radically innovative spirit of capitalism. Weber did not claim that Calvinism was necessary to sustain contemporary capitalism, only that Calvinist ideas had encouraged the origin of capitalism. Nevertheless, he did point to contemporary patterns that display the imprint of Calvinism, even though such patterns are fully divorced from particular Calvinist doctrines or organizations. Comparing the reserved Englishman or mechanically friendly American with the sentimental, emotional, *gemütlich* (South) German, Weber speculated that the contrast reflects the impact of Calvinist Puritanism on England and America versus the Catholic and Lutheran influence on Germany. In Benjamin Franklin he detected another example of the effect of Calvinism. He was well aware that Franklin was no practicing Calvinist, yet he saw in Franklin's frugality and rationality a reflection of a milieu strongly influenced by its Calvinist origins. Besides Franklin, of course, numerous other American prototypes of the Protestant Ethic character could be described; Sinclair Lewis's portrait of a captain of industry, Dodsworth, can serve as an example:

> He always wore large grave suits, brown or gray or plain blue, expensively tailored and not very interesting, with decorous and uninteresting ties of dull silk and no jewelry save a watch chain. . . .
> He made his toilet like a man who never wasted motion—and who, incidentally, had a perfectly organized household to depend upon. His hand went surely to the tall pile of shirts (Fran ordered them from Jermyn Street) in the huge Flemish armoire, and to the glacial nest of collars, always inspected by the parlor maid and discarded for the slightest fraying. He tied his tie, not swiftly but with the unwasteful and extremely unadventurous precision of a man who has introduced as much "scientific efficiency" into daily domesticity as into his factory.
> . . . He would certainly (so the observer assumed) produce excellent motor cars; he would make impressive speeches

to the salesmen; but he would never love passionately, lose tragically, nor sit in contented idleness upon tropic shores.[6]

Weber's Protestant Ethic Thesis has been criticized on a variety of grounds. Although we agree that certain problems plague Weber's arguments, we also believe that many of the common criticisms [7] miss his point, distort his views, and obscure the usefulness of his thesis.

"Weber is wrong since many contemporary capitalists are not Calvinists or even practicing Protestants" is a frequently heard criticism. Weber's thesis, however, was not that Calvinism is necessary for capitalism today, only that Calvinism was the creative force behind the first capitalistic societies. Therefore, his thesis is not refuted by citing the numerous examples of non-Calvinist, non-Protestant capitalists of today. Besides, statistics show that in general Protestant nations are even today significantly more successful at capitalism than non-Protestant (*e.g.,* Catholic, Buddhist, Muslim) nations * and that within at least one major city of Protestant America, Protestant groups tend to be more capitalistic than Catholic groups.†

Students of history sometimes argue that Weber's thesis is incorrect because in pre-Reformation and post-Reformation periods there were many successful non-Calvinist capitalists.‡ But Weber's

---

* David C. McClelland, *The Achieving Society,* pages 50–52; Gerhard Lenski, *Human Societies,* chapter 10, table 25. The table in Lenski's book shows that the present median per capita income of predominantly Protestant nations is approximately six times the median for non-Protestant nations (including not only Eastern Orthodox and Roman Catholic, but also Buddhist, Muslim, and other nations). The median of Protestant nations is approximately three times the median of Eastern Orthodox and Roman Catholic nations.

† Gerhard Lenski, *The Religious Factor* (1963). Although Lenski's study covers only one city, Detroit, there is evidence that it could be generalized to numerous other American cities.

‡ Brentano, one critic who raised this issue, comes from a family that produced successful Catholic capitalists about the time of the Reformation. Misconstruing Weber's thesis as saying that only Calvinists could be good capitalists, he took it as a maligning of his ancestors.—Samuelsson, 1961, page 12.

central point was not that Calvinism was required to spur each individual or family to capitalistic feats, but that Calvinism was the driving force behind whole societies as they became organized capitalistically. In Weber's view, the difference between traditional and capitalistic societies was qualitative rather than quantitative. Capitalistic society did not result merely from the presence of numerous capitalists, but also from the organization of a complex of legal, governmental, educational, scientific, and economic institutions in such fashion as to facilitate capitalistic enterprise. Traditional societies were organized in such a way as to hamper capitalism; thus even if numerous capitalists were present, these had to work against the grain of society.

Some scholars suggest that capitalist societies existed before Calvinism—as in medieval Italy and Flanders. However, were these so-called pre-Calvinist capitalistic societies capitalist in Weber's sence of the word? Did they consist of a complex of governmental, educational, scientific, and economic institutions that were oriented toward facilitating the conduct of rational, ascetic, bureaucratic capitalism? Or were they simply traditional societies containing numerous capitalists? Anti-Weberians often claim that capitalism was present before Calvinism, but their definition of capitalism differs from Weber's. Obviously, to show that capitalism of type X is present when the Protestant Ethic is absent is not to prove that Weber's capitalism of type Y could flourish without the Protestant Ethic. To show that X occurs without Z is not to disprove the correlation between Y and Z.

A final criticism is that Calvinist leaders (*e.g.,* Calvin, Baxter, Wesley, Penn) explicitly preached against the accumulation of wealth; hence, say the critics, Calvinism discouraged rather than encouraged capitalism.[8] Actually, Weber himself went to some pains to show that Calvinist leaders such as Calvin and Baxter preached against the accumulation of wealth, particularly the accumulation of wealth for its own sake. Weber was fully aware that Calvinist theologians did not intend to encourage capitalism. But their attitude certainly does not disprove Calvinism's unintentional encouragement of capitalism. Weber argued that, regardless of the *intent* of Calvinist preachers, the pattern of Calvinist belief was such as to foster a drive toward salvation that found expression in capitalist action and institutions.

We should note in passing that Weber's critics have usually dealt exclusively with his analysis of Calvinism and capitalism in the West, although this is only a fragment of his work. His full analysis deals with Asia as well as Europe; it inquires not only why capitalism flourished in the West, but also why it did *not* flourish in the East. His approach to China in these terms has already been mentioned; we will shortly consider post-Weberian studies that extend the question to Japan.

Defense of Weber should not obscure legitimate questions that can be raised concerning his views. We shall propose a few questions we regard as legitimate because they derive from and build on Weber's penetrating insights and are amenable to empirical research.

Weber regarded England and the United States as the best examples of the modern capitalistic pattern, and Calvinism was certainly an important force in molding the institutions and values of both. Calvinism, however, was only a part of the Reformation, and England and America are only two capitalist societies among many. Can so limited a phenomenon as Calvinism account for so general a phenomenon as capitalism? Did Weber overlook important contributions to capitalism and modernism flowing from the total Reformation movement? After all, the entire Reformation, not Calvinism alone, transformed old social images, overturned the old feudal order, and rejected the church hierarchy. Perhaps the widespread, Reformation-inspired rejection of a single, legitimate, hierarchical authority opened the door for a pluralism and dissent of modern society, which insistently refuses any single authority the right to decree the truth.

In the face of competing systems of belief and value—those of traditional Christianity and of non-Calvinistic Protestantism—how could the beliefs and values of Calvinism prevail and become the basis of a new society? Were the Calvinistic ideas intrinsically more compelling and forceful than the competing ones? Did they frighten even non-Calvinist Christians into adopting Calvinist methods for salvation? At a more secular level, did Calvinistic institutions, such as the contract, inspire such successful business transactions that competitors were forced to adopt at least the institutions, if not the underlying doctrines? Confrontations like these between Calvinism and the non-Calvinist world may have stimulated the spread of Calvinist values without necessarily transforming the world's peoples into card-carrying Calvinists. Indeed, such confrontations might even have encouraged the secularization of Calvinist ideas: individuals who began acting like Calvinists, but who, religiously, remained non-Calvinist, would tend to deny the religious base of their actions and values.

Broad historic questions emerge from the Weberian studies. Although Weber focused primarily on the economic impact of Calvinism, later scholars have traced the effects of Calvinism on politics and on science. Much remains to be done in analyzing the impact of Calvinism on philosophy, but it is clear that Calvinistic notions seeped into the minds of Locke, Hobbes, and Adam Smith, to mention only a few.

A further elaboration of Weberian analysis is of pressing contemporary concern. What can the Weber thesis say about the prospects of modernization of the non-Western nations of today? Let us turn to Japan first, then to Indonesia, to illuminate this question.

THE PROTESTANT ETHIC THESIS AND THE
INDUSTRIALIZATION OF JAPAN

The development of early-modern society in the West was, of course, a gradual and lengthy process, but eventually the capitalistic, industrial early-modern pattern did spread throughout Western Europe and European settlements, such as America. It has proved remarkably difficult to export the pattern to non-Western societies.

The efforts of missionaries, colonists, and, more recently, development agencies have hardly met with dazzling success. Although contact with the West has always elicited some modernization, almost no society has successfully modernized. Japan, one of the few that has, to a degree, been successful in modernizing is therefore of special interest.

In a remarkably short time, Japan managed to transform herself from a basically feudal-agrarian society into one of the most industrial societies of the world. That feat was the more striking because it was accomplished without great natural and economic resources. In terms of raw material, surplus population to employ in industry, and availability of capital to entrepreneurs, Japan was less favored than some of the other non-Western societies, such as neighboring China. Yet

> with an almost complete absence of internal blood-letting, the Japanese altered their governmental system, maintained their national independence, formed effective capital at an astonishing rate and virtually without foreign loans, and by the fourth decade of this century had become one of the five or six most "highly modernized" and powerful nations in the world.[9]

How was Japan able to achieve so much so fast? For one thing, Japan could profit from the experience of the West—emulate its successes, avoid its mistakes. With no model before it, the West, by contrast, had struggled toward capitalism through painful trial and error, guided by religious ideologies, the economic implications of which were unclear even to their believers.

But this advantage was open to all non-Western societies. The model of the West was there for all to see. Why, then, was it Japan, and not the others, who successfully industrialized? Could it be something special about Japan's sociocultural patterning? We might ask, with Robert Bellah, "Was there a functional analogue to the Protestant Ethic in Japanese religion" that contributed significantly to Japan's unique success in industrialization? [10]

Prior to its industrialization, Japan experienced almost unprecedented stability and peace for over two hundred and fifty years, during the Tokugawa period (1600–1868). Tokugawa society was composed of semi-independent feudal fiefs united under the *shogun* ("military ruler"), who wielded his power in the name of the emperor. The emperor himself, lacking power, lived neglected and ignored at his court in Kyoto, while the actual operations of government were centered at the shogun's court in Edo (present-day Tokyo).

Tokugawa society was rigidly stratified into a hierarchy of classes. At the apex were the emperor, the shogun, and the feudal lords who ruled the great fiefs. Immediately below these were the samurai, or Bushi, who were nominally warriors but who also served as officials and administrators of the fiefs. Separated from these elite by a wide gulf were the masses who, like the elite, were stratified. Peasant-farmers were at the top because they furnished food to the elite; artisans ranked next because they provided objects of beauty and utility for the elite; merchants were near the bottom because they were unproductive—they were mere middlemen distributing goods produced by others. At the bottom slunk the outcaste groups, the Eta and the light-skinned hairy Ainu. Although mobility within each class was common, mobility between classes was difficult if not impossible.

Although Japan had borrowed much from China (*e.g.,* Mahayana Buddhism, Confucianism, and a writing system), its values were its own. The Japanese placed overwhelming emphasis on political values—values pertaining to the attainment of collective goals. Membership in a collectivity was essential since all blessings (*on*) were thought to flow from the various collectivities to which the individual was attached. For example, a person's parents and family provided life and identity, and his fief and lord gave status and protection. For blessings (*on*) received, the individual was expected to return blessings (*hoon*), particularly his loyalty, to the group.

Yet loyalty alone was not enough. The Japanese demanded performance as well. Only continuous performance in the service of group goals validated one's position. Even the group's head was accountable for his performance; the emperor himself had to report periodically to his ancestors and the gods on his performance while in office. The strong emphasis on performance did not allow passive devotion or docile subordination; it demanded active service.

Given the central values of loyalty and performance, it is not surprising that the military (samurai), who strikingly manifested these values, were very prestigious. Even during the long period of Tokugawa peace, the samurai managed to retain their prestige. Indeed, Bushido ("the way of the warrior") came to symbolize the ideal life style for Japanese of all classes. All Japanese were influenced by the military notion of self-sacrifice in the interest of the overlord.

Of course, economic activities could serve social goals, and when they did they were regarded as legitimate and essential. All classes were urged to maximize production and, at the same time, to minimize consumption—to live frugally so that resources could be diverted toward collective ends. When work did not serve collective ends, it was not valued. Hence, the farmer and the warrior were praised because they produced for fief and lord, but the merchant was suspected of working for his own interests and was consequently ranked low in the hierarchy.

Education was highly regarded, but not, as in China, for its own sake. Learning was valued primarily for its social contribution. The learned man had to be first and foremost a loyal man, exploiting his knowledge for the good of the group. Education thus contributed to conformity, rather than providing independent standards that might lead to critical comparison and perhaps rebellion.

Nor did a person's private emotions escape society's emphasis on loyalty and performance. Yearnings for romantic love were not satisfied by marriage since the elders, who expected the young to subordinate their feelings to the needs of the family, arranged their children's marriages. That such sacrifice was not always easy is demonstrated by the Japanese tradition of love suicides, prominent in literature, art, and even in life. Lovers could not simply elope; only through death could they violate loyalty to the group.

Japanese values were inspired and sanctified by Tokugawa religion, a composite of Confucianism, Mahayana Buddhism, and Shinto. These religions postulated a bond between man and the supernatural that paralleled the ideal bond between man and the group whereby the group conferred blessings (*on*) and man reciprocated with loyalty and performance (*hoon*). Shinto stressed the *on-hoon* relationship between the people and the national gods who oversaw their fate. Since the emperor represented the gods, loyalty to the emperor was loyalty to the gods. To repay the gods for blessings they bestowed, one performed for the emperor. Japanese Confucianism also emphasized loyalty to ruler and polity; but, in contrast to Chinese Confucianism, loyalty to ruler and polity ranked even higher than loyalty to the family. Mahayana Buddhism obliquely reinforced the same theme in that it preached the believer's dependency on a particular Buddha figure (*bhoddhisattva*) through whose grace one could attain heavenly reward; this figure could be a political superior. All religions, then, placed major emphasis on service and loyalty to the group and the leader. If the individual's service were sufficiently disciplined and ascetic, he could purify himself of his evil impulses and desires.

This Japanese attitude paralleled the ascetic-activist attitude of the Protestant Ethic, and probably served Japan as the Protestant Ethic had served the West: to inspire continuous, methodical, diligent work within a capitalistic economy. But whereas the Western Protestant Ethic encouraged achievement for God and self, Tokugawa religion encouraged achievement for emperor and state. It was this motive which Japan harnessed in the service of industrialization.

By the late nineteenth century the Tokugawa regime was at an end and the post-Tokugawa leaders, drawn mainly from the old samurai, faced the threat of the West. They clearly saw that, because of the West's superior technology, Japan would be crushed in a military contest, that colonialism threatened and that Japanese tradition could be eroded by Western capitalism. To maintain her autonomy and identity, Japan would have to transform herself into an industrial state capable of competing with the industrial nations of the West. The first order of business was to abolish the old feudal system and create a national state. The leaders accomplished this with the aid of the Shinto concept *Kokutai* ("national polity"), which sanctified the state by identifying service to the emperor with service to the gods. Disseminating the concept of *Kokutai* through the schools and shrines, the leaders successfully elevated loyalty to emperor and state above all else and mobilized all loyalties and efforts to implement national goals, among which was the establishment of an industrial economy similar to that of the West.

Japan's industrialization differed from that of the West not only in being faster and more government-directed, but also in proceeding from a different cultural base. The Japanese managed to erect an early-modern techno-economic system on an essentially archaic sociocultural foundation: the Japanese emperor, like the Egyptian pharaoh, was identified with divinity. But a more general difference between Japan and the West was that in the West economic and political revolution followed religious reformation, whereas in Japan a similar economic and political revolution utilized ancient religious patterns, revitalizing them to fit new demands.

THE NEW NATIONS: POLITICAL RELIGION IN INDONESIA

Since the end of World War II, which marked the end of the colonial empires, many new nations have been established. These nations are presently struggling to achieve some measure of parity with the long-established industrial nations, and, as part of that struggle, they aim to incorporate into their diverse traditions certain facets of the early-modern pattern.

In the West a radical cultural transformation, the Protestant Reformation, was a prelude to the emergence of early-modern society. In quite a different manner, Japan was able to incorporate many early-modern features without radically transforming her basic cultural patterns. But in both Japan and the West, cultural systems—systems of values and ideas—played a central role in socioeconomic modernization. These did more than render socioeconomic modernization meaningful: they made it seem as though such modernization flowed inevitably from the nature of existence.

Socioeconomic change in the new nations has not proceeded as smoothly as it did in Japan. Admittedly, the economic and political conditions confronted by the new nations differ from those confronted by Japan in the nineteenth century. A fundamental problem is the lack, among most new nations, of cultural systems that are readily harnessed to modernization. The new nations must undergo deep-seated cultural changes similar to those of the European Reformation before modernization can proceed at a significant rate. Perhaps they can learn even more from the European experience than from the Japanese one.

It is noteworthy that the leaders of many new nations are charismatic figures who, like Reformation preachers, proclaim a vision of a new society. With their millenarian quality, these visions lend urgency to exhortations aimed at inflaming the masses. Leaders like Gandhi, Mao, Sukarno, Kenyatta, U Nu, Nkrumah, Nehru, and Sihanouk have preached what may be called a new species of religion—"political religion," [11] a system of values, ideas, and symbols often divorced from and hostile to the supernatural beliefs of conventional religion. Yet like conventional religion, the new ideologies offer hope of salvation and immortality for the believer by promising a secure future in a life not yet experienced by mortal man.

Political religion also promises new identity through the union of the individual with a system larger and more powerful than any he has experienced. This system, be it the nation or something wider and deeper, draws the citizen away from traditional attachments to kinship, ethnic, or local groups. Youth is especially vulnerable to such appeals, for the young crave identity and are more ready than their elders to forsake the securities of traditional loyalties.

Exciting new goals are created by political religion. Citizens are urged to work and struggle to actualize in five-year plans the vision of the charismatic leader. By "retooling" themselves as instruments for the fulfillment of that pure vision, the citizens are supposed to feel cleansed and purified. A political religion can foster a political puritanism paralleling Calvinistic puritanism.

The problems the new nations encounter as they seek to transform their old societies are unbelievably complex. Americans, deeply grounded in their own culture with its peculiar Calvinist-capitalist-democratic warp, are necessarily biased in their perception of these problems. Typically, the American view is that if the new nations would simply repair their economies, stable political and social orders would automatically follow. Many of the new leaders—who are presumably sensitive to the needs of their societies—view the situation differently. They not only treat economic reform as a secondary problem, but even brutally manhandle their economies. Perhaps they sense that a stable economic, political, and social order cannot be achieved without first establishing a cultural order that wins inner as well as outer commitment of the citizenry. Democracy emerged from the Reformation, and Americans should entertain the possibility at least that from the current ferment may emerge cultural systems that inspire governmental systems different from any we now imagine.

A sketch of the rise of political religion in one new nation—Indonesia—may render these general remarks more meaningful. The sketch will cover the period from 1949, when Indonesia became an independent nation, to 1965, when Sukarno's fall signalled the collapse of political religion in Indonesia.[12]

When Indonesia gained its independence in 1949, Hatta, who was prime minister, was more powerful than Sukarno, who was president. The next few years bore the stamp of Hatta's rational but humdrum rule. The press was free; a constitutional democracy, with a parliament, operated with reasonable effectiveness; courts were not overly entrapped in politics; rice production soared and exports increased; and education expanded enormously at every level.

Unfortunately Hatta's regime could not sustain the loyalty of the people and the political parties. The uncharismatic Hatta, who could not bear the touch of the crowd and who scorned ideology and symbolism, failed to satisfy those who "had come to expect government and politics to provide their personal lives with meaning." [13] For this and other reasons, Hatta lost support, and in 1953 the last pro-Hatta cabinet fell and was replaced by a pro-Sukarno cabinet. Then began an era of revolutionary Indonesian political religion centering on such mythical symbols as Sukarno's Pantjasila, the charter of the Indonesian nation. Unlike Hatta, Sukarno and his colleagues were willing to sacrifice economic prosperity for nationalist-revolutionary spirit and meaning. Thus, to encourage deeper sentiments of national unity, Sukarno "Indonesianized" the economy by replacing important Dutch enterprises with Indonesian ones, a step that caused incredible inflation and serious decline in production.

Economic disruption and political turbulence marked the years from 1953 to 1956. Ideological conflicts, stimulated by intense and bitter electioneering that drew the energy of the parties away from socioeconomic reform, divided the nation. The basic schism was between the Muslims and the Nationalist-Communists. The Muslims, represented by the Masjumi and Nahdatul Ulama parties, were favored by businessmen and by the people of the outer islands (such as Hatta's Sumatra). The Nationalist-Communist faction, represented by the Indonesian Nationalist Party (PNI) and the Indonesian Communist Party (PKI), was favored especially by bureaucrats, workers, and the people of the central island, Java (Sukarno's homeland).

As conflicts worsened and civil war threatened, Sukarno proposed a solution to strife: his concept (*konsepsi*) of Guided Democracy. Guided Democracy, unveiled in 1957, called for the formation of a single cabinet, in which all major parties would cooperate harmoniously, and a national council that would unite the various functional groups—workers, peasants, and national businessmen—through consensus rather than the vote. Sukarno's idea was to abandon the free-for-all democracy of the West, which had led to conflict, and to replace it with a system patterned after the government-by-consensus supposedly practiced in ancient and idyllic Indonesian villages. With the nation in danger of shaking apart, Sukarno's Guided Democracy loomed as the one hope for unity and order. In the late fifties Sukarno and the army acted to institute Guided Democracy.

Sukarno dissolved the elected parliament and the cabinet responsible to the parliament—agencies that restrained his power—and instituted a 616-member People's Consultative Assembly, which seldom met, appointed a parliament, and set up a cabinet responsible to him alone. He also created a 75-member National Planning Council, a 45-member Supreme Advisory Council, and a National Front Organization enrolling two hundred political parties, mass organizations, and functional groups, and encompassing, by 1962, a membership of thirty-three million.

By mid-1958 political parties were "no longer leading actors on the Indonesian stage." [14] By its "guiding actions" the army had banned Communist political meetings, labor union activities, and activities of parties opposing Sukarno. The decline of parties and parliamentary apparatus was accompanied by a marked diminution of civil liberties: strikes and newspapers were banned and legal guarantees were brushed aside.

Once Guided Democracy was under way, Sukarno turned his attention to political religion as the means of sanctifying the new social order. He made clear that he was not just a politician: he was a prophet attempting to improve "values and standards," to bring about "spiritual changes," and to set in motion a "mental momentum" that would culminate in "spiritual revolution." He claimed to pattern his speeches after the narrations spoken by the *dalang,* priestly narrator of the sacred Javanese puppet play, the *wajang.* He developed street-cleaning rites to signify retooling for the future. He portrayed the Constitution of 1945 as a "magically-sentimentally-nationally-loaded" creature that occupies a "throne" and has a "soul and spirit." He verbally transformed mosquito-ridden West New Guinea into a land of paradise to be wrested from Dutch imperialists by lady paratroopers emulating the mythical heroine Srikandi. And he appointed a poet to formulate a plan for economic development, which, when completed, consisted of eight major sections, each composed of seventeen subsections, to symbolize the August 17 birthdate of Indonesia. Sukarno enthusiastically praised the plan for its "symbolic richness."

The central ideology of Guided Democracy was Manipol-Usdek. Manipol-Usdek, an acronymn coined by Sukarno and his associates, stood for several exalted objectives: to attain, in Sukarno's phrases, the "Just and Prosperous" society organized under "Socialism à la Indonesia," financed by "Guided Economy," in keeping with "The Indonesian Personality." Taught in schools, preached by newspapers, and propagated by song and dance, billboards, shantytown gates, and movie commercials, Manipol-Usdek was supposed to elicit absolute loyalty. Editors, professors, and other intellectuals were made to swear allegiance to it. Civil servants who did not display sufficient allegiance were "retooled," *i.e.,* demoted or dismissed, and their successors were made aware that their positions depended on active loyalty to the current political leadership and to Manipol-Usdek.

The symbolism of political religion always appeals to youth, and in Indonesia youth was both the target and the source of such symbolism. Sukarno preached that Indonesia began with a nationalist declaration by the Congress of Indonesian Youth in 1928, and that the Indonesian nation itself was a youth. Passing through a "transition period" like that of "puberty," Indonesia was trying to show the "whole world that . . . we are a nation of men with the spirit of a bull" and at the same time that it had to "search for and attain our own identity." [15] Like Indonesia, Sukarno himself took on the imagery of youth; he often preferred to be called not "father" (*bapak*), in accordance with traditional custom, but rather "peer" (*bung*), in accordance with his role of symbolic youth within the gang of actual and symbolic youths of which he was the leader. Nor was youth imagery restricted to Sukarno's speeches and labels. Important streets and buildings bore the names "Youth Street" and "Youth Hall," and youths were prominent in congresses, clean-ups, and other public actions. Indeed, the youth possessed real power since each major political party had its youth wing—that of the Communist Party being the only Communist appendage directly financed by the central committee.

Although Indonesian political religion did inspire dynamism and creativity, it was carried to such a point that it interfered with practical economics and government. Government money was diverted from practical tasks into the purchase and construction of such prestige symbols as bombers, destroyers, missiles, nuclear generators, giant stadiums, luxury hotels, and the National Monument. More important, political religion sanctified the rule of symbol wielders, such as Sukarno, rather than rational administrators, such as Hatta. At all levels of Indonesian government, positions were awarded in recognition of charisma and fervor rather than of technical qualifications. Even those rational administrators who retained their positions found it difficult to bring about practical reforms because practical reforms possessed little merit under the ideologies of the day.

With the decline in rational administration came hardship and corruption. As prices tripled yearly and government salaries did not rise to match, bureaucrats saw themselves obliged to make ends meet by stealing and accepting bribes. Even though salaries within the bureaucracy decreased in buying power, the political power of the bureaucracy rose sharply owing to the decline in power of business groups. The banning of the Muslim "business" party removed the one major nonbureaucratic group that heretofore had counterbalanced the authority of the bureaucracy. By the 1960's, bureaucracy had become a law unto itself, and politics had become simply bureaucracy bolstered by political religion.

Certain parallels can be seen between Indonesian political re-

ligion and European-American Protestantism, that is, between Sukarnoism and Calvinism. Both undercut hierarchy. Calvinism erased
the hierarchies that extended from man to God. Sukarnoism col-
lapsed those that, in traditional lowland Southeast Asia, had
extended from peasant to god-king. Sukarno's assumption of the
role of peer (*bung*) instead of father (*bapak*) symbolized this
transformation, as did the replacement of the Javanese language
with a new national language, Indonesian, which was egalitarian in
that it dispensed with the Javanese rule of employing special
vocabularies when speaking to persons of high rank. Indeed, although Sukarno's Guided Democracy accented "guidance" more
than "democracy," even this development signified a rejection of
the hierarchical order in favor of a vision of communal equality.
Guided Democracy conceived of Indonesian society not as an
archaic hierarchy but as an incredibly complex system of crosscutting voluntary groups—congresses, parliaments, parties, movements—united by loose consensus. Guided Democracy differed
from early-modern democracies of the West in that the various
groups had only limited power to challenge the state. The Indonesian bureaucracy, encompassing all interest groups, was a law
unto itself rather than an instrument of commerce, science, education, or the pursuit of happiness.

Calvinism inspired free enterprise, in many senses: business for
business's sake, science for science's sake, and art for art's sake
were encouraged by Calvinism and early-modern society. Work of
any kind was good, production of any kind was good. "What's
worth doing is worth doing well" was a guiding motto, and "What
can be done well is worth doing" was a basic value. To the pious
Calvinists, such work was directed toward God's glory; few felt
strongly that it should be harnessed to the glory of the state. Sukarnoism, on the other hand, nourished the attitude that business for
business's sake or science for science's sake was not sufficient. It
behooved the businessman or scientist to demonstrate at all times
that his enterprise served Sukarno, and frequently such a demonstration of loyalty took precedence over or interfered with the enterprise

itself. Perhaps the danger of interference with accomplishment is greater when the object of ultimate loyalty is a real person than when it is a spiritual symbol, whose requirements, according to some points of view, can be tailored by the believers to fit their desires. In Calvinism demonstration of spiritual loyalties could be scheduled at the convenience of the worker, whereas in a political religion such demonstration is decreed by an earthly leader.

A system such as Sukarno's Guided Democracy is obviously more immanent in the state and the world than is God's Kingdom. Therefore, political and economic chaos, corruption and stagnation, could and did tarnish the image of Guided Democracy, and Indonesians became disillusioned not only with the worldly reality but with the utopian image as well. By contrast, the image of God's Kingdom retained its purity however terrible earthly conditions became, and wickedness in the state and in the world only intensified the Calvinist's resolve to fulfill his calling and build God's Kingdom on earth. Nor could any man prove that God's Kingdom was impure, for no man had been there and returned to report. Calvinism thus possessed certain psychological advantages over Sukarnoism. Undoubtedly, some of the problems of Indonesia and Sukarnoism are rooted in the psychological contradictions that are intrinsic to political religion.

OVERVIEW

Archaic religion was monistic, historic religion dualistic. Archaic man conceived of one world, inhabited by both gods and men. Historic man envisioned two worlds: an otherworldly realm of the gods (or other ultimate entities) and a this-worldly realm of men. Linking the historic otherworld and the real world were symbolic-social hierarchies, which, because of their sacred aura, historic man was disposed neither to view objectively nor to change.

Calvinism, the prototype of early-modern religion, swept away the hierarchies. With Calvinism, the real world and the otherworld were linked only through the faith and commitment of individuals. The real world, wicked and devoid of sanctity, was regarded as a chaotic jungle through which moved committed individuals guided by purposes and plans issued from the otherworld. No longer sacred, the real world could be viewed and criticized from the perspective of these divine purposes and plans. Should The Divine call for worldly change, the world would be *changed*. Since Calvinism denied the efficacy of ritual, such change could come about only through the rational action of active work and reform.

Historic society was significantly more universalistic than primitive or archaic societies, for in historic society at least most *religious* statuses could be achieved by all men, regardless of their status at birth. But in nonreligious sectors, even in historic society, particularism was still the rule. Thus, the feudal system of Europe, rooted in such images as the Great Chain of Being and the Organic Analogy, decreed that every man should stay in his inherited place. The destruction of feudal particularism was in part the work of Calvinism, which denied any earthly power or authority the right to dictate what status an individual should occupy. For Calvinists, the individual's rank was determined solely through his covenant with God.

Calvinism regarded the relationship between God and the individual as a contract voluntarily made by each party. This contractual pattern spread from the religious to the secular realm and became dominant in early-modern life. No longer did the individual accept without question his inherited and fixed bond to another; he was expected actively to seek contractual relations. Even marriage became a contract. The kinsmen of the marrying couple, who were not party to the contract, were not bound to each other by the marriage. The extended network of kinship was weakened, therefore, and concern shifted from extended kinship to the nuclear family and to the marriage tie itself.

Early-modern society is composed of myriad voluntary groups to which each individual relates contractually. Each person's relation to a group is functionally specific rather than diffuse. Each group asks its members to perform roles which, being specialized, exploit only a part of each member's personality; that is, each member spreads his personality among a number of specialized roles. Conflict among such roles inevitably arises. Being a worker gets in the way of being a father, being a Democrat interferes with being an industrialist, being a Quaker with being a soldier. The task of integrating conflicting, specialized roles into an organized self is greater for the early-modern personality than for the archaic or primitive personalities.

Primitive society was one-class, archaic society two-class, and historic society was structured around a hierarchy of three classes. Calvinism undermined this class structure. Where Calvinism became dominant, kingship, aristocracy, and class hierarchy were either eroded or destroyed and replaced by a flexible, multicentered pattern of crosscutting voluntary groups. In early-modern society, firms, factories, unions, parties, and associations all compete for a share of power, and no single authority, such as church or state, monopolizes all power. Bureaucratization, mass media, and giant national parties are among the mechanisms that have emerged to centralize the diversified voluntary groups of early-modern society.

The very complexity of early-modern society stimulates change, for conflicts and strains among diversified interest groups inevitably result in change. A thrust toward change is also part of early-modern *culture*. Early-modern culture, derived from Calvinism, denied the sacredness of the world and affirms the need to reform the world in order that it may approach the transcendent model of the Kingdom of God. Because the discrepancy between the model and the reality is unceasing, the individual feels incessantly driven to change the reality. Although the majority of early-modern men no longer recognize the specifically religious substance of this pattern, its secular manifestations remain strong. Built into the very core of ideologies governing early-modern law, government, education, science, business, social welfare, and community life is the notion that reforming reality to match transcendental models is necessary and desirable. The resulting drive to change makes early-modern society a self-revising system. Regardless of outside stimulation, its inner dynamic sustains an incessant process of change. In this, it is more "modern" than primitive, archaic, or historic society.

Since we have treated early-modern society and culture as products of the Protestant Reformation and especially of Calvinism, it is not surprising that America and Western Europe should be viewed as prototypes of early-modern society and culture. Tendencies toward early-modern society have appeared sporadically in Buddhist and Muslim cultures; only in the West, however, was the early-modern pattern successfully instituted in a total society.

Japan, which has established certain early-modern socioeconomic institutions while at the same time managing to retain an archaic cultural base, contrasts instructively with India. In elite spheres of Hinduism, India displayed a movement toward historic religion (some might even say, toward modern religion), but these ideas did not penetrate deeply and widely enough to transform India from an essentially archaic society. Japan, on the other hand, exploited its archaic god-king religion in such a way as to industrialize and nationalize with great speed, but these changes in the socioeconomic order did not suffice to transform Japanese culture from its archaic form.

Indonesia and other new nations face problems that are, in one respect, more like those of the medieval West than they are like those of Japan. Just as the West underwent a radical religious reformation before it successfully modernized its society and economy, so the new nations are undergoing radical cultural transformations, which are apparently necessary for successful socioeconomic modernization to occur. Cultural reformations in the new nations are led by charismatic prophets, such as Sukarno, who strive to create political religions. Political religion seeks to capture the loyalty of its citizens, to free them from traditional identities, and to provide a new sense of purpose. It aims to provide a moral basis for transforming and modernizing a nonmodern society in order to create a system better adapted to the contemporary world. Although political religions are of fundamental importance in the struggle of the new nations, they do create contradictions and problems. As was suggested in the analysis of Indonesia, political religions tend to create disillusionment to a greater degree than conventional religions such as Calvinism. Nevertheless, they have an increasingly valuable function, for with the decline of supernaturalism throughout the world, conventional religion is becoming less and less capable of serving as a framework for modernization. Political religion is the first postsupernaturalist attempt at sanctifying and rendering meaningful the process of modernization.

TOPICS FOR DISCUSSION

This chapter has suggested a number of areas for further exploration of the Weber thesis. For example, the student might consider more fully the impact of the total Reformation movement on the development of early-modern Western society. The root causes of the Reformation itself might be considered. Did some radical disjunction between the way medieval men conceived of their society and their actual experience of that society goad them to change their religious views and ultimately their society? The success of Japan in grafting early-modern patterns on a basically archaic foundation poses further questions. Was the success of Japan a unique occurrence, the result of its peculiar value system? Or can the Japanese accomplishment provide a model for other societies undergoing modernization? In contemporary Japan the rise of a number of new religions is causing considerable religious ferment. Are these new religions modifying the Japanese value system to accord better with the conditions of an industrialized society? More generally, why are religious or quasi-religious movements (the political religions are an example) so common during periods of great social upheaval and change? Exploring this question, the student may discover significant facts about human existence and character.

It is also interesting to consider the relative advantages and disadvantages of the Protestant Ethic pattern and of other sociocultural patterns that man has evolved. For example, how do primitive religion and some of the early-modern substitutes for conventional religion, such as political religion, compare with the Protestant Ethic in their consequences for human stability, productivity, creativity, and happiness? The student might try to design a substitute for the Protestant Ethic which would satisfy the conditions of today, yet provide the same psychological and social benefits that the Protestant Ethic apparently provided in the past.

THE PROTESTANT ETHIC

The Protestant Ethic and the Spirit of Capitalism (paperback, 1958) by Max Weber. The basic source for this chapter.

The Structure of Social Action (paperback, 1968) by Talcott Parsons. Part III provides an excellent summary and evaluation of the Weber thesis.

Max Weber: An Intellectual Portrait (paperback, 1962) by Reinhard Bendix. Part II supplies a first-rate summary and evaluation of the Weber thesis.

Religion and the Rise of Capitalism: A Historical Study (paperback, 1961) by Richard Tawney. Expands the historical basis of the Weber thesis.

The Protestant Ethic and Modernization: A Comparative View (paperback, 1968) edited by S. N. Eisenstadt. Extends Weberian analysis into new areas outside the West.

The Religious Factor: A Sociological Study of Religion's Impact on Politics, Economics, and Family Life (paperback, 1963) by Gerhard Lenski. A careful test and extension of the Weber thesis in an American city.

Protestantism and Capitalism: The Weber Thesis and Its Critics (paperback, 1959) edited by Robert Green.

Religion and Economic Action: A Critique of Max Weber (paperback, 1961) by Kurt Samuelsson. A suggestive if misguided critique.

"Puritanism, Pietism, and Science" in *Social Theory and Social Structure* (1957) by Robert Merton. Shows the implications of Calvinism for science.

The Revolution of the Saints: A Study in the Origins of Radical Politics (paperback, 1968) by Michael Walzer. Shows the implications of Calvinism for politics. Chapter 5 provides a more detailed discussion of medieval imagery from the perspective of the Weber thesis than is given in our text.

"Mystics and Merchants in Fourteenth Century Germany" (1969) by James L. Peacock. Amplification of our discussion of medieval imagery from the perspective of the Weber thesis.

MODERNIZATION IN CHINA AND JAPAN

Tokugawa Religion: The Values of Pre-Industrial Japan (1957) by Robert Bellah. On the cultural basis of the industrialization of Japan.

"Contrasting Factors in the Modernization of China and Japan" (1953) by Marion J. Levy, Jr.

"Some Aspects of 'Individualism' and the Problem of Modernization in China and Japan" (1962) by Marion J. Levy, Jr.

"Reflections on the Protestant Ethic Analogy in Asia" (1963) by Robert Bellah.

POLITICAL RELIGION AND THE NEW NATIONS

The Politics of Modernization (paperback, 1965) by David Apter.

Old Societies and New States (1963) edited by Clifford Geertz.

The Ideologies of the Developing Nations (paperback, 1963) by Paul E. Sigmund.

"The Ideologies of Delayed Industrialization: Some Tensions and Ambiguities" (1962) by Mary Matossian.

Religion and Progress in Modern Asia (1965) edited by Robert Bellah. See especially the epilogue, which synthesizes many of the modernizing trends in the world today in terms of the framework underlying the present book.

INDONESIA

"The Dynamics of Guided Democracy" (1963) by Herbert Feith. On Indonesia as a new nation embracing political religion.

Indonesia (1963) edited by Ruth T. McVey. Provides general background on Indonesia. Chapters are available separately in paperback.

The Religion of Java (paperback, 1964) by Clifford Geertz. A basic book on Java, the largest ethnic group in Indonesia and the dominant source of its political religion.

Rites of Modernization: Symbolic and Social Aspects of Indonesian Proletarian Drama (1968) by James L. Peacock. An analysis of Indonesian modernization as experienced via certain symbols by a particular group.

7

America: an emerging
modern society and culture

Carrying forward the thrust of the argument in the last chapter, this chapter will sketch the penetration of early-modern patterns into American life and the movement beyond the early-modern, which America is now experiencing. The focus on America is certainly not meant to imply that the latest sociocultural advances are to be found only, or even primarily, in America. Full analysis would certainly include the total world system, of which American trends are a part. Nevertheless, since American trends are currently influential in the world, understanding of America will contribute significantly to understanding of other parts of the world. More important, for the purposes of this book America is the proper system on which to center the *American* reader's attention at the end of a far-ranging survey. Now that he has progressed through various alien patterns, with opportunities for comparison, he should be prepared to perceive America in a more distant and objective fashion.

Extension of the anthropological perspective to include the anthropologist's own society is neither new nor unusual. Anthropologists have dissected American communities (*e.g.,* Hortense Powdermaker, *After Freedom: A Cultural Study in the Deep South*); they have emulated sociologists in analyzing American class structure and popular culture (*e.g.,* Lloyd Warner, *American Life: Dream and Reality*); and they have even attempted sweeping assessments of the American character (*e.g.,* Margaret Mead, *And Keep Your Powder Dry,* and Geoffrey Gorer, *The American People: A Study in National Character*). Of course, the anthropologist is not the only one who has trained his sights on American society. The anthropologist who analyzes America can consult the writings of journalists, essayists, social critics, social scientists, and others concerned with the contemporary scene. Indeed, since the focus of this chapter is on emerging trends rather than on the enduring patterns that have most attracted anthropological attention, we shall rely more on those social prophets who undertake to fathom emerging trends than on the anthropologists themselves.

SHAPING A NEW SOCIETY

A new society emerged from the religious reformation and political revolution of sixteenth- and seventeenth-century Europe. Freed from explicit ties to conventional religion, this new society could, despite its origins in religious reformation, be characterized as *secular*. Politically it might be deemed *nationalistic,* for it was based on the nation-state that had replaced the narrower feudal forms. Thanks to its great technological and economic advance, it was *industrial*. Because its population had shifted to the cities, and its cities had become the center of affairs, it was *urban*. And since its various segments and processes were bound together by large-scale, rationally and universalistically based organizations, it was certainly *bureaucratic*.

In Europe the shaping of the new society was influenced by the existing old forms. Monarchical traditions, institutions of nobility, craft and guild organizations, and local rivalries remained to alter and mask the emerging structure. In America, on the other hand, the new patterns emerged with special clarity because the old forms were absent and because many of those who helped found America were radical dissenters from the old European society who had deliberately repudiated the traditional order and who consciously sought to establish a new society in a new land.

From the beginning, American society deviated from the feudal and postfeudal pattern of Europe. Although aristocratic ideas crossed the Atlantic to the South and to portions of New England, values emphasizing equality of opportunity and of rights were more widely held. Hereditary elite groups, whether religious, political, or economic, were viewed with suspicion. This egalitarianism did not, of course, deny that there were significant differences in social status among men, but it denied that those awarded by birth and inheritance were binding and immutable. Each man had the opportunity to demonstrate by deeds his claims to status and power. The idea that the right to govern depended on the voluntary consent of the governed, a concept similar to the Puritan notion of the covenant, had a strong influence on American politics. An obvious extension of this idea was the belief that the will of the majority should prevail. These democratic convictions opened effective channels for changing the government without destroying it, thereby encouraging a politics of persuasion and consensus instead of force and tyranny. The Puritan base of democratic concepts is clearest in New England, where such democratic institutions as the town meeting flourished. The town meeting, which fostered a sense of individual participation and of collective morality, was in many respects a secular form of the Puritan congregation.

As the nation expanded westward and the population grew, government too expanded at every level. Its function, however, remained restricted. Government was regarded as merely a facilitating service to smooth the functioning of community, school, and court in a but-recent wilderness. In marked contrast to Europe, few in America expected or desired government to penetrate deeply into daily life or dictate the direction of social development. Only after the industrialization of America had progressed quite far was government seen not only as a facilitating service, but also as a protector of a collective public interest which might overrule certain private interests.

Despite the eventual commercial importance of a few ports such as Boston, New York, and New Orleans, the early American economy was even more predominantly agricultural than was the European economy. Initially, then, Europe, with its extensive commercial network and a nascent industrial system originating in medieval times, had a more complex economy than did early America. America, however, did not have the disadvantages of traditional structures to inhibit the development of new and progressive industries, and in agriculture, too, innovation was easier in America than in Europe. In Europe, the development of large-scale commercial agriculture was hampered by the necessity of destroying feudal enclosures or relocating tenants in order to consolidate lands. In America, especially in the South, great plantations could be carved out of a virgin wilderness. The result was that large-scale farming, geared to production of commercial crops and raw materials for European industries, flourished in America. Subsistence, as well as commercial, agriculture took on a distinctly American pattern. In Europe, farmers lived clustered together in villages, going forth each day to cultivate the surrounding fields. Although they were no longer serfs, they *were* peasants, bound to their land and locale. Each generation succeeded the previous one, with little expectation of either geographic or social mobility. In America, however, the farmer typically lived in an isolated farmhouse set in the midst of wide fields—a pattern of living which both reflected and encouraged American individualism. The American farmer did not feel bound to a particular locale. The pioneer could not have pulled up stakes and gone West to tame vast frontiers had he been hobbled by the traditional values of the European peasant. The mastery of successive frontiers became itself a potent influence on American culture and character, and the "frontier ethos" came to pervade all realms of American life.

Although America remained predominantly agricultural during the taming of the frontier, the expanding needs of the spreading populace also stimulated extensive industrial growth. Textile mills, wagon factories, and other industries sprang up, aided by the emergence of centers of commerce and trade routes along strategic rivers and roads as well as on the coasts. To a degree, the regions specialized—the South in production of agricultural raw materials for Northeastern industries, the West in food production and mining. With the growth of regional specialization and the expansion of commercial, communications, and transportation networks linking the various areas, the tendency to centralization increased, with resultant economic ramifications. The building of railroads, for example, encouraged the development of heavy industries and mining to supply rolling stock, rails, and coal. And since the railroads were left in the hands of private entrepreneurs, these entrepreneurs were forced to abandon the traditional family firm and partnership modes of organization and create corporations in order to cope with the complexities of coast-to-coast transportation systems. Thus, big business grew, and big government was encouraged to grow as well to serve as counterbalance and mediator.

The remarkable growth in American productivity is indicated by measures of *work output*. In 1850, work output per person per year was an estimated 435 horsepower hours—a figure not much in excess of that of the average agrarian-historic society. By 1950, the figure was an estimated 4,470 horsepower hours, with the increase coming primarily from innovations in technology which tapped new sources of energy. In 1850, 65 percent of the energy consumed by work in the United States was supplied by men and animals, another 28 percent by wind, water, and wood. A century later, these traditional agrarian-historic sources of energy supplied only one and a half percent of the energy; the remainder came from the fossil fuels (*e.g.,* coal, oil) and hydroelectric power. The new sources of energy increased productivity in the established industries and stimulated the creation of new industries, such as mining and petro-chemicals.[1]

A general cultural theme that helps account for the statistics is the American readiness to *innovate* in technology. It is striking that, unlike Europe, America chose for its folk heroes inventors as frequently as it did political or military leaders. Eli Whitney, Cyrus McCormick, Thomas Edison, George Washington Carver, and Henry Ford are some of the better-known examples. The American values emphasizing individual achievement and constant change are apparent in this phenomenon.

With economic growth and industrialization came, of course, population growth (attributable, in part, to the massive influx of migrants, whose assimilation was facilitated by American universalism and emphasis on individual achievement). Even more dramatic, however, was the shift in the distribution of population. Early America conformed to the typical agrarian-historic pattern, with 90 percent of the populace living in the country and only 10 percent in the cities. By 1960, however, only 30 percent of the American population lived in rural areas. The shift was made possible through the growth of urban industry and the mechanization of farming. With greatly increased agricultural productivity, a few farmers could produce enough for hordes of urbanites. By 1962, only 9 percent of the American labor force was engaged in agriculture, yet great surpluses were still produced. With the mechanization of agriculture, the family farm tended to be replaced by the large commercial farm—the rural counterpart of the urban factory. The demise of the family farm and the movement of rural people (often the farmer's children) to the cities meant that "the whole fabric of rural and small town social organization [was] disappearing throughout the rural Midwest, West, and South." [2]

Most of the early urban population growth was in the city proper. In recent years, however, much urban growth has really been suburban. Bedroom suburbs on the outskirts of the city have flourished, and with these, the commuter syndrome. In the city itself, formerly respectable downtown neighborhoods have deteriorated into dingy ghettos as rural migrants and ethnic or racial minorities came to dominate the city's core. The great downtown mansions have been transformed into museums, offices, and headquarters for foundations.

The flight from the center city to residential suburbs has been paralleled by a movement of business to industrial exurbs. Even the *Wall Street Journal,* whose very name indicates its urban affiliation, has moved its major offices to the New Jersey countryside. Major arteries encircling the city or leading directly to its heart are now preferred locations for industries wishing to avoid urban congestion (for example, Route 128 in Boston is a favored site for electronics and other light industries). Still more exurban are the industrial park complexes that attract industries into the virtual wilderness (an example is the Research Triangle of Raleigh-Durham-Chapel Hill, North Carolina).

The movement of population and business away from the center city might suggest at first that America is becoming decentralized, rather than increasingly centralized as the modernization theory would predict. Actually, the movement outward from the center, instead of allowing the former urbanites to escape from centralization, is serving to integrate the countryside into the centralized society. Indeed, the ruralization of business and living has required and stimulated the development of complex systems of transportation and communication. Increasingly complex highways, telephone systems, radio, television, high-speed trains, airports, traffic planning and control have made possible the shift to the country, and at the same time have widened the network linking the country to the urban centers.

America's shift from agrarian-rural to industrial-urban (suburban) patterning produced significant changes in the patterning of social relations, especially relations of family and kinship. In the days of the family farm, the family was typically an economic as well as a kinship and residential unit. The rural family was like a small corporation, a family firm, whose task was to run the farm. The family was large and often consisted of several generations, with still more relations living nearby. Producing its own food, it was self-sufficient and ruggedly independent, yet it could rely on nearby relatives and neighbors for special occasions: harvest time, a house-raising, a birth or death, a financial crisis. Local affairs dominated its attention, and except during elections or wars, the nation and the world were far removed from the family farm.

With increasing industrialization, the members of the rural family were drawn away from the farm to work for industries in the cities. In the industrial-urban family, the father's role became sharply segregated into occupational and familial components—the former associated with the factory or office, the latter with the home—in contrast to the family-farm pattern, where the two components are fused. The industrial-urban family is smaller, its generational depth shallower, since parents, grandparents, uncles, aunts, and other kinsmen are left behind or scattered far and wide. It is cut off from the nexus of neighbors and relatives on whom the farm family can depend in time of crisis, and, as a result, it is forced to turn to impersonal, large-scale, bureaucratic organizations—public welfare agencies, finance companies, hospitals, and banks. Because these bureaucratic agencies are closely bound to supralocal affairs, the family's interests naturally move away from the local toward the national and international.

The farm child of early America could expect to live a life rather similar to that of his parents; like his father, the son would also be a farmer, and he would live in the same or a similar rural locale. Parents could, therefore, serve as direct models of what the children would grow up to be. At an early age, children began learning to be like their parents, by milking the cow, feeding the chickens, and plowing the fields. Formal schooling was often limited to the learning of the three R's in the traditional one-room schoolhouse. Parents had few doubts on how to raise their children to fit them for adult life. They were raised "naturally" to emulate their parents.

Very different is the situation in industrial society. Since the father is away at his job and the child is away at school, the father is not immediately available as a model for emulation. Both the occupational and the educational systems thus decrease the opportunity for parents to serve as role models for their children. Parental role models become less relevant anyway, since industrial society changes so rapidly that children are unlikely to follow in their parents' footsteps, hence find it unprofitable to emulate their parents. With the decline in the role-model function of parents, schools and other bureaucratic organizations become increasingly important in preparing children for adult roles.

As their child-rearing responsibilities decrease, parents, paradoxically, become increasingly anxious about whatever responsibilities they do have. In the absence of traditional guides to child-rearing, they turn to Doctor Spock and to faddish "scientific" programs for instruction in proper "socialization." Since parents can teach the child little of vocational importance, they concentrate on that area where they can still have impact—the formation of the child's personality. Attempting to treat this delicate and subtle process scientifically, however, transforms the character of the parent-child bond. The child's progress is measured against norms established statistically by researchers. Instead of the myths of Santa Claus and the Easter bunny, the child must be taught scientific "facts" to prepare him for "real life." Now the parent is advised not to say simply, "Do this," and expect the child to do it, but to provide technical (rather than formal or traditional) explanations so that the child understands why he should do as he is told.*

American society has become increasingly centralized owing to the development of large-scale bureaucratic organizations, which serve to coordinate the increasingly differentiated and specialized units that compose the society. American Telephone and Telegraph currently employs three quarters of a million people—more than the half million people employed in the imperial bureaucracy of archaic China—and it is simply one gigantic example of the organizations essential for the operation of a complex industrial society. As in business, mass organization and bureaucratization exist and are apparently necessary in virtually all other spheres of industrial society—politics, religion, education, medicine, science, and the arts.

Bureaucracies are able to integrate and coordinate great populations and differentiated activities by clearly delineating specialized duties and specific lines of authority. It is this mode of organization, designed to insure efficient functioning, that endows bureaucracies with a distinctive structure. Bureaucracies are composed of three strata: a small elite of professional managers, a larger group of white-collar workers and middle managers, and the mass of skilled, semiskilled, and unskilled workers. Although the standards of recruitment and reward vary, they tend to be universalistic for all strata of bureaucracy, reflecting the American emphasis on individ-

---

* One reflection of this technical approach to child-rearing is the "conditional love" pattern reported by various American analysts (*e.g.,* Geoffrey Gorer, *The American People,* p. 174). Instead of loving their children unconditionally (formally, particularistically)—that is, simply because they are their children—American parents tend to love them conditionally (technically, universalistically)—responding affectionately to them only when they achieve designated goals.

ual achievement. Thus, new recruits are expected to show evidence of either training or proved or potential competence for their specific duties, while promotion depends on output, creativity, and dependability.

The development of bureaucracy is not, of course, unique to America or even to industrial-modern society. What *is* unique in America is the degree to which bureaucracy has penetrated all levels and spheres of life. America has also uniquely contributed to a particular form of bureaucracy—the industrial form. The distinctly American development of mass-production industrial organization, linked with the name Henry Ford,* is essentially the application of bureaucratic principles to the productive process.

Another distinctively American bureaucratic form is the labor union exclusively concerned with the material condition of the worker. Unlike European workers, American workers have never become a separate political faction; there is no labor party in the United States, and although union leaders commonly endorse one party or another, the ability of union leaders to deliver the votes has never been demonstrated. In striving for the worker's economic betterment, however, the American unions have had notable results. The American worker's wages rose more than fourfold between 1871 and 1944 and 300 percent between 1939 and 1959 despite shortened work weeks.

With bureaucratization, formal education has become increasingly important in America. Modern bureaucracy calls for literacy: workers must be able to read the instructions, manuals, and memos that serve as the instruments of bureaucratic functioning. Bureaucratic specialization of tasks calls for highly specialized training, whether on the production line or in research and design. Personnel offices, faced with huge numbers of applicants for jobs, depend on such standardized ways of assessing competence as diplomas

---

* Ford's achievement, of course, built on earlier American developments, such as Eli Whitney's remarkable advances in creating interchangeable and standardized parts for machinery (see Jeannette Mirsky and Allan Nevins, *The World of Eli Whitney*).

or degrees. Thus, schools and other educational agencies have been called upon to fill the distinctive needs of a complex, industrialized, bureaucratic society. And American education has flourished. More than 90 percent of all American children, aged seven to thirteen, attend school; and 18 percent of college-age youths attend college. (America produces a higher percentage of college graduates than any other nation.) American universities, however, now face serious problems derived from the very trends that encouraged their development. Like other institutions of American life, American universities have become increasingly bureaucratized in order to accomplish the increasingly complex tasks that the bureaucratized society has demanded of them. This bureaucratization has bred an impersonality that contributes to students' feelings of alienation and discontent, and ultimately to strikes, riots, and serious disruption of the educational process.

Schools provide more than training in specialized technical skills and knowledge. The school is a microcosm of the larger society, and it helps to instill in the young the larger society's central values, attitudes, and orientations. Thus, the American school inculcates values underlying bureaucratic, industrial America. The school separates the child from the family unit, just as the American factory or office does the adult. Like other bureaucracies, the school is organized along clear-cut lines of authority and responsibility. The school divides time and work into differentiated and specialized periods and courses. It teaches that the individual is responsible for his own work and that achievement is differentially rewarded according to universalistic standards. In these and other ways, the school teaches values of universalism, specialization, and achievement that the modern American must assimilate in order to function successfully in virtually all of his society's statuses and jobs.

The increasing bureaucratization of America has aroused concern among many observers. One of the most provocative of these is C. Wright Mills, who expresses the view that the major leaders of American bureaucracy, *i.e.,* big businessmen, politicians, and the military, have united to form a single, tyrannical "power elite." [3]

From their strategic "command posts," the power elite make the crucial decisions that determine the direction of American life, and remain uninfluenced by the mass democratic process. Indeed, the democratic games of the masses, such as elections, serve the interests of the power elite: they keep the people at play in the yard while the decisions are made upstairs.

Although the power elite exercise their control through bureaucracy, Mills feels that they gained that control through ownership of wealth and property. They are the very rich Americans whose wealth has grown disproportionately by comparison with the earnings of their countrymen. Mills is alarmed by this situation because he believes that the great wealth of the elite effectively frees them from legal or governmental constraints. They are free to act irresponsibly in pursuing power.

Mills associates the rise of the power elite with the decline of an independent middle class whose economic and political security were anchored in small, local businesses and properties. He estimates that small businessmen and entrepreneurs today form only 40 percent of the entire American middle class (20 percent of the labor force as a whole). They have been replaced by the Organization Man, the white-collar bureaucrat, who, unfortunately, enjoys no independence from the bureaucracies controlled by the power elite because he is employed by them and, therefore, cannot effectively oppose their policies. According to Mills, the faithful remnant of the independent entrepreneurial-business group is carrying on constant battle against the ever-increasing centralization and control of the bureaucracies and the power elite, but their efforts are vain.

Mills's theory is of special interest because it resembles those of left-wing and right-wing radicals, both of whom believe that a governmental-industrial-military complex exercises tyrannical power over the rest of the country. The issue is worth serious discussion, and a few statistics and analytical remarks may serve as a beginning.

In the United States, the number of independent entrepreneurs (men owning and operating their own business) dropped from 11.4 percent of the labor force in 1870 to 6 percent in 1954. Even more significant, the relative power of this group has declined drastically, as is demonstrated by a study of the nation's two hundred largest corporations, which control nearly half of its corporate wealth.[4] The study shows that 44 percent of these companies are now controlled or directed by hired managers rather than by their owners. Ownership of the corporations has become more broadly based through the issuance of stocks; and professional managers, rather than stockholders, make the decisions. Other studies reveal that, increasingly, hired managers, rather than the children of owners or founders, run the firms. Ownership and managership of corporations tend to be separate, with the independent entrepreneur who is both owner and manager becoming a rarity. The trend is made more complex, however, by the practice, among high-ranking managers, of obtaining stock options which give them partial ownership of the firms that employ them.

Regardless of how little stock they may own, professional managers wield great power. They can, for instance, set their own salaries. Not surprisingly, these are very high, especially when compared to the salaries paid to men with comparable education and ability employed in nonbusiness spheres. A survey of 939 non-family-owned American corporations showed that the median income of chief executives was $68,000 per year during 1959; salaries exceeding $800,000 were reported. These highly advantaged managers seem to be replacing some of the big business owners in the ranks of Mills's power elite. Perhaps a symptom of this trend is the tendency for high government offices to be awarded to elite managers, whereas formerly they went to big business owners. Charles Wilson, former president of General Motors Corporation, became President Eisenhower's Secretary of Defense; more recently, Robert McNamara, former president of Ford Motor Company, held the same post under Presidents Kennedy and Johnson. This may signal a tendency toward more universalism in recruiting members of the power elite, since hired managers are more likely to reach the top through ability than are individuals who simply inherit ownership. At the same time, according to one study, approximately 50 percent of the managers themselves come from the propertied or wealthy class.

Membership in the political elite may also be financially rewarding. A study of twenty American city "bosses" carried out a generation ago showed that, although none came from wealthy families, at least nine left estates valued at a million dollars or more, and only three had failed to accumulate a substantial fortune. To take an example at a higher level: President Johnson, though a politician and not a businessman most of his life, managed to amass approximately nine million dollars by 1964. Such wealth is not ordinarily acquired by chicanery or corruption; perfectly legal opportunities to accumulate wealth are afforded by political office. In recent years, however, these opportunities have declined, owing to the increasing bureaucratization of government and the civil service. As recruiting and operating procedures have been depersonalized, opportunities for politicians to turn personal power into profit have decreased. A great deal of power has moved from the politicians to the bureaucrats. Just as the managerial elite—the business bureaucrats—are replacing Mills's entrepreneurs, so are government bureaucrats tending to replace politicians with the power elite.

What of the military, the third faction of the power elite? Has the almost continuous military crisis of current times placed great power in the hands of the military? The answer is, of course, yes, but it must be recognized that the military have exercised marked restraint in certain areas. By contrast to most new nations, America has experienced neither military coups nor blatant corruption by the military. This is especially striking in view of their remarkably low salaries. As recently as 1958, only a handful of top officers received more than $20,000 per year, less than half the minimum paid to superintendents of large school systems. These facts suggest that the picture of the military as exclusively power hungry is exaggerated.

Certainly the bureaucratic-managerial elite do command great power, and Mills is correct in pointing to the potential dangers of tyranny. On the other hand, Mills underemphasizes both internal and external restraints on the power of this elite. It is not naive and Pollyannaish to assume that the religious and ideological traditions that have shaped American culture have exercised some influence on the consciences of the elite, causing them to restrain at least some of their lust for power in deference to the rights of the majority. It must also be kept in mind that the military, the government, and big business are not a single organization, but a cluster of many, each with its own interests. Competition among diverse interests is bound to check and balance the selfish interests of any single organization. Finally, although the power elite doubtless are to a degree a chummy clique of kinsmen and former Ivy League classmates, universalistic selection criteria probably have a sharper cutting edge than Mills admits. In a certain measure, incompetent and irrational individuals are doubtless lopped from the circle of the power elite.

Despite tendencies to exaggeration, a radical analysis such as Mills's helps toward a more penetrating and objective view of the power structure than is afforded by conventional opinion. Mills, for example, touches among other things on the important American trend toward ever greater bureaucratization and centralization —some cultural correlates of which we shall now examine.

TRENDS IN AMERICAN CULTURE

Instrumental activism and *institutionalized individualism* are, according to the social theorist Talcott Parsons, the two fundamental American values.[5] Parsons believes that both are rooted in the New England Puritanism that so heavily influenced American culture.

Activism refers to the American conviction that society should aggressively exploit its environment, rather than passively adjust to it. *Instrumental* refers to the American view that society is an instrument made to serve the ends of its members, rather than an end in itself. According to Parsons, American values of instrumental activism are most clearly expressed in the drive to produce *generalized resources, i.e.,* resources (human as well as material) potentially mobilizable to achieve a wide variety of goals. Americans frantically produce anything and everything, from hula hoops to electronic computers, without much concern about the way these resources will ultimately serve society. To produce is good, for it is activism, and society should serve this activism rather than vice versa. The underlying Soviet value—that production should serve social goals defined by five-year plans—is distinctly un-American.

Instrumental activism can be traced to the Puritan traditions of early America, which held that society was not an end in itself, but merely an instrument to be employed by man in serving God. Man, aided by society, was called to produce and create incessantly in order to build on earth a kingdom like God's Kingdom. Today, although the Puritan beliefs are fast disappearing, the drive to produce and to employ society as an instrument toward production, remains. Some critics of the sprawling affluent society, which has resulted from the unchanneled productivity, exhort Americans to harness their productivity to specific social goals and policies. Although America is moving in this direction, it is far from a socialistic society.

Institutionalized individualism can also be traced to Puritan roots. The Puritans saw each moral individual as called on by God to undertake a special task. This notion encouraged a society of specialized roles, each performed according to the individual's interpretation of God's special command to him. Though the individual might join a group, God, not the group, dictated his calling. The individual joined the group voluntarily, and was free to leave if it did not facilitate his service to God. A secularized version of this pattern is reflected in America's bewildering assortment of voluntary groups, any of which the individual may join or leave according to his special needs.

American individualism is *institutional* in that it functions within the context of organizations. Americans organize everything: production, business, war, politics, child-rearing, Sunday school, bowling. America has nourished the Red Cross, United Fund, Heart Association, Cancer Society, and Community Chest, to name only a few organizations within the single sphere of charity. When Americans think of a job to be done, their next thought is, "Let's organize." This attitude reflects not a Romantic view that the individual is the be-all and end-all, but a Puritan view that the individual is an instrument toward some larger end for which he must organize social instruments even as he follows his own conscience.

Instrumental activism and institutionalized individualism clearly are basic and important American values. Yet social commentators warn of deviations from this cherished pattern.

The Organization Man syndrome [6]

In *The Organization Man,* William H. Whyte, Jr. argues that the Protestant Ethic had already begun to decline in America by the turn of the century. Whyte maintains that as the big business and big government bureaucratic Organization grew and spread, the Protestant Ethic became ever more irrelevant to work and life. The employee does not need Protestant attitudes of thrift, for the Organization is thrifty for him; the personnel and payroll departments automatically provide pension plans, group health plans, and low interest loans. Even more significantly, the total orientation of the Organization is toward spending, not thrift. Whyte argues that one of the talents most in demand is that of persuading the public to deviate from the Protestant Ethic and spend.

The Organization Man directly reverses the Protestant Ethic by feeling guilty not about sloth, but about work. Work brings ulcers or (as in *The Man in the Gray Flannel Suit*) neglect of family. Work should be carefully separated from the rest of life, rather than be the whole of life as the Calvinists believed. The Organization

Man reserves weekends for leisure activities in the club, the boat, or the suburban home. Rugged Protestant individualism is also out, says Whyte. Conferences, committees, and administration are the keys to success within the Organization. Achievement is through harmony with others, not through lonely struggle.

Whyte admits that the small businessman is likely even today to adhere to the doctrines derived from the Protestant Ethic of free enterprise and rugged individualism, but he asserts that small business is of decreasing importance in the American economy. The small businessman is fighting a losing battle against the Organization, and he

> can smell the future as well as anyone else. The bland young man the Organization sent to town to manage the plant is almost damnably inoffensive; he didn't rent the old place on the hill but a smaller house, he drives an Olds instead of a Caddy, and when he comes to the Thursday luncheons he listens more than he talks. But he's the future just the same.[7]

A similar decline of Protestant Ethic individualism is observed by another popular commentator, David Riesman, but Riesman sees the mass media as the culprit that has transformed the American character from an inner-directed Protestant Ethic type toward an other-directed Organization Man type.

According to Riesman, in the inner-directed Protestant societies after 1600, the medium of print concentrated especially on success in business. Benjamin Franklin's *Poor Richard's Almanack*—the text selected by Max Weber as a typical self-inspirational document of the period of the Protestant Ethic—taught attitudes conducive to commercial achievement. Riesman considers even Defoe's *Robinson Crusoe,* with its elaborate descriptions of food, clothing, shelter, and money transactions, to have encouraged a business-like approach to life. Pious biographies as well as fictional works encouraged a spirit of Calvinist capitalism. A biography of George Washington preached that if a child worked hard, did not lie, and kept a firm character, he would succeed. The story of Booker T. Washington provided a similar model for the black child.

With the advent of other-directed values in American culture, observes Riesman, child-oriented media changed. Rather than train children to be thrifty and productive, the new media trained "the young for the frontiers of consumption—to tell the difference between Pepsi-Cola and Coca-Cola. . . ." [8] And they taught conformity. To mark this shift in attitude, Riesman cites the old nursery rhyme:

> This little pig went to market;
> This little pig stayed at home.
> This little pig had roast beef;
> This little pig had none.
> This little pig went wee-wee-wee
> All the way home.

In the Protestant Ethic era, suggests Riesman, this rhyme symbolized inner-directed individualism. In the other-directed era of the twentieth century, however, "all the little pigs go to market; none stay home; all have roast beef, if any do; and all say 'we-we.' " [9]

Riesman notes that the child-reader of the other-directed era is rarely alone. Before the spread of television, he was typically lying on the floor with his peers, trading comics, or listening to the "Lone Ranger" on the radio. Riesman feels that the other-directed child is too aware of his real-life peers to identify deeply with fictional heroes in the way the inner-directed child could—a change reflected in the media of the two eras:

> Think of the Count of Monte Cristo's years in jail, his suffering, his incredible patience, and the industry and study of the abbé's teaching. . . . he is an old man when, after many chapters, he wins.[10]

By contrast, the comic book or radio drama detective or superfigure might get roughed up and kicked around during the story, but he did not undergo a deep and gradual development of character in the process. Therefore, unlike the story of the Count of Monte Cristo, comic book and radio tales did not encourage their audiences vicariously to undergo sustained transformations of character. Extending Riesman's arguments to today, much of what he says would seem to apply to television. Characters do not ordinarily mature and develop in the television drama, which typically covers only one episode in a life. Not only is television often viewed by groups, but the heroes themselves often are groups (*e.g.,* teams of scientists or a family of cowboys). Presumably, this emphasis on the group reflects and encourages collectivism, an attitude of other-direction rather than individualism.

Riesman's analysis concentrated on media that are enjoyed passively. More active modes of entertainment, however, seem to reflect the same trend toward other-direction. Thus, in suburbia lives the "participative purist," [11] the enthusiastic joiner of folkdance, hi-fi, or recreation clubs. Even a seemingly private hobby such as painting may surrender to the guidance of the painting association. Children are organized at play through Little League baseball, eurythmics, and violin instruction by the Suzuki *group* method; bureaucratized recreation replaces the old hopscotch, marbles, and hide-and-seek; and universities offer degrees in "recreation administration."

Beyond the suburbs have emerged the flash and dazzle of New York pop, Las Vegas honky-tonk, and California hot-rod culture—the subjects of Tom Wolfe's *The Kandy-Kolored Tangerine-Flake Streamline Baby.* Baby Jane Holzer in her jumpsuit and with her mane of hair, teen-age tycoons of hard rock, and middle-aged frantic types like Murray the K are "what's happening" in Wolfe's New York pop world. Fat-fannied old "babes" are the devotees of Las Vegas slot machines. The Kandy-Kolored Tangerine-Flake Streamline Baby itself is a California hot-rod automobile treated as an *objet d'art.* These patterns reflect a group sensuality which is a significant change from the Protestant asceticism of early America, a sensuality clearly connected to the gigantic entertainment-world Organization, which, in turn, is related to the collectivism and conformism observed by Riesman and Whyte.

Perusal of *Dissent, Partisan Review, Harper's, The Atlantic Monthly, Saturday Review,* and *Esquire* will unearth abundant commentary on the other-direction, bureaucratization, popularization, and commercialization. Loss of individuality and the rise of a herd-like conformism are observed. Cheapening and vulgarization of culture and character are seen as the result. These two trends are perceived as mutually supportive: through constant exposure to cheap culture, the public is deprived of its critical capacities and is thereby prepared for an unthinking conformity to the group and ultimately to totalitarian power elites.

Many of the criticisms and fears are, of course, justified. Many of the remarkable qualities of Puritan early America *are* disappearing with the rise of other-direction and the Organization. The strident voices of the critics, however, should not obscure alternative interpretations such as the one presented by Winston White in his *Beyond Conformity.*

White takes issue with the social critics for their assumption of a *zero-sum* social system, that is, one in which the quantity of choices available within the society and culture is fixed, so that a given trend's gain is automatically another's loss. In this view, loss of individuality follows directly from increase in conformity. If only X amount of individuality is available, an increase in conformity necessarily means a decrease in that X amount of individuality. As an alternative to the zero-sum assumption, White suggests an interpretation much like the theory of modernization. Societies evolve toward greater and greater functional specialization and differentiation. In primitive society, a single unit (*e.g.,* a lineage or clan) may perform all functions (economic, political, religious, etc.); therefore, primitive society is essentially a set of identical, unspecialized units (*e.g.,* a set of clans). Modern society, on the other hand, is a coordinated system of dissimilar units, each with its own speciality—religious, economic, educational, political, etc. —and these units cooperate to form a workable system. Primitive man has basically one choice open to him: to be a nonspecialist and perform all functions that others of his age and sex perform. Modern man, on the other hand, can choose to specialize in religion, education, politics, art, or any other field. About the only choice not open to modern man is to be a nonspecialist.

This modern pattern increases the range of choices open to the individual and also increases the flexibility of society as a whole. Modern society, consisting of a variety of relatively independent units, can shuffle these into new combinations—say, religious businesses or educational churches.

True, modern man loses freedoms that primitive man enjoyed. White argues, however, that the freedoms lost are of a lower order than the freedoms gained. The modern worker loses the primitive man's freedom to schedule his own hours on the job, but he gains the freedom to change the job itself. He also gains freedom to choose his own activities after working hours; he can theoretically devote his leisure hours to any of a range of creative endeavors. Organization and standardization of the lower-order categories of life—*i.e.,* work schedules and bureaucratic procedures—free the individual to devote his time and energy to higher-order creativity and development. Thus, far from depriving the individual of his individuality, White concludes, the low-order conformism demanded by bureaucracy and the Organization sets the stage for creative individuality on a wide scale.

A final question that White raises is whether the increasing complexity of modern society and the increasing opportunity for high-order creativity may not force man drastically to transform his personality. Basic human character itself may change, perhaps toward a more complex, creative, and sophisticated type.

The media explosion

"The electric light," says Marshall McLuhan, "may prove illuminating." [12] Although the electric light does not say anything (unless it should spell out words on a sign), it carries a message. That is, the light affects minds and introduces "a change in scale, pace, or pattern" [13] into human affairs. The light bulb is simply one of many media—radio, television, movies, telephones, typewriters, computers—which, according to McLuhan, have impact on thought and life simply by virtue of their distinctive forms. "The medium is the message!" [14] shouts McLuhan. He means that, regardless of the particular words uttered, stories told, or lessons taught via a given medium, that medium carries a distinctive punch and impact solely because of its *form*.

Print, for example, has a distinctive form. In the West, print is arranged in straight lines across a page. McLuhan asserts that with the introduction of print in the West, men's lives were flooded with printed lines, and men began to think linearly. Such linearity is reflected in Western patterns of designing cities, economies, and wars: "For the West, literacy has long been pipes and taps and streets and assembly lines and inventories." [15] "Print taught men to say, 'Damn the torpedoes, Full steam ahead.' " [16]

McLuhan asserts that because in the West physics and mathematics are taught by print, Western physicists are barely capable of comprehending nonlinear notions of time and space. They find it difficult to understand post-Newtonian physics. In order to overcome linear biases, McLuhan proposes the teaching of physics by telephone. The telephone is oral and oral media induce configurational, participational orientations, as opposed to the linear, analytical ones of print. Oral media absorb the fullness of one's being rather than concentrating a mere segment of one's attention along a sequential line of print.

The oral, participational, configurational orientation is spreading in the West thanks to television, McLuhan argues. The TV image is not as clear as the movie image, for it is composed of roughly connected dots on the screen. The viewer is urged to "close" the spaces between the dots by a "convulsive sensory participation that is profoundly kinetic and tactile." [17] (For McLuhan, tactility is, like the auditory and oral, participational and configurational.) Television viewers presumably feel moved mentally to crawl inside the set and gambol in the spaces between the dots.

As evidence that television induces a sense of participation, Mc-Luhan cites the fact that, although movie fans are fascinated with the private lives of movie stars, television viewers show little interest in the private lives of television stars. Even though they identify with a particular TV character, they are so strongly involved with his on-screen roles that they would even prefer not to see the real person behind the character. This, at least, is McLuhan's theory. Like many of his observations, these "facts" about television are open to alternative explanations. Might not the difference between movie and television fans stem from differences in programming? Television stars frequently play in serials, movie stars commonly appear in one-shot stories. Playing in a variety of one-shot stories, the movie star naturally stands above any single role as a personality in his own right. The television star who plays a single character in a serial does not so easily transcend his screen personality. And television's availability at home is sufficient to explain why it should lend itself to serials. Its fuzzy image is not necessary to explain the viewer's identification with the characters on screen.

Although McLuhan's interpretation of television may be questioned, he is suggestive in his perception of a new, configurational, participational attitude in America. America has reached the end of the line! Lineality is out, along with the Protestant Ethic and the straight and narrow path. The lonely, inner-direction of the Calvinist gives way to gregarious, other-directed participationality. The trend is reflected in the new hirsute pattern. Young men and women now grow great manes of hair in which they engulf themselves, rejecting the antiseptic crew cuts of linear epochs. The tiny "wrap-around" automobiles reflect a similar shift in attitude. In the American "Big Buick," one sat in cold and solitary splendor, while in the Volkswagen, one enjoys cozy, intimate participationality. Best of all, with the new participationality, B.O. is back. "B.O., the unique signature and declaration of human individuality, is a bad word in literate society," but since odor is the "most iconic" of the human senses in that it involves the "entire human sensorium," [18] it should naturally come on strong in the new era of participationality.

"The World's a sage," declares McLuhan, alluding to the fast flow of information in the world of today. He forecasts that the world will become a giant village whose inhabitants are cozily plugged in on one another via the electronic media.[19] Early-modern society may have been organized as a system of specialized "lines" of work, but in the world village specialized units will melt into a communal participationality of sensuous delight. Of course, linear thinkers might protest that without rationality, specialization, universalism, and the other modern values, technology cannot advance and complex technology cannot function. By this argument, McLuhan's electronic village will institute antimodern values that would soon force its technological base to crumble; the villagers would not long enjoy their communal bliss, for all those electric circuits would soon break down. Yet this may be an overly conservative view. Self-repairing machines may be developed, or perhaps an elite of ascetic eunuchs could administer the orgy which the rest of society would enjoy, as in Aldous Huxley's *Ape and Essence.*

Certainly the values governing McLuhan's new society would differ from those of the Protestant Ethic. The Calvinist, suppressing carnal appetites to attain salvation and restraining the acquisitive instinct to insure profit, forwent immediate gratification in the interest of long-range goals. Future, plans, and career were important American symbols derived from Calvinism. But this is no longer the case, according to McLuhan, for with television has come a new emphasis on immediate, depth participation and a de-emphasis on linear paths toward future goals: "The TV child cannot see ahead." [20] This interpretation agrees in part with Riesman's. What Riesman had to say about radio failing to draw the viewer through the same sustained progression as the classical novel could also be applied to television. The television drama is episodic, a succession of "nows."

In McLuhan's new, television-schooled, electronically integrated society, there will be no distance between present situation and future goal. The automated and computerized world will resemble Al Capp's schmoo. One had only to look at the schmoo and "think longingly of pork chops or caviar," and the schmoo ecstatically transformed itself into the object of desire. Similarly, the new man will program his wishes into the computer, and they will be immediately fulfilled. No time lag will exist between wish and outcome. The world will be one of immediacy and simultaneity.

To be sure, many objections can be raised against McLuhan's theories. The assertion that print gave birth to linear thinking in the West is surely an exaggeration. In the first place, non-Western print (*e.g.,* Arabic or Chinese) is also linear, yet to these cultures McLuhan often attributes nonlinear thought. Secondly, the West possessed linear thought long before print. The linear grammatical structure of Western languages and the linear conceptions of time and history found in Judeo-Christian thought existed many centuries before Gutenberg. Nevertheless, many of McLuhan's assertions fit into our framework. The Protestant Reformation *was* connected with the rise of print and reading (especially of the Bible). The imagery of Protestantism *was* very linear, as in the progress of the pilgrim, the voyage of the ship of state, and the straight and narrow path toward success and salvation. And the trend toward immediate participation does currently seem a reality. Certainly, McLuhan is tracing a significant transformation of early-modern patterning. One "line" of analysis that he does not pursue, however, is that of religious systems which may serve to render this new world meaningful. Perhaps one movement toward such a system is the movement that proclaims the Death of God.

The Death of God movement

Historic Christianity filled the gulf between God and man with a sacred hierarchy of offices, symbols, and rites. Calvinistic Christianity swept away and desanctified this mediating hierarchy, concentrating all sacredness on a single symbol, God. The Death of God movement seeks to further the progress of religion by removing sacredness from even this symbol. To the young and radical "Atheistic Christian" theologians who proclaim the death of God, no symbol, not even the symbol God, is sacred, because every symbol is a mere product of the human mind. Therefore, to regard God or any other symbol as sacred is idolatry. Jesus fought idols with vigor, and the Atheistic Christians, carrying his campaign further, would topple what they consider the God idol.

Repudiating God, the Atheistic Christians also repudiate the traditionally sacred Christian goals of Heaven and salvation. They place their hope in immediate situations, not in distant goals, and preach that the Christian should operate from situation to situation in search of immediate participational experience. They see life as a floating crap game, with the Christian as a gambler who wagers anew each day. Enduring human relationships such as the *I–Thou* bond are idolatrous, as well as inconvenient since they promote plans and promises that distract from the immediate experience. The *I–You* encounter on the street is more valuable.

Emphasizing the immediate present at the expense of the distant future, the Atheistic Christians redefine the thrust of the Protestant Ethic. The Calvinist is under continuous pressure to progress toward the idealized future, which holds Heaven, salvation, and the Kingdom of God. To move toward that future and to transform the present in its image is man's calling. More important than immediate encounters—be they sensory, social, or aesthetic—is the fulfillment of that calling. Immediate participationality is at best distracting, at worst sinful and productive of eternal damnation. McLuhan's new society is hardly sanctioned by the Protestant Ethic; perhaps the theology of God's Death comes closer to providing a sanction.

For a more concrete view of the Atheistic Christians, let us briefly summarize some distinctive ideas of the movement's leading figures, including those of Gabriel Vahanian, Harvey Cox, Thomas J. J. Altizer, William Hamilton, and Paul M. van Buren.*

Gabriel Vahanian illustrates God's irrelevance to modern culture by referring to the opening scene of Fellini's film, *La Dolce Vita,* in which a huge crucifix suspended from a helicopter hovers incongruously over an indifferent sunbathing woman below. Vahanian and Harvey Cox argue that the transcendental essence formerly symbolized by God and His Kingdom is now manifest in the secular world—in art, in social change, and in the fleeting I–You encounters of the modern secular city. Embracing this world in all its participational immediacy, man must evaluate and appreciate human relationships for their own sake, without reference to abstract, God-given standards. Both Vahanian and Cox seek a transcendent being, but a being to be encountered in the pulsating secular life "where the action is." [21]

Professing the principle of the *coincidence of opposites,* Thomas Altizer concludes that the way to encounter the otherworld is to welcome fully this world. To discover the transcendent, man should deny the transcendent. As stated by the poet and mystic William Blake, man should dare to "name God as Satan" and to "identify the transcendent Lord as the ultimate source of alienation and repression." [22] According to the principle of the coincidence of opposites, this procedure will result in the discovery of the true God. Altizer, therefore, does not deny the existence of the transcendent, but simply claims (as did mystics such as Meister Eckhart) that the transcendent exists beyond the conventional symbol, God. He differs from the mystics in that he hopes to discover and know this transcendental being not by probing the inner recesses of the soul or by direct communion with the ultimate, but by embracing the world in all its chaos, filth, and flux.

---

* The following quotations from the Atheistic Christians were, for convenience, taken from a single source, John Warwick Montgomery's *The "Is God Dead?" Controversy.* Although Montgomery's book is polemical, a survey of various writings by the Atheistic Christians indicates that these particular passages accurately reflect their thought.

William Hamilton calls for a new optimism that will "say Yes to the world of rapid change, new technologies, automation, and the mass media." [23] In these realms may lurk Jesus. Hamilton, therefore, calls on man to move from his anguished quest for salvation toward a confident, optimistic stance "in the world, in the city, with both the needy neighbor and the enemy." For "Jesus is in the world as masked." [24]

Paul van Buren believes that modern life is irrevocably pluralistic and relativistic, the source of a multitude of "language games." Theology is simply one of these languages and is appropriate in some situations, irrelevant in others. It does not speak about God, but is "a dated way, among a number of ways," of talking about "man and human life and human history." [25] What theology says can also be said by other languages, such as psychology. Thus, van Buren interprets Gospel accounts as a reporting of psychological experiences—for example, the gaining of new insights into life's meaning by the disciples after Christ's death.

OVERVIEW

In many respects, American society is simply a perfection (or monstrous exaggeration) of trends toward modernization: it maximizes characteristics far less pronounced in premodern societies, such as specialization of units, specificity of social relationships, centralization, bureaucratization, universalization, conjugalization, technological advance, mobility, and rapidity of change.

Consider bureaucratization. Nonmodern societies, of course, developed extensive and effective bureaucracies. Such bureaucracies—for example, the Mesopotamian city-state, the Buddhist state-church, the Chinese scholar-bureaucrat system—made possible the integration and control of large populations. Yet the nonmodern bureaucracies never administered more than a fraction of a society's activities. Modern American bureaucracies administer a much larger proportion of American activities.

At the same time, American bureaucrats perform roles much more specialized than did nonmodern bureaucrats. An archaic priest-councillor or temple scribe experienced many facets of his life in terms of his office. Whom he married, where he resided, what recreation he indulged in, were strongly determined by his office. It was a diffuse status—covering many strands of life. The American bureaucrat's office is much more specific and specialized; his nonbureaucratic roles are much more separate from his bureaucratic one.

The great specialization and specificity of the American bureaucratic role make possible efficient bureaucratic organization toward some single, limited goal. A firm specializing in the manufacture of toothpicks can hire and fire solely on the basis of the individual's talent and interest in making toothpicks. It is acceptable to ignore other personal characteristics since the concept and pattern of the specialized, specific bureaucratic role is well established in American society and culture.

American society is composed of a variety of more or less autonomous specialized organizations, each built to cope effectively with a particular need or problem. Such a system of specialized organizations is far more flexible than, for example, an archaic one consisting of a single politico-religious organization. The archaic system's functions are so intimately entwined that change in any one function provokes turbulence and confusion throughout the system. The tendency is, therefore, to avoid change by being inflexible.

The flexibility of America's bureaucratic system depends on several patterns rarely considered by business or government planners. For example, the nuclear family, the typical American pattern, is more mobile than the extended family of the family-farm type. Business and government would experience much greater difficulty in transferring employees if the extended family of early America rather than the nuclear family of today were prominent.

Individuals, as well as families, move freely about the American landscape. Partly because of the incessant creation of new specialties, few parents expect their children to inherit their jobs. Many children leave home and their home town in search of jobs different from those of their parents. Such mobility is aided by the highly bureaucratized school system, which provides universalistic systems of recruitment and transmits skills, knowledge, and values that equip the youth, mentally and emotionally, for a wide range of American occupations.

The mass media enable Americans of widely varying backgrounds to share common experiences and symbols and to gain skill in empathizing with one another. Such a psychocultural base is essential for the workable centralization of American society. Yet if analysts such as Marshall McLuhan are right, these mass media are at the same time undermining the present society. The media are subtly, but powerfully, shaping American personalities so that the populace will demand a different type of nation—one that allows immediacy, participationality, and "now democracy." The hippies and yippies, riots in the cities, civil rights movements, student violence, and the New Left doubtless reflect broad changes in the national character as well as particular political grievances.

The student protestors, for example, demand not only the old, liberal quantitative achievements of wider distribution of privilege, wealth, and freedom, but also qualitative advances in human experience. They call for creative, participatory, depth encounters in art and life to replace the shallow efficiency of the technocracy. They revolt against uniformity and standardization, worshipping in its place the exotic and unique, even the quaint and the queer. They foresee a life of continual openness and development, such that the individual's unfolding never ceases, and he is always "with it" and in step with the present. They propose a participational democracy through which they themselves will take part in the decisions that affect their own education and maturation. They

crave human relationships which, though short-lived, are meaningful and deeply involving of the whole self.*

A partial explanation for these new attitudes (and for their popularity among great numbers of the young, instead of merely among
a restricted bohemian elite) is simply that America is an affluent
society—that in America, as well as in Germany, Japan, and other
centers of the "qualitative" student revolution, there is so much
material abundance. Productivity is not a challenging problem for
the affluent young. Deprived of deprivation, they cannot find meaning and satisfaction in harnessing themselves to production aimed
at overcoming want. The old ideologies of productivity, such as
the Protestant Ethic and traditional Communism, have lost their
power to give life legitimacy and meaning. Participationality, not
productivity, is what counts. Among the ideologies that grope
toward making life meaningful in terms of the new participational
goals, one of the most intriguing is the Death of God movement.

Consider the relationship of God's Death to bureaucracy. Although the Atheistic Christians explicitly side with the antibureaucratic radicals of America, their theology, ironically, sanctifies
bureaucratic values by calling for the removal of a personal deity.
Bureaucracy also calls for a depersonalization (since regulations,
manuals, and examinations replace personalistic modes of adminis-
tering and recruiting). Perhaps the Organization Man who comes
to think in depersonalized, bureaucratic categories would find very
meaningful a religion that denies the existence of a personal deity.

In other respects, however, the Death of God movement resonates
with profoundly antibureaucratic sentiments and values and could
potentially reinforce radical antibureaucratic protests. The Now
Democrat rejects bureaucratic democracy, which gives all men equal
opportunity to achieve, but which assumes that, since achievement
takes time, older men will always have more power than younger

* This formulation follows Kenneth Keniston, "You Have to Grow Up in
Scarsdale to Know How Bad Things Really Are," pp. 122–130. Keniston's
article is an excellent statement of conditions underlying American student
protest.

men of equal talent. The Now Democrat (and this label could apply to numerous protest movements, especially those led by students) will have none of this inequality; in his extreme demands, he wants communal, participational equality among all men *now,* regardless of achievement, age, or ability. He scorns the bureaucratic democrat's offer of equal opportunity, for this offer distinguishes between present opportunity and future rank or reward. Thus, the Now Democrats erase the linear distinction between present and future just as the Atheistic Christians (some of whom explicitly favor Now Democracy) erase it. In this oblique way, by lending meaning to new attitudes, the Death of God movement could frame and sanctify some of the most radical trends in America.

God's Death, however, carries even broader implications. The reformist, flexible, self-revising character of American society is, we have suggested, inspired in part by the Calvinist belief in a duality between this world and the otherworld such that this world must be constantly remodelled to fit the other. Since the time of Kant, this dualistic world view has been repeatedly challenged. The notion has emerged that, instead of merely two worlds, as many worlds exist as man can apprehend. Why stop with imagining merely a Heaven and a Hell? Why not imagine an infinity of worlds? The Atheistic Christians encourage this view by offering to free men from the preoccupation with any single symbol, such as God, or Heaven, or Hell. They maintain that these symbols possess no special sanctity, and that others might just as well be imagined. Incessant production of new images of transcendent worlds would seem to be the consequence of current theological trends.

Such constant cultural ferment and creativity might, paradoxically, yield social stagnation. The Calvinist could strive continuously for a better world because he had a secure place to stand. Rigidly adhering to an image of God's Kingdom, which he perceived as an eternal and unchanging model of the ultimate, he insisted that the world change. Avant-garde proponents of cultural creativity must consider the possibility that by constantly multiplying images of the ideal, they deprive men of a constant cultural ideal that can inspire continuous social reform. Stagnation is not, of course, inevitable. Rapid change of ideal images, any one of which can arouse temporary passion to remake the social order, seems more likely.

A highly significant current trend is the movement away from social reform, toward psychological exploration. "The New Religion is finding out about yourself," proclaims the young singer-poet Rod McKuen, and disciples of psychoanalysis, Zen Buddhism, existential psychiatry, and the mind-expanding drugs all agree. Such modern "religions" are significant in that their adherents worship not the symbols that man has created, but the very consciousness of man himself. In this they parallel the Atheistic Christians.

TOPICS FOR DISCUSSION

A central topic for discussion suggested by this chapter is the place of sociocultural analysis in *modern* contexts. Consider the following argument. Core values of modern society call for endless evaluation and revision of the society itself. Therefore, scientific analysis of the society is religious worship in the sense that it expresses the ultimate values of the social scientist's society. If science is a rite expressing modern social values, traditional social analysts were less religious than modern social scientists. For example, the ancient Indian grammarian Panini was not, by his analytical performances, worshipping core values of his society. His society's values were anti-analytical. Unlike the modern social scientist, Panini was a radical and a nonconformist.

But are the core values of modern society themselves so profoundly antireligious that to call the expression of these values "worship" is sacrilege? After all, the genuinely religious attitude is one of unconditional commitment. To regard a symbol as sacred or ultimate is to be unconditionally committed to that symbol, to sacrifice all for its sake. Modern men tend to regard all symbols as conditional. God and Heaven are seen as human creations, hence dependent on human conditions. Social scientists such as Marx and Freud argue that as these conditions change, the symbolism of religion also changes. Should social science be seen, then, as undermining unconditional commitment to all symbols by revealing them as products of changing conditions? If the answer is yes, social analysis, far from constituting worship, should be regarded as a profoundly antireligious action. The worshipful attitude that sometimes pervades the analytic endeavor would be viewed as merely an abortive clutching after ultimate commitments within a framework of thought that renders such commitment logically impossible.

AMERICAN CULTURE

The American People: A Study in National Character (paperback, 1964) by Geoffrey Gorer. A readable and perceptive anthropological analysis of American life by a British anthropologist.
And Keep Your Powder Dry (paperback, 1965) by Margaret Mead. Readable and perceptive anthropological analysis of American life by a well-known American anthropologist.
American Life: Dream and Reality (paperback, 1964) by W. Lloyd Warner. American society and symbolism viewed from a Durkheimian perspective by an expert on the Australian aborigine.
"The Dominant Value Profile of American Culture" (1955) by Cora DuBois.
"National and Regional Cultural Values in the United States" (1955) by John Gillin.
"The American Cultural Configuration" in *Anthropology: An Introduction* (1965) by Lowell D. Holmes.
"Body Ritual Among the Nacirema" (1956) by Horace Miner. Useful if somewhat heavy-handed satire on American culture.
Culture Against Man (paperback, 1963) by Jules Henry. Provocative and bitter anthropological critique of American culture.

Power and Privilege: A Theory of Social Stratification (1966) by Gerhard Lenski. A useful synthesis of information on technological, demographic, and social trends in America. Provides detailed references to other sources.

"Population Growth in the United States" (1965) by Donald J. Bogue. A readable essay on population trends.

THE CHANGING SHAPE OF
AMERICAN SOCIETY AND CULTURE

The Power Elite (paperback, 1956) by C. Wright Mills.

The Lonely Crowd: A Study of Changing American Character (abridged paperback, 1953) by David Riesman, Nathan Glazer, and Reuel Denney.

The Organization Man (paperback, 1957) by William H. Whyte, Jr.

Mass Culture (paperback, 1957) edited by Bernard Rosenberg and David Manning White.

Beyond Conformity (1961) by Winston White.

The Kandy-Kolored Tangerine-Flake Streamline Baby (paperback, 1966) by Tom Wolfe. A particularly enjoyable commentary.

America as a Civilization (paperback, 1957) by Max Lerner. An encyclopedic synthesis with an extensive bibliography.

The First New Nation: The United States in Historical and Comparative Perspective (1967) by Seymour Martin Lipset. Elaborates many of the present authors' points about America.

THE MC LUHAN THESIS

Understanding Media (paperback, 1964) by Marshall McLuhan. A basic source.

The Medium Is the Massage (paperback, 1967) by Marshall McLuhan and Quentin Fiore. Presents the McLuhan thesis through pictures as well as words.

"The Medium Is the Massage" (Columbia Stereo C5 9501). To insure that the message is properly mediumed, McLuhan has made it audible in this bizarre and entertaining phonograph record.

THE DEATH OF GOD

The "Is God Dead?" Controversy (paperback, 1966) by John Warwick
    Montgomery.
The Meaning of the Death of God (1967) edited by Bernard Murch-
    land.
The Death of God Debate (paperback, 1967) edited by Jackson
    Lee Ice and John J. Carey.

8

Sociocultural evolution
and the future

Evolutionary theory has provided a viewpoint and framework in terms of which to confront various issues, generalizations, cultures, and behavioral processes. If nothing else, it is a useful pedagogical and organizational device. But it may be more than this. If its premises are valid, evolutionary theory should lead toward a better comprehension of world trends and even help predict the shape of the future.

Two broad evolutionary trends can be discerned. The first is apparent in the increased maximization, with the passage of time, of such features as specialization of units, specification of social relations, bureaucratization, centralization, mobility, and changeability. From this standpoint, the evolutionary process has been a gradual, but continuously accelerating, spread and intensification of modern traits. Assuming that this process will continue, the future will display these traits of modernity more extensively and intensively than the present does.

The second trend is evolution by a series of "leaps" from one level to another. Instead of merely spreading and intensifying a *fixed* set of traits, evolution has created a series of patterns, each displaying radically *different* traits. Archaic patterns differ radically from primitive ones, historic from archaic, early-modern from historic, modern from early-modern. Since each level is so radically different from the others, it is particularly difficult to predict what the patterning of the next level will be.

CONTINUOUS EVOLUTIONARY TRENDS

By simply assuming that the spread and intensification of modern traits will continue into the future—that the future will be like the present but that there will be "more of it"—we can hazard numerous speculations about the future. Several caveats should be issued, however. First, the very traits and dimensions that we

have employed in constructing an evolutionary scheme are con-
ditioned by our present position in the evolutionary process. Our
view of the future is severely limited by our image of present and
past. For example, we imagine the future in terms of images such
as "world government," yet "government" may well appear to
future theorists as outmoded an image as the medieval "social
body" appears to us today.

Secondly, one of the very features that is increasingly salient
renders the task of prediction increasingly difficult. The rate of
sociocultural change is increasing. Because patterns are changing
faster and faster, they are more and more difficult to perceive and
analyze. A related trend is toward greater freedom of choice. The
freer men are to choose, the more complex becomes the task of
predicting what they will choose.

Finally, the assumption that certain evolutionary trends are continuous is an oversimplification. All evolutionary changes are in
kind as well as in degree. Nevertheless, it is useful and defensible
to treat some trends as merely quantitative, as simply tending toward more specialization, greater centralization, and faster change.

Rates of change

The trend of sociocultural evolution throughout human history has
been toward a faster overall rate of change. The trend is clearest
in the realm of technology, but it is also apparent in other spheres
of life. Especially with the advent of early-modern society, change
becomes a positive value. Early-modern science, education, and
government are built to insure incessant and rapid change, and
since the early-modern pattern is spreading around the world, the
world's overall rate of change will continue to increase—barring
holocaust and catastrophe.

The dynamism of early-modern society was inspired in part by a
cultural pattern delineating a single, transcendent cosmos in whose

image the world must be incessantly re-ordered and re-formed. With the Death of God movement and associated cultural developments, the single transcendent cosmos of early-modern culture is being replaced with a multiplicity of transcendental images. This multiplicity might encourage a confusion resulting in stagnation. More likely, however, it will result in wild diversification of reformist impulses, as swarms of provocative images are propagated by prophets of every conceivable type.

Advances in mass communications and world transportation can be expected to encourage cultural exchange and hybrid union, with associated increases in excitement and creativity. Exploding population alone will insure a large number of creative minds, and if all these minds remain on earth (instead of migrating to another planet), the density of high-level thought guarantees continuous cross-fertilization and ferment.

To what point can change accelerate before man reaches his limit of tolerance? Sociocultural patterns threaten to set a pace that the human organism itself cannot endure. Advances in genetics, neurology, and psychology may increase the organism's capacity to tolerate rapid change. Yet even if the organism can adapt, can the society do so? So far man has managed to evolve social and technological systems to meet each new demand for faster change. Bureaucratic organization, high-speed automation, and computers are among the significant responses to such demands. Some problems, however, are difficult to solve organizationally or technologically. One of these is the "generation gap." The world changes so fast that parents must rear their children for an unknown future. The alternative is to train children for a way of life that is extinct by the time they are adolescent. Trained in this manner, adolescents feel confused and alienated. They protest, revolt, and in other ways incite social change and ferment—perpetuating the very conditions that produced their alienation. Social planning could break this cycle by providing parents with a firm view of the future. Yet rigid social planning may hamper a society's ability to adapt to rapidly changing environments.

Social differentiation and specialization

The general trend of history is toward societies that are increasingly differentiated into specialized units. This trend aids adaptation to accelerating change. As specialties and skills change and multiply faster and faster, it becomes impossible for the individual to master all of them; and the mastery is accordingly divided among numerous specialists and specialized groups.

The consequence for the individual is that he divides his time and energy among increasingly specialized and disconnected roles. His existence becomes more and more fragmented. How does this affect him? How far can fragmentation go before it reaches the limits of psychic tolerance? Men are, apparently, evolving new modes of neurosis in response to social fragmentation. Obsessive-compulsive neurosis was a frequent response to early-modern fragmentation in the West; the obsessive-compulsive's preoccupation with scheduling of roles and with separating technical jobs from emotional pleasures was simply an exaggeration of early-modern values. Neurotics today, however, complain of other symptoms. They feel "alienated," they feel they have no "identity," and they find no "meaning in life." These are perhaps more serious symptoms than the old ones in the sense that the neurotic individuals are, at a deep level of the psyche, reacting *against* the fragmented society instead of overconforming to its values.

A workable, viable society requires a degree of mutual empathy and solidarity among its members. In the primitive village, rites draw all villagers into a mutual empathy and solidarity. In the archaic community, public dramas serve the same function. In modern society, such rites and dramas unfortunately do not, perhaps cannot, flourish. Groups and individuals are too differentiated to join together as a total community on the village green.

Mass media partially fill the vacuum left by the demise of ritual and drama; but the media do not provide the kind of empathetic experience the rites offered. The rite or drama, occurring within a community of diffusely bound individuals, projected a diffuse empathy—an empathy with others that touched many levels of the self. The media, in a society bound together by one-dimensional ties, provide only shallow empathy. The contrast between the modern man's empathy with a stranger on a screen and the primitive's empathy with a kinsman during a rite is clear. Is it possible that the more one-dimensional social relations become, the more shallow empathetic experience will become? Future empathy might shrink into a ghastly shadow of what we know even today. In the film *Barbarella,* for example, future sexual union is depicted as touching hands after taking a pill. But as this film also suggests, technological advance might allow the dispensing of specialized empathy in highly condensed doses.

Centralization and bureaucratization

Social differentiation is always accompanied by a balancing trend toward centralization and bureaucratization, so that the differentiated units will perform in harmony. Therefore, if the world becomes more differentiated, it will likely also become more centralized and bureaucratized.

As this occurs, the individual will probably become more alienated. The more levels between the coordinating center of bureaucracy and the specialist bureaucrat, the more alienated the individual is likely to feel (as vividly illustrated in Kafka's *The Trial*). The alienation that comes with increasing bureaucratization is, of course, an old problem, and it will doubtless continue to be one. As in the present, future solutions will oscillate between anarchy and fascism, both of which aim at restoring a sense of belonging that bureaucracy destroys. The new dimension of future fascism will doubtless be an elaborate technology of tyranny. As science fiction predicts, electronic devices may control the public mind with great precision.

Will the future world centralize itself into a single society? Multinational governmental or economic unions such as NATO, the

Warsaw Pact, the European Common Market, and the United Nations are indicative of a trend in that direction. But these organizations themselves raise questions about the chances for a world society. In the United Nations, for instance, the poor nations are at a disadvantage, and this is likely to be so in any world organization. Unfortunately, despite great strides by the poor nations, they are becoming relatively poorer as the rich nations become richer. Development of the underdeveloped nations must proceed at a much faster rate than it is doing in order to produce a union of equal nations.

It is conceivable that there could emerge some radically new governmental system which manages to coordinate unequal nations in a viable union, or perhaps such unity could be achieved by a system other than a governmental one. One thinks of possible advances in the media of exchange. The invention of money allowed fantastic innovations in economic exchange; perhaps some supergeneralized medium could do the same for international relations. One can imagine a political credit card that would allow politicians to move effortlessly among the nations, arranging pacts, treaties, and coalitions as easily as a housewife shops in a supermarket. To unite or not to unite with a given nation would be decided instantly by the assessment (facilitated by lightning-fast computers) of how much political credit the nation possesses at the moment of decision. Laborious negotiations would be a thing of the past, as would wars. This whimsy rests, of course, on an oversimplified analogy between economic and political media of exchange. Still, it is quite possible that treaties and diplomacy as they are currently known will give way to a much more flexible and quantitative system.

Family and kinship

The importance of kinship units and of the parent-child bond on which such units are based is declining. Since this trend is connected to the trends of increased universalism, specialization, and centralization, if these continue, it will too.

Even in the last decades, the family in modern society has decreased its contribution to the education of the child—just about the only important function still served by the modern family. Children enter nursery school at an increasingly early age and stay in school to an increasingly advanced age. Eventually, the task of educating the child for an unknown future may simply prove too much for parents, and the child's education may be placed fully in the hands of specialized and bureaucratized organizations, guided by the latest research and expertise. Motivational problems might arise, as studies of children raised in orphanages suggest. Perhaps a compromise arrangement could be established, with the child allowed to sleep at home in order to receive and reciprocate parental love, but the parent forbidden by law to attempt to educate the child. The parent might then be merely a pal, entrusting the difficult task of educating the child in skills, knowledge, character, and ethics to the experts.

Relieved of their child-rearing responsibilities, man and wife would also be relieved of a keystone of marital permanence and stability: shared obligation to a child. Marital permanence would be much less important; marriage would no longer be a sacrament, nor even a long-term contract. Perhaps it would become no more than a courtship or date, and today's computerized dating systems could be extended to include all men and women, of all ages, all over the world.

Personal identity

With sociocultural evolution the self has become a more and more distinct unit. Presumably this trend will continue; but what will this future self be like? Some current social commentators maintain that the ascetic, goal-directed Protestant Ethic character, supposedly dominant in earlier times, is being supplanted by a hedonistic, participational, sensuous character—what the Calvinists would call a good-for-nothing type. This may be partly true, but the evolutionary argument suggests an alternative diagnosis.

With evolution, the self becomes more distinct and it also assumes more responsibility for its own deeds. The individual may indeed cease to suppress sensual drives, but he will not simply remove his trousers and indulge his drives whenever a suitable object appears. Instead, assuming that the evolutionary trend toward rationality continues, he will *rationally* decide when, where, and how to indulge his *irrational* drives. This is not to say that technical measurements and calculations will go into each decision of whether or not to copulate, but it does imply that the individual will feel compelled to consider carefully whether a particular experience will properly develop the self and contribute to his work. None of the Protestant Ethic taboos will be available to provide the individual with an absolute and categorical "no," so the individual must decide "yes" or "no" on rational grounds. Such freedom of choice is hardly likely to yield a joyous animal spontaneity.

THE FUTURE AND LEVELS OF SOCIOCULTURAL EVOLUTION

Certainly the predictions hazarded so far are tentative, general, and to some extent fanciful. But if the extrapolations from continuing trends must be speculative, forecasts about the nature of an utterly new level of sociocultural patterning must be even more so. If a trend can be anticipated to continue, it is reasonably safe to extrapolate from that trend and predict "the present, but more of it." But if the next level of sociocultural evolution is to be drastically different from the present one—different not merely in degree but in kind—simply predicting more of the present would be grossly misleading.

Let us imagine a Martian who, during his visit to the earth, rides in an automobile. He observes the driver shift into first, then second, then third gear. On the principle of "the present, but more of it," the Martian would predict that the trend will continue, and that the driver will shift into fourth, fifth, sixth . . . n gears. His prediction would, of course, be incorrect. If he is intelligent, however, he will base his prediction on more than mere observation of a trend. He will inquire about the mechanism that operates the automobile. With sufficient understanding of the mechanism, he could predict that stubbornly trying to shift a three-gear automobile into fourth gear would result in a new pattern, that is, a breakdown. He might even be able to predict the particulars of this new pattern: what happens to the clutch, the gears, the engine.

This analogy warns that plotting a trend in "history so far" is simply not adequate for predicting the character of an emerging sociocultural level (a breakdown or breakthrough). At the same time, it suggests that understanding the mechanism by which society moves from one level to the next may substantially aid such prediction.

Ordinarily, the three analytically distinguishable life processes that we have called *cultural, social,* and *psychological* are more or less in harmony. The patterning of values, symbols, and ideas in terms of which the individual defines his existence, the patterning of his society, and his own personal patterning are mutually supportive. Myth, self, and kinship reflect and reinforce each other among the Australian aborigine, as do cosmology, self and kingship among the ancient Egyptians.

Nevertheless, there have been epochs when the cultural, the social, and the psychological were not in harmony. The city's commercial clamor did not harmonize with medieval man's organic imagery and pastoral disposition. For the Organization Man, the American dream is not in accord with other-directed passivity and the bureaucratic maze. Sensing such discrepancies, the populace is disquieted and expresses this disquietude in riots, crime, withdrawal, neurosis, millenarianism, and civil disobedience. Men speak of chaos, anxiety, and meaninglessness. Out of the chaos emerge new ideologies, cosmologies, theologies, and myths that can make sense of the forces of society and give them order, and that can harness and integrate the urges of the self.

How and why do cultural, social, and psychological systems get out of mesh? And how does such disharmony excite radical, *i.e.,* evolutionary, sociocultural change? Despite the importance of the questions, surprisingly little is known about the precise mechanisms that bring about the disharmony; nor is it clear precisely how much is tolerable before radical change must occur. Yet both the disharmony and the change have appeared throughout human history, in circumstances so varied that they must derive from characteristics intrinsic to sociocultural systems and to the human condition itself.

Cultural systems and social systems differ in their manner of integration. The beliefs, values, and ideas in terms of which men direct their actions, interpret their experiences, and render their lives meaningful are integrated by a unity of style and a consistency of logic. Mathematical systems, artistic compositions, religious theologies, even political ideologies and informal philosophies of life work toward such integration. These cultural systems tend toward *logico-meaningful* integration. The roles, groups, and relationships involved in ongoing processes of interaction, alliance, and conflict tend more toward *causal-functional* integration. They are connected in sequences of cause and effect, condition and consequence, and by interdependencies of supply and demand, goal and function. Social systems such as economies, governments, communities, and societies tend toward causal-functional integration.

Tendencies toward logico-meaningful integration are inevitably in disharmony with tendencies toward causal-functional integration. The idealist's drive toward an aesthetically pleasing and logically consistent five-year plan interferes with the practical arrangements necessary for an economy that *works*. The true believer's premise that "devotion to the otherworld is the only moral act" cannot be applied with perfect consistency to all men if the operational requirements of a functioning society—for example, that commerce proceed and that procreation occur—are to be met.

Perceiving the discrepancy between the two modes of integration, the individual feels disillusionment, even nostalgia—a feeling due partly to the psychology of growing up. Especially in complex modern societies, the individual tends to acquire basic culture—beliefs, values, religion, world view—mainly in childhood, whereas he tends to learn adult roles—that of job-holder, family-head, property-owner—mainly in adulthood. These tendencies may suggest why cultural systems and their characteristic modes of thought and patterning recall the warmth, innocence, and magic of childhood, social systems the harsh realities of adulthood. A special sadness and a sense of loss of childhood and of youth may be evoked, at varying levels of consciousness, by the realization that the cultural (the logico-meaningful) must be compromised and sacrificed for the sake of the working system (the causal-functional). The process of growing up is not, of course, the only psychological dynamic that lends poignance to the perception of dissonance between the cultural and social systems, but it is an important one, for the adult's attitude is rooted in the earliest experiences of life. Because of this and other psychological processes, the drive to order social reality, to render it meaningful by subsuming it within a cultural framework, is a fundamental force within the human personality.

The drive toward meaningfulness is often expressed by a belief that culture is constant, even as society changes. As with the aborigines, mythical, totemic, and other symbolic frameworks are imagined as eternal, constant, and static systems in terms of which ongoing and changing events of society can be classified, hence rendered orderly and meaningful. In actual fact, of course, neither culture nor society is entirely static. Instead, societies are constantly changed to match cultural ideals. And all societies boast specialists in elaborating and modifying the cultural order to accommodate social changes. In primitive societies, this is the task of the teller of tales; in modern society, of theologians, scientists, educators, and politicians. Paradoxically, the very attempt to elaborate the cultural that it may better fit the social may intensify the dissonance between the two, because cultural elaboration proceeds logico-meaningfully, social change proceeds causal-functionally.

External factors may also contribute to the cultural-social dissonance. When modern and nonmodern societies come in contact, modern elements are invariably introduced in the nonmodern societies—whether deliberately, as by missionization, colonialization, and foreign aid, or unintentionally, as by trade and tourism. For the recipient society, the new elements abruptly create discrepancies between cultural traditions and contemporary realities. For example, myths may venerate stone axes, but now the natives are actually using steel knives. Theologies may rank the priestly caste above the artisan caste, but in daily life it is the talents of the latter that, because of the influx of new machinery, are in demand. The resulting discrepancies between traditional culture and modern society precipitate tensions which find myriad expressions— an important one being religio-political movements that attempt radical modernization.

Whether precipitated by external contacts (as in the case with most of the movements of radical social and cultural reformulation that are emerging among colonized peoples) or by internal dynamics (as was broadly the case with the Protestant Reformation), these religio-political movements display certain common features. Either they dig deep into native traditions to select old elements suitable for a new order, as in the Reformation's claim to reestablish the original and pristine Christianity; or they project a fantasied future utopia, as in the millenarian movements of the Middle Ages and in political religions such as Communism. In both instances, the results are the same: the undermining of established values, the creation of new loyalties, the harnessing of dormant energies, and the shaping of modern forms of consciousness. Some of the movements (*e.g.*, those that originated the historic religions) have deeply affected the whole of human history, others have so far had only local effects. All have contributed some sense of order and meaning to an existence suddenly rendered complex by modernization.

We may now draw on some of the above considerations, as well as others mentioned throughout the book, to formulate a basic mechanism of sociocultural evolution. We suggest that *each new cultural pattern that renders meaningful an advance in social mo-*

dernity and complexity "transcendentalizes" the old cultural pattern from which it derives. The mechanism of transcendentalization has already been exemplified by the various stages of evolution. Archaic Egypt, Mesopotamia, Swaziland, and Southeast Asia replaced primitive cosmic orders, existing in their respective regions, with more transcendent ones; their gods and god-kings transcended man and his world more than did the primitive spirits, totems, and heroes. Historic Buddhism, Islam, and Christianity replaced archaic cosmologies, whose gods and god-kings lived in the world, with conceptions of gods and ultimate orders existing outside and above the world, in a transcendent otherworld. Calvinism rendered this otherworld even more transcendent by sweeping away the mediating hierarchies, which, under historic Christianity, had connected it to this world. And now modern religion, represented by such schools as the Death of God, bids to transcendentalize the cosmic even more, pushing it to a level above God, Heaven, and the other idolatrous symbols of traditional Protestantism.

At each new level, there was an increase in social complexity. Therefore, it is reasonable to expect that the cosmic (cultural) order should be transcendentalized to render meaningful the new complexity and chaos of social existence. The old cosmology is too much wedded to the differentiated complexity of this existence to stand above it and subsume it, thereby rendering it meaningful. A broad prediction of the future, then, is that from current advances in modernization and complexity of society will emerge a cosmology more transcendent than any yet imagined. Otherwise the basic human drive toward meaning will be thwarted.

The Death of God disciples suggest one direction of this future transcendentalization: the placing of ultimate being far above and beyond God and other concrete symbols. Whatever form is assumed by the substance of such a religion, it will not be a visible, personified form, such as God or the Virgin Mary. Indeed, this substance may have no form at all; it will be that which the visible symbols have heretofore represented. Discovery of this "that," this ultimate essence, will be the aim of believers.

Given the positivist warp of modern culture, it is unlikely that

believers will accept an ultimate essence inhabiting some fourth
dimension unknowable except by mystics. Nor will they be satisfied
by tracing the ultimate to a set of nerve endings and brain cells in
the neurologist's laboratory. At present, the clearest trend, suggested at the close of the last chapter, is toward a searching within
the self. Yet the self as a unit of consciousness is no more visible
than the mystic's fourth dimension. Accordingly, should this mysterious self become an object of worship, many cults and theories,
speculating about its nature and destiny, will arise. As the cults
and theories multiply, the self will become ever more mysterious
and complex, expanding in rhythm with the worship lavished upon
it by those faithful who seek the transcendent within the self. As
seeker seeks to transcendentalize the sought, and the sought is
within the seeker's self, this self will assume an odd shape. A world
of such *selves* could be radically different from the world we know
today.

Notes

Preface

1. Robert N. Bellah, "Religious Evolution."
2. V. Gordon Childe, *Man Makes Himself,* chapter 5.
3. Abraham Kaplan, *The Conduct of Inquiry,* p. 11.

Chapter 1

1. Raymond Firth, *We, the Tikopia,* p. 2.
2. Walter Goldschmidt (ed.), *Exploring the Ways of Mankind,* p. 15.
3. Lynn White, Jr., "World View and Technology in the European Middle Ages," p. 2.
4. Weston LaBarre, "The Cultural Basis of Emotions and Gestures," pp. 49–68.

* Full facts of publication for sources cited in the Notes are supplied in the Bibliography.

5. Clyde Kluckhohn, *Mirror for Man,* pp. 153–154.
6. Kluckhohn, p. 155.
7. This broadcast was reported in *True: The Man's Magazine,* 49 (September, 1968), p. 20.
8. Edward T. Hall, *The Silent Language,* chapters 1, 4, 9, 10.
9. James George Frazer, *The Golden Bough,* pp. 12–52.
10. Dorothy Lee, "Lineal and Nonlineal Codifications of Reality," p. 97.
11. John Gillin, *The Ways of Men,* pp. 295–296.
12. Hall, chapter 9.
13. Marion J. Levy, Jr., *Modernization and the Structure of Societies,* vol. I, p. 29.
14. The Navaho and Hopi examples cited below come from Weston LaBarre, *The Human Animal,* pp. 197–198.
15. John B. Carroll and Joseph B. Casagrande, "The Function of Language Classifications in Behavior."
16. From a letter by Franklin to the Abbé Morellet, quoted in Robert K. Merton, *Social Theory and Social Structure,* p. 38.
17. George Herbert Mead, "The Psychology of Punitive Justice," p. 591.
18. George Devereux, "Art and Mythology."
19. Tom Wolfe, *The Kandy-Kolored Tangerine-Flake Streamline Baby,* pp. 42–43.
20. Dorothy Baker, *Young Man with a Horn.*

Chapter 2

1. Godfrey Lienhardt, *Social Anthropology,* p. 13.
2. Lienhardt, p. 14.
3. Marvin Harris, *The Rise of Anthropological Theory,* pp. 171–173.
4. L. T. Hobhouse, G. C. Wheeler, and M. Ginsburg, *The Material Culture and Social Institutions of the Simple Peoples* (London, 1915). Quoted in Lienhardt, *Social Anthropology,* p. 43.
5. Personal communication, Marion J. Levy, Jr.
6. Much of this section is based on Levy, *Modernization and the Structure of Societies.*
7. These levels are derived from Robert Bellah, "Religious Evolution."

8. Bronislaw Malinowski, *Argonauts of the Western Pacific.*
9. Daniel Lerner, *The Passing of Traditional Society.* The subsequent examples of empathy in the Near East come from this work.
10. J. K. Campbell, *Honour, Family, and Patronage,* pp. 217–247.
11. Campbell, pp. 59–88.
12. Edmund Leach, in *Rethinking Anthropology,* pp. 8–21.
13. Bronislaw Malinowski, *Sex and Repression in Savage Society.*
14. Campbell, p. 145.
15. James L. Peacock, *Rites of Modernization,* chapter 15.
16. Bellah, "Religious Evolution."
17. Ernest Nagel, *The Structure of Science,* pp. 107–117.
18. Robert Redfield, *The Primitive World and Its Transformations,* chapter 5.
19. Harold F. Blum, "On the Origin and Evolution of Human Culture," pp. 211, 219.

Chapter 3

1. This paragraph and the diagram follow Robin Fox, *Kinship and Marriage,* p. 183.
2. This section follows W. E. H. Stanner, "The Dreaming."
3. Stanner, p. 514.
4. Stanner, p. 517.
5. Claude Lévi-Strauss, *The Savage Mind,* p. 89.
6. A. P. Elkin, *The Australian Aborigines,* p. 211.
7. Lévi-Strauss, *The Savage Mind,* pp. 233–234.
8. Edmund Leach, *Political Systems of Highland Burma,* pp. 73–74.
9. See Rodney Needham, *Structure and Sentiment.*
10. Godfrey Lienhardt, *Social Anthropology,* p. 113.
11. Needham, p. 96.
12. Needham, p. 99.
13. This account is taken from Victor W. Turner, "A Ndembu Doctor in Practice," pp. 230–263.
14. Turner, pp. 260–261.
15. Max Gluckman, "Les Rites de Passage," p. 24.
16. Leach, *Political Systems of Highland Burma.*
17. Harold F. Blum, "On the Origin and Evolution of Human Culture," pp. 211, 219.

Chapter 4

1. This section follows the research of Hilda Kuper, reported in *An African Aristocracy*.
2. Kuper, p. 69.
3. Kuper, p. 141.
4. Kuper, p. 203.
5. Kuper, p. 204.
6. Kuper, p. 205.
7. Kuper, p. 217.
8. Kuper, p. 217.
9. Kuper, pp. 217–218.
10. Kuper, p. 206.
11. Max Gluckman, "Rituals of Rebellion in Southeast Africa."
12. T. O. Beidelman, "Swazi Royal Ritual."
13. Beidelman, p. 397.
14. Most of the following material on Egypt comes from John A. Wilson, *The Culture of Ancient Egypt*. The material on Mesopotamia comes from a variety of sources, especially Sabatino Moscati, *The Face of the Ancient Orient*. Some suggestions for comparing the Egyptian and Mesopotamian patterns derive from Talcott Parsons, *Societies: Evolutionary and Comparative Perspectives*, chapter 4.
15. Wilson, *The Culture of Ancient Egypt*, p. 48.
16. Wilson, p. 49.
17. See Thorkild Jacobsen, "Mesopotamia."
18. Jacobsen, pp. 189ff.
19. Much of the material presented here can be found in Robbins Burling, *Hill Farms and Padi Fields*, chapters 4 and 5.
20. Burling, p. 66.
21. Karl A. Wittfogel, *Oriental Despotism*.
22. Robert J. Braidwood and Gordon R. Willey (eds.), *Courses Toward Urban Life*, pp. 350–358.

Chapter 5

1. Much of the material on Buddhism and Thailand comes from A. Thomas Kirsch, "Phu Thai Religious Syncretism."

2. The following remarks on Indian prehistory follow Sir Mortimer Wheeler, *Early India and Pakistan: To Ashoka.* The analysis of Hinduism owes much to Max Weber, *The Religion of India,* and Talcott Parsons, *Societies,* chapter 5.
3. The following analysis of Islam is primarily based on Gustave von Grunebaum, *Medieval Islam.*
4. Carl Brockelmann, *History of the Islamic Peoples,* pp. 8ff.
5. von Grunebaum, *Medieval Islam,* p. 215.

Chapter 6

1. Michael Walzer, *The Revolution of the Saints,* p. 167.
2. The following account of Weber's Protestant Ethic Thesis owes much to Talcott Parsons, *The Structure of Social Action,* part III. The other major source is Max Weber, *The Protestant Ethic and the Spirit of Capitalism.*
3. Weber, *Protestant Ethic,* p. 51.
4. Weber, p. 116.
5. Reinhard Bendix, *Max Weber: An Intellectual Portrait,* p. 72.
6. Sinclair Lewis, *Dodsworth,* p. 10.
7. Several of the following criticisms are expressed in Kurt Samuelsson, *Religion and Economic Action.*
8. Samuelsson, pp. 27–42.
9. Marion J. Levy, Jr., "Some Aspects of 'Individualism' and the Problem of Modernization in China and Japan," p. 230.
10. Robert N. Bellah, *Tokugawa Religion,* p. 2. The following discussion derives from this work.
11. David E. Apter, *The Politics of Modernization,* chapter 8.
12. The interpretation of Indonesia presented here basically follows Herbert Feith, "The Dynamics of Guided Democracy." However, most comments and examples regarding Sukarno's imagery and the role of youth come from direct observation by Peacock during a 1962–1963 sojourn in Indonesia.
13. Feith, p. 313.
14. Feith, p. 325.
15. These images are taken from several utterances by Sukarno, some of which are briefly described in James L. Peacock, *Rites of Modernization,* p. 101, note 9.

Chapter 7

1. These and other statistics cited in this chapter are, except where noted otherwise, taken from Gerhard Lenski, *Power and Privilege.*
2. Donald J. Bogue, "Population Growth in the United States," p. 385.
3. Full exposition of Mills's argument appears in his *Power Elite.*
4. These statistics, those that follow, and some of the implications drawn from them derive from Lenski, *Power and Privilege,* pp. 347–363.
5. Parsons set forth this analysis in the course of lectures on the "Social Structure of the United States" at Harvard University in 1964.
6. The following argument is taken from William H. Whyte, Jr., *The Organization Man,* pp. 4–24.
7. Whyte, p. 22.
8. David Riesman, Nathan Glazer, and Reuel Denney, *The Lonely Crowd,* p. 122.
9. Riesman, p. 122.
10. Riesman, p. 127.
11. Reuel Denney, *The Astonished Muse,* p. 28.
12. Marshall McLuhan, *Understanding Media,* p. 8.
13. McLuhan, p. 8.
14. McLuhan, pp. 7–21.
15. McLuhan, p. 86.
16. McLuhan, p. 178.
17. McLuhan, p. 314.
18. McLuhan, p. 136.
19. McLuhan, p. 332.
20. McLuhan, p. 346.
21. Cited in John Warwick Montgomery, *The "Is God Dead?" Controversy,* p. 21.
22. Cited in Montgomery, p. 24.
23. Cited in Montgomery, p. 29.
24. Cited in Montgomery, p. 29.
25. Cited in Montgomery, p. 33.

Bibliography

An asterisk (*) at the beginning of an entry means either that the edition cited is in paperback or that it is available in paperback.

*Apter, David E. *The Politics of Modernization.* Chicago: University of Chicago Press, 1965.

Baker, Dorothy. *Young Man with a Horn.* Boston: Houghton Mifflin, 1938.

Baldus, H. "Curt Nimuendaju, 1883–1945." *American Anthropologist* 48 (1946):238–243.

*Beattie, John. *Bunyoro: An African Kingdom.* New York: Holt, Rinehart and Winston, 1960.

Beidelman, T. O. "Swazi Royal Ritual." *Africa* 36 (1966):373–405.

Bellah, Robert N. "Reflections on the Protestant Ethic Analogy in Asia." *Journal of Social Issues* 19 (1963):52–60.

———. "Religious Evolution." *American Sociological Review* 29 (1964):358–374.

———. *Tokugawa Religion: The Values of Pre-Industrial Japan.* New York: Free Press, 1957.

Bellah, Robert N., ed. *Religion and Progress in Modern Asia.* New York: Free Press, 1965.

*Bendix, Reinhard. *Max Weber: An Intellectual Portrait.* Garden City, N. Y.: Doubleday, 1962.

Bloomfield, Leonard. *Language.* New York: Holt, 1933.

*Blum, Harold F. "On the Origin and Evolution of Human Culture." In Wilbert E. Moore and Robert M. Cook, eds., *Readings on Social Change.* Englewood Cliffs, N. J.: Prentice-Hall, 1967.

Bogue, Donald J. "Population Growth in the United States." In Edward C. McDonagh and Jon E. Simpson, eds., *Social Problems: Persistent Challenges.* New York: Holt, Rinehart and Winston, 1965.

Bohannan, Paul J. *Justice and Judgment Among the Tiv.* London: Oxford University Press, 1957.

————. *Social Anthropology.* New York: Holt, Rinehart and Winston, 1963.

*Bowen, Elenore S. *Return to Laughter.* Garden City, N. Y.: Doubleday, 1964.

*Brace, C. Loring. *The Stages of Human Evolution: Human and Cultural Origins.* Englewood Cliffs, N. J.: Prentice-Hall, 1967.

Braidwood, Robert J., and Willey, Gordon R., eds. *Courses Toward Urban Life: Archeological Considerations of Some Cultural Alternatives.* Chicago: Aldine, 1962. (Viking Fund Publications in Anthropology, 32)

*Brockelmann, Carl. *History of the Islamic Peoples.* New York: Putnam, 1960.

Bunzel, Ruth. "Introduction to Zuni Ceremonialism." In *47th Annual Report of the Bureau of American Ethnology.* Washington, D. C.: U. S. Government Printing Office, 1932.

*Burling, Robbins. *Hill Farms and Padi Fields: Life in Mainland Southeast Asia.* Englewood Cliffs, N. J.: Prentice-Hall, 1965.

Campbell, John K. *Honour, Family and Patronage.* New York: Oxford University Press, 1964.

Carroll, John B., and Casagrande, Joseph B. "The Function of Language Classifications in Behavior." In Alfred G. Smith, ed., *Communication and Culture: Readings in the Codes of Human Interaction.* New York: Holt, Rinehart and Winston, 1966.

*Casagrande, Joseph B., ed. *In the Company of Man: Twenty Portraits of Anthropological Informants.* New York: Harper & Row, 1964.

*Childe, V. Gordon. *Man Makes Himself.* New York: New American Library, 1956.

*————. *Social Evolution.* Cleveland: World, 1951.

*————. *What Happened in History.* Baltimore: Penguin, 1946.

*Clark, W. E. Le Gros. *History of the Primates.* Chicago: University of Chicago Press, 1965.

*Coe, Michael D. *Mexico.* New York: Praeger, 1962.

Coedès, George. *Angkor: An Introduction.* New York: Oxford University Press, 1963.

————. *The Making of Southeast Asia.* Berkeley: University of California Press, 1966.

*Cox, Harvey. *The Secular City.* New York: Macmillan, 1965.

*Deetz, James. *Invitation to Archeology.* New York: The Natural History Press, 1967.

*Denney, Reuel. *The Astonished Muse.* Chicago: University of Chicago Press, 1957.

Devereux, George. "Art and Mythology: A General Theory." In Bert Kaplan, ed., *Studying Personality Cross-Culturally.* New York: Harper & Row, 1961.

Dewey, Alice G. *Peasant Marketing in Java.* New York: Free Press, 1962.

Douglas, Mary. *Purity and Danger: An Analysis of Concepts of Pollution and Taboo.* New York: Praeger, 1966.

DuBois, Cora. "The Dominant Value Profile of American Culture." *American Anthropologist* 57 (1955):1232–1239.

*Durkheim, Emile. *The Elementary Forms of the Religious Life*. New York: Free Press, 1965.

*————, and Mauss, Marcel. *Primitive Classification*. Chicago: University of Chicago Press, 1963.

*Eisenstadt, S. N., ed. *The Protestant Ethic and Modernization: A Comparative View*. New York: Basic Books, 1968.

*Elkin, A. P. *The Australian Aborigines*. London: Angus and Robertson, 1966.

Evans-Pritchard, E. E. *Kinship and Marriage Among the Nuer*. London: Oxford University Press, 1951.

*————. *The Nuer*. London: Oxford University Press, 1940.

————. *Nuer Religion*. London: Oxford University Press, 1956.

*————. *Social Anthropology and Other Essays*. New York: Free Press, 1964.

*————. *Theories of Primitive Religion*. London: Oxford University Press, 1965.

*Fallers, Lloyd. *Bantu Bureaucracy*. Chicago: University of Chicago Press, 1965.

Fei, Hsiao-t'ung. *Peasant Life in China: A Field Study of Country Life in the Yangtze Valley*. New York: Oxford University Press, 1946.

Feith, Herbert. "The Dynamics of Guided Democracy." In Ruth T. McVey, ed., *Indonesia*. New Haven, Conn.: Human Relations Area Files Press, 1963.

Firth, Raymond. *Primitive Polynesian Economics*. London: Routledge, 1939.

*————. *We, the Tikopia: A Sociological Study of Kinship in Primitive Polynesia*, 2nd abr. ed. Boston: Beacon Press, 1963.

*Forde, Daryll, ed. *African Worlds: Studies in the Cosmological Ideas and Social Values of African Peoples*. London: Oxford University Press, 1954.

Fortes, Meyer. "The Structure of Unilineal Descent Groups." *American Anthropologist* 55 (1953):17–41.

*Fortes, Meyer, and Evans-Pritchard, E. E., eds. *African Political Systems*. London: Oxford University Press, 1940.

*Fox, Robin. *Kinship and Marriage*. Baltimore: Penguin, 1967.

*Frankfort, Henri. *Ancient Egyptian Religion*. New York: Harper & Row, 1961.

————. *Kingship and the Gods*. Chicago: University of Chicago Press, 1948.

*————, et al. *Before Philosophy: The Intellectual Adventure of Ancient Man*. Baltimore: Penguin, 1967.

*Frazer, James George. *The Golden Bough: Study in Magic and Religion*, abr. ed. New York: Macmillan, 1958.

Geertz, Clifford. *Islam Observed: Religious Development in Morocco and Indonesia*. New Haven, Conn.: Yale University Press, 1968.

*————. *Peddlers and Princes: Social Change and Economic Modernization in Two Indonesian Towns*. Chicago: University of Chicago Press, 1963.

*————. "Religion as a Cultural System." In Michael Banton, ed., *Anthropological Approaches to the Study of Religion*. London: Tavistock, 1966.

*————. *The Religion of Java*. New York: Free Press, 1964.

————, ed. *Old Societies and New States*. New York: Free Press, 1963.

Geertz, Hildred. *The Javanese Family: A Study of Kinship and Socialization*. New York: Free Press, 1961.

*Gibb, H. A. R. *Mohammedanism: An Historical Survey*. New York: Oxford University Press, 1962.

Gillin, John. "National and Regional Cultural Values in the United States." *Social Forces* 34 (1955):107–113.

————. *The Ways of Men: An Introduction to Anthropology*. New York: Appleton-Century-Crofts, 1948.

Gluckman, Max. *The Ideas in Barotse Jurisprudence*. New Haven, Conn.: Yale University Press, 1965.

Gluckman, Max. *The Judicial Process Among the Barotse of Northern Rhodesia.* New York: Free Press, 1955.

―――. "Les Rites de Passage." In Max Gluckman, ed., *Essays on the Ritual of Social Relations.* Manchester: Manchester University Press, 1962.

―――. "Rituals of Rebellion in Southeast Africa." In Max Gluckman, ed., *Order and Rebellion in Tribal Africa.* New York: Free Press, 1963. (Bobbs-Merrill reprint A–368)

Goldschmidt, Walter, ed. *Exploring the Ways of Mankind.* New York: Holt, Rinehart and Winston, 1960.

*Goode, William J. *Religion Among the Primitives.* New York: Free Press, 1964.

―――. *World Revolution and Family Patterns.* New York: Free Press, 1963.

Goodenough, Ward H. "Residence Rules." *Southwestern Journal of Anthropology* 12 (1956):22–37.

Goody, Jack, ed. *The Developmental Cycle in Domestic Groups.* London: Cambridge University Press, 1958. (Cambridge Papers in Social Anthropology, 1)

*Gorer, Geoffrey. *The American People: A Study in National Character.* New York: Norton, 1964.

*Granet, Marcel. *Chinese Civilization.* New York: Meridian Books, 1958.

*Green, Robert, ed. *Protestantism and Capitalism: The Weber Thesis and Its Critics.* Boston: Heath, 1959.

*Greenberg, Joseph H. *Anthropological Linguistics: An Introduction.* New York: Random House, 1968.

*Hall, Edward T. *The Silent Language.* Greenwich, Conn.: Fawcett, 1961.

Harris, Marvin. *The Rise of Anthropological Theory.* New York: Crowell, 1968.

*Hart, C. W. M., and Piling, Arnold R. *The Tiwi of North Australia.* New York: Holt, Rinehart and Winston, 1960.

*Hays, H. R. *From Ape to Angel*. New York: Putnam, 1964.

Heider, Karl G. *Films for Anthropological Teaching*. Cambridge, Mass.: Program in Ethnographic Film, 1968.

Heine-Geldern, Robert. *Conceptions of State and Kingship in Southeast Asia*. Ithaca, N. Y.: Cornell University Southeast Asia Program, 1956. (Data paper, 18)

*Henry, Jules. *Culture Against Man*. New York: Random House, 1963.

*Herberg, Will. *Protestant, Catholic, Jew*. Garden City, N. Y.: Doubleday, 1955.

*Herskovits, Melville J. *Economic Anthropology*. New York: Norton, 1965.

Hockett, Charles F. *A Course in Modern Linguistics*. New York: Macmillan, 1958.

————, and Ascher, Robert. "The Human Revolution." *Current Anthropology* 5 (1964):135–168.

*Hoebel, E. Adamson. *The Law of Primitive Man: A Study in Comparative Legal Dynamics*. New York: Atheneum, 1968.

Holmes, Lowell D. *Anthropology: An Introduction*. New York: Ronald, 1965.

Homans, George C., and Schneider, David M. *Marriage, Authority, and Final Causes*. New York: Free Press, 1955.

Honigmann, John J. *Personality in Culture*. New York: Harper & Row, 1967.

*Hsu, Francis L. K. *Under the Ancestor's Shadow*. Garden City, N. Y.: Doubleday, 1948.

————, ed. *Psychological Anthropology: Approaches to Culture and Personality*. Homewood, Ill.: Dorsey Press, 1961.

Hubert, Henri, and Mauss, Marcel. *Sacrifice: Its Nature and Function*. Chicago: University of Chicago Press, 1964.

Hymes, Dell, ed. *Language in Culture and Society: A Reader in Linguistics and Anthropology*. New York: Harper & Row, 1964.

*Ice, Jackson Lee, and Carey, John J., eds. *The Death of God Debate.* Philadelphia: The Westminster Press, 1967.

*Jacobsen, Thorkild. "Mesopotamia." In Henri Frankfort *et al., Before Philosophy.* Baltimore: Penguin, 1967.

Johnson, Harry M. *Sociology: A Systematic Introduction.* New York: Harcourt, Brace & World, 1960.

*Kaplan, Abraham. *The Conduct of Inquiry: Methodology for Behavioral Science.* San Francisco: Chandler, 1964.

*Kardiner, Abram, and Preble, Edward. *They Studied Man.* New York: New American Library, 1965.

Keniston, Kenneth. "You Have to Grow Up in Scarsdale to Know How Bad Things Really Are." *The New York Times Magazine* (April 27, 1969):27–28, 122–130.

Kirsch, A. Thomas. "Phu Thai Religious Syncretism." Unpublished doctoral thesis, Harvard University, 1967.

*Kluckhohn, Clyde. *Mirror for Man: The Relation of Anthropology to Modern Life.* Greenwich, Conn.: Fawcett, 1968.

*————, and Leighton, Dorothea. *The Navaho,* rev. ed. Garden City, N. Y.: Doubleday, 1962.

Kroeber, Alfred L. *Anthropology,* rev. ed. New York: Harcourt, Brace, 1948.

————. *Configurations of Culture Growth.* Berkeley: University of California Press, 1944.

*————, and Kluckhohn, Clyde. *Culture: A Critical Review of Concepts and Definitions.* New York: Random House, 1963.

Kuper, Hilda. *An African Aristocracy: Rank Among the Swazi.* London: Oxford University Press, 1965.

*————. *The Swazi: A South African Kingdom.* New York: Holt, Rinehart and Winston, 1963.

LaBarre, Weston. "The Cultural Basis of Emotions and Gestures." *Journal of Personality* 16 (1947):49–68.

*————. *The Human Animal.* Chicago: University of Chicago Press, 1960.

Landon, Kenneth. *Southeast Asia: Crossroad of Religions.* Chicago: University of Chicago Press, 1949.

*Lanning, Edward P. *Peru Before the Incas.* Englewood Cliffs, N. J.: Prentice-Hall, 1967.

*Leach, Edmund. *Political Systems of Highland Burma.* Boston: Beacon Press, 1965.

*————. "The Structural Implications of Matrilateral Cross-Cousin Marriage," *Rethinking Anthropology.* New York: Humanities Press, 1966.

Lee, Dorothy. "Lineal and Nonlineal Codifications of Reality." *Psychosomatic Medicine* 12 (1950):89–97.

*Lehman, F. K. *The Structure of Chin Society.* Urbana: University of Illinois Press, 1963.

Lenski, Gerhard. *Human Societies: A New Introduction to Sociology.* New York: McGraw-Hill, 1970.

————. *Power and Privilege: A Theory of Social Stratification.* New York: McGraw-Hill, 1966.

*————. *The Religious Factor: A Sociological Study of Religion's Impact on Politics, Economics and Family Life.* Garden City, N. Y.: Doubleday, 1963.

*Lerner, Daniel. *The Passing of Traditional Society: Modernizing the Middle East.* New York: Free Press, 1965.

*Lerner, Max. *America as a Civilization.* New York: Simon and Schuster, 1957.

Lessa, William A., and Vogt, Evon Z., eds. *Reader in Comparative Religion,* 2nd ed. New York: Harper & Row, 1965.

*Lévi-Strauss, Claude. *The Elementary Structures of Kinship.* London: Eyre and Spottiswoode, 1969.

*————. "The Family." In Harry L. Shapiro, ed., *Man, Culture, and Society.* New York: Oxford University Press, 1956.

————. "The Future of Kinship Studies." *Proceedings of the Royal Anthropological Institute* (1965):13–22.

*Lévi-Strauss, Claude. *The Savage Mind.* Chicago: University of Chicago Press, 1966.

*———. *Totemism.* Boston: Beacon Press, 1963.

*———. *Tristes Tropiques.* New York: Atheneum, 1964.

Levy, Marion J., Jr. "Contrasting Factors in the Modernization of China and Japan." *Economic Development and Culture Change* 2 (1953):161–197.

*———. *The Family Revolution in Modern China.* New York: Atheneum, 1968.

*———. *Modernization and the Structure of Societies: A Setting for the Study of International Affairs,* 2 vols. Princeton, N. J.: Princeton University Press, 1966.

*———. "Social Patterns (Structures) and Problems of Modernization." In Wilbert E. Moore and Robert M. Cook, eds., *Readings on Social Change.* Englewood Cliffs, N. J.: Prentice-Hall, 1967.

———. "Some Aspects of 'Individualism' and the Problem of Modernization in China and Japan." *Journal of Educational Development and Cultural Change* 10 (1962):225–240.

*Levy, Reuben. *The Social Structure of Islam.* New York: Cambridge University Press, 1962.

*Lewis, Sinclair. *Dodsworth.* New York: Harcourt, Brace, 1929.

Lienhardt, Godfrey. *Divinity and Experience: The Religion of the Dinka.* London: Oxford University Press, 1961.

*———. *Social Anthropology.* London: Oxford University Press, 1965.

*Lipset, Seymour Martin. *The First New Nation: The United States in Historical and Comparative Perspective.* New York: Doubleday, 1967.

Llewellyn, K. N., and Hoebel, E. Adamson. *The Cheyenne Way: Conflict and Case Law in Primitive Jurisprudence.* Norman, Okla.: University of Oklahoma Press, 1941.

Lowie, Robert H. *The History of Ethnological Theory.* New York: Holt, 1937.

*McClelland, David C. *The Achieving Society.* New York: Free Press, 1967.

*McDonagh, Edward C., and Simpson, Jon E., eds. *Social Problems: Persistent Challenges.* New York: Holt, Rinehart and Winston, 1966.

*McLuhan, Marshall. *Understanding Media.* New York: McGraw-Hill, 1964.

*————, and Fiore, Quentin. *The Medium Is the Massage.* New York: Bantam Books, 1967.

McVey, Ruth T., and Pelzer, Karl J., eds. *Indonesia.* New Haven, Conn.: Human Relations Area Files Press, 1963.

*Maine, Henry. *Ancient Law: Its Connection with the Early History of Society and Its Relations to Modern Ideas.* Boston: Beacon Press, 1963.

*Malinowski, Bronislaw. *Argonauts of the Western Pacific: An Account of Native Enterprise and Adventure in the Archipelagoes of Melanesian New Guinea.* New York: Dutton, 1961.

*————. "Myth in Primitive Psychology," *Magic, Science and Religion, and Other Essays.* Garden City, N. Y.: Doubleday, 1954.

*————. *Sex and Repression in Savage Society.* Cleveland: World, 1968.

*Matossian, Mary. "The Ideologies of Delayed Industrialization: Some Tensions and Ambiguities." In J. H. Kautsky, ed., *Political Change in Underdeveloped Countries: Nationalism and Communism.* New York: Wiley, 1962.

*Mauss, Marcel. *The Gift: Forms and Functions of Exchange in Archaic Societies.* New York: Norton, 1967.

Mead, George Herbert. "The Psychology of Punitive Justice." *American Journal of Sociology* 23 (1918):577–602.

*Mead, Margaret. *And Keep Your Powder Dry.* New York: Apollo Editions, 1965.

Merton, Robert. *Social Theory and Social Structure.* New York: Free Press, 1957.

Michael, Donald N. "The Problems of Automation." In Edward C. McDonagh and Jon E. Simpson, eds., *Social Problems: Persistent Challenges*. New York: Holt, Rinehart and Winston, 1966.

Middleton, John, and Tait, David, eds. *Tribes Without Rulers*. London: Routledge, 1958.

*Mills, C. Wright. *The Power Elite*. New York: Oxford University Press, 1956.

Miner, Horace. "Body Ritual Among the Nacirema." *American Anthropologist* 58 (1956):503–507.

*Mirsky, Jeannette, and Nevins, Allan. *The World of Eli Whitney*. New York: Macmillan, 1952.

Montgomery, John Warwick. *The "Is God Dead?" Controversy*. Grand Rapids, Mich.: Zondervan, 1966.

*Moore, Wilbert, and Cook, Robert M., eds. *Readings on Social Change*. Englewood Cliffs, N. J.: Prentice-Hall, 1967.

*Morgan, Lewis Henry. *Ancient Society*. Cleveland: World, 1963.

*Moscati, Sabatino. *The Face of the Ancient Orient*. Garden City, N. Y.: Doubleday, 1962.

*Murchland, Bernard, ed. *The Meaning of the Death of God*. New York: Random House, 1967.

*Murdock, George Peter. *Social Structure*. New York: Free Press, 1965.

Nagel, Ernest. *The Structure of Science: Problems in the Logic of Scientific Explanation*. New York: Harcourt, Brace & World, 1961.

Nash, Manning. *The Golden Road to Modernity*. New York: Wiley, 1965.

———, ed. *Anthropological Studies in Theravada Buddhism*. New Haven, Conn.: Yale University Southeast Asia Studies, 1966. (Cultural Report, 13)

Needham, Rodney. *Structure and Sentiment*. Chicago: University of Chicago Press, 1962.

Norbeck, Edward. *Religion in Primitive Society.* New York: Harper & Row, 1961.

*Parsons, Talcott. *Societies: Evolutionary and Comparative Perspectives.* Englewood Cliffs, N. J.: Prentice-Hall, 1966.

*————. *The Structure of Social Action.* New York: Free Press, 1968.

————, Shils, Edward, Naegele, Kaspar D., and Pitts, Jesse R., eds. *Theories of Society: Foundations of Modern Sociological Theory,* 2 vols. New York: Free Press, 1961.

Peacock, James L. "Mystics and Merchants in Fourteenth Century Germany." *Journal for the Scientific Study of Religion* 8 (1969):47–59.

————. *Rites of Modernization: Symbolic and Social Aspects of Indonesian Proletarian Drama.* Chicago: University of Chicago Press, 1968.

Penniman, T. K. *A Hundred Years of Anthropology,* rev. ed. London: Duckworth, 1965.

*Peterson, Frederick. *Ancient Mexico.* New York: Putnam, 1959.

*Piggott, Stuart. *Approach to Archaeology.* New York: McGraw-Hill, 1965.

*Potter, J. M., Diaz, M. N., and Foster, G. M., eds. *Peasant Society: A Reader.* Boston: Little, Brown, 1967.

*Powdermaker, Hortense. *After Freedom: A Cultural Study in the Deep South.* New York: Atheneum, 1968.

*Radcliffe-Brown, A. R., and Forde, Daryll, eds. *African Systems of Kinship and Marriage.* London: Oxford University Press, 1950.

*Redfield, Robert. *The Primitive World and Its Transformations.* Ithaca, N. Y.: Cornell University Press, 1953.

*Riesman, David, Glazer, Nathan, and Denney, Reuel. *The Lonely Crowd: A Study of Changing American Character,* abr. ed. Garden City, N. Y.: Doubleday, 1953.

*Rosenberg, Bernard, and White, David Manning, eds. *Mass Culture.* New York: Free Press, 1957.

*Saggs, H. W. F. *The Greatness That Was Babylon.* New York: New American Library, 1968.

*Samuelsson, Kurt. *Religion and Economic Action: A Critique of Max Weber.* Stockholm: Scandinavian University Books, 1961.

*Sapir, Edward. *Language.* New York: Harcourt, Brace, 1921.

*Schneider, David M. *American Kinship: A Cultural Account.* Englewood Cliffs, N. J.: Prentice-Hall, 1968.

————, and Gough, Kathleen, eds. *Matrilineal Kinship.* Berkeley: University of California Press, 1961.

*Service, Elman R., *Primitive Social Organization.* New York: Random House, 1962.

*Sigmund, Paul E. *The Ideologies of the Developing Nations.* New York: Praeger, 1963.

*Spiro, Melford E., ed. *Burmese Supernaturalism.* Englewood Cliffs, N. J.: Prentice-Hall, 1967.

*Spuhler, James N., ed. *The Evolution of Man's Capacity for Culture.* Detroit: Wayne University Press, 1959.

Stanner, W. E. H. "The Dreaming." In W. A. Lessa and E. Z. Vogt, eds., *Reader in Comparative Religion,* 2nd ed. New York: Harper & Row, 1965.

*Stebbins, G. Ledyard. "Pitfalls and Guideposts in Comparing Organic and Social Evolution." In Wilbert E. Moore and Robert M. Cook, eds., *Readings on Social Change.* Englewood Cliffs, N. J.: Prentice-Hall, 1967.

Stevenson, H. N. C. *The Economics of the Central Chin Tribes.* Bombay: Times of India Press, 1943.

Steward, Julian H. *The Theory of Culture Change: The Methodology of Multilineal Evolution.* Urbana: University of Illinois Press, 1955.

*Swanson, Guy E. *The Birth of the Gods: The Origin of Primitive Belief.* Ann Arbor: University of Michigan Press, 1960.

*Tawney, Richard. *Religion and the Rise of Capitalism: A Historical Study.* New York: New American Library, 1961.

True: The Man's Magazine 49 (September, 1968).

Turner, Victor W. *The Drums of Affliction: A Study of Religious Processes Among the Ndembu of Zambia.* London: Oxford University Press, 1968.

————. *The Forest of Symbols: Aspects of Ndembu Ritual.* Ithaca, N. Y.: Cornell University Press, 1967.

————. "A Ndembu Doctor in Practice." In Ari Kiev, ed., *Magic, Faith and Healing: Studies in Primitive Psychiatry Today.* New York: Free Press, 1964, pp. 230–263.

————. *Schism and Continuity in an African Society.* Manchester: Manchester University Press, 1957.

Underhill, Ruth M. *Ceremonial Patterns in the Greater Southwest.* New York: Augustin, 1948. (Monographs of the American Ethnological Society, 13)

Vergouwen, J. C.. *The Social Organization and Customary Law of the Toba-Batak of Northern Sumatra.* The Hague: Nijhoff, 1964.

*von Grunebaum, Gustave E. *Medieval Islam.* Chicago: University of Chicago Press, 1961.

Wales, H. G. Quatritch. *Ancient Siamese Government and Administration.* New York: Paragon, 1965.

Wallace, Anthony F. C. *Religion: An Anthropological View.* New York: Random House, 1966.

*Walzer, Michael. *The Revolution of the Saints: A Study in the Origins of Radical Politics.* New York: Atheneum, 1968.

*Warner, W. Lloyd. *American Life: Dream and Reality.* Chicago: University of Chicago Press, 1964.

* ————. Black Civilization. New York: Harper & Row, 1964.

*Weber, Max. *The Protestant Ethic and the Spirit of Capitalism.* New York: Scribner, 1958.

* ————. *The Religion of China.* New York: Free Press, 1951.

* ————. *The Religion of India.* New York: Free Press, 1958.

*West, James. *Plainsville, U. S. A.* New York: Columbia University Press, 1945.

Wheeler, Sir Robert Eric Mortimer. *Early India and Pakistan: To Ashoka.* New York: Praeger, 1959.

*White, Jon E. M. *Everyday Life in Ancient Egypt.* New York: Putnam, 1967.

*White, Leslie A. *The Evolution of Culture.* New York: McGraw-Hill, 1959.

*White, Lynn, Jr. *Medieval Technology and Social Change.* New York: Oxford University Press, 1962.

————. "World View and Technology in the European Middle Ages." Paper presented at Wenner-Gren Summer Symposium no. 41, Burg Wartenstein, Austria, August, 1968.

White, Winston. *Beyond Conformity.* New York: Free Press, 1961.

*Whorf, Benjamin Lee. *Language, Thought, and Reality: Selected Writings of Benjamin Lee Whorf,* ed. John B. Carroll. Cambridge, Mass.: The M. I. T. Press, 1956.

*Whyte, William H., Jr. *The Organization Man.* New York: Simon and Schuster, 1957.

Willey, Gordon R. *An Introduction to American Archaeology,* vol. I: *North and Middle America.* Englewood Cliffs, N. J.: Prentice-Hall, 1966.

*Wilson, John A. *The Culture of Ancient Egypt.* Chicago: University of Chicago Press, 1956.

*Wittfogel, Karl A. *Oriental Despotism.* New Haven, Conn.: Yale University Press, 1957.

*Wolf, Eric. *Peasants.* Englewood Cliffs, N. J.: Prentice-Hall, 1966.

*Wolfe, Tom. *The Kandy-Kolored Tangerine-Flake Streamline Baby.* New York: Pocket Books, 1966.

Zimmer, Heinrich. *Philosophies of India.* New York: Meridian Books, 1956.

Film bibliography

The Ancient Egyptian. (International Film Foundation)
Ancient Mesopotamia. (New York University)
Apu Trilogy: Pather Panchalli, Aparajito, The World of Apu. (Audio
Film Center)
The Baboon Troop (Amboseli Reserve).
Bear and the Hunter.
Dead Birds. (Contemporary Films; University of California)
Djalambu. (Australian Institute of Aboriginal Studies)
Dynamics of Male Dominance in a Baboon Troop. (Educational
Services)
The Exiles. (Contemporary Films)
Fincho. (Audio Film Center)
Four Families. (New York University)
Glooscap County. (Canadian Consulate)
The Great Unfenced. (Contemporary Films)
The Hunters. (Contemporary Films; New York University)
Journey to Mecca. (Radim Films)
The Loon's Necklace. (New York University; University of Cali-
fornia)

Moulay Idriss. (Radim Films)

The Navaho as Filmmaker.

North Indian Village. (International Film Bureau; University of California)

Primitive People. (University of California)

Tjuringa: The Story of Stone Age Man. (Australian News and Information Bureau)

Trance and Dance in Bali. (New York University; University of California)

Trobriand Islanders. (University of California)

Walkabout: A Journey with the Aborigines. (Australian News and Information Bureau)

ADDRESSES OF FILM DISTRIBUTORS

Audio Film Center, Inc.
10 Fiske Place
Mount Vernon, N. Y. 10550

The Secretary
Australian Institute of Aboriginal Studies
P. O. Box 553
Canberra, A. C. T., Australia

Australian News and Information Bureau

Films Officer
636 Fifth Avenue
New York, N. Y. 10020

Press and Information Officer
Australian Consulate General
350 Post Street
San Francisco, Calif. 94108

Canadian Consulate

University of California Extension Media Center
2223 Fulton Street
Berkeley, Calif. 94720

Contemporary Films Inc.

267 West 25th Street, New York, N. Y. 10001
614 Davis Street, Evanston, Ill. 60201
1211 Polk Street, San Francisco, Calif. 94109

Educational Services, Inc.
39 Chapel Street
Newton, Mass. 02158

International Film Bureau, Inc.
332 South Michigan Avenue
Chicago, Ill. 60604

International Film Foundation
475 Fifth Avenue
Suite 916
New York, N. Y. 10017

The Film Library
New York University
26 Washington Place
New York, N. Y. 10003

Radim Films, Inc.
220 West 42nd Street
New York, N. Y. 10036

actual pattern   a pattern of behavior formulated by the objective scientific observer but not necessarily recognized by the performer. *Cf.* IDEAL PATTERN.

affine   a person related to another by marriage, *e.g.,* an "in-law." *Cf.* KINSMAN.

age-grade   a group or status that includes all members of a society of a given age and sex.

avoidance custom   culturally prescribed inhibition of social contact.

bilineal kinship   a relationship established according to a pattern of tracing descent more or less equally through both paternal and maternal lines. *Cf.* UNILINEAL KINSHIP.

bureaucracy   an organization in which positions are ranked along explicit lines of authority and responsibility, one staffed according to universalistic standards and requiring of its personnel the performance of explicitly defined duties.

centralization   a trend toward coordinating the units of society under a central control.

circulating connubium a system whereby prescribed marriage of matrilateral cross cousins results in a regular exchange of women and goods between unilineal descent groups.

cultural relativism the view that a society should be evaluated only in terms of the standards held by that society.

clan a sizable unilineal descent group, ordinarily composed of a number of related lineages.

classificatory kinship terms label given by Lewis Henry Morgan to a nomenclature in which a single term is applied to several kin types (lineal and collateral, maternal and paternal, etc.), with the effect of lumping them into one category; *e.g.,* the English term "uncle" is classificatory in that it may refer either to a maternal or to a paternal relative. *Cf.* DESCRIPTIVE KINSHIP TERMS.

cross cousin a child of one's parents' siblings of unlike sex, *e.g.,* one's mother's *brother's* daughter, one's father's *sister's* daughter. *Cf.* PARALLEL COUSIN.

culture a system of logically related ideas and values shared by members of a social system.

descriptive kinship terms label given by Lewis Henry Morgan to a nomenclature in which distinct terms or combinations of basic terms are used to designate specific relationships; *e.g.,* the terms "father" and "father's brother" distinguish lineal from collateral kin. *Cf.* CLASSIFICATORY KINSHIP TERMS.

diffuseness the tendency to leave implicit the rights and obligations entailed by a given social relationship. *Cf.* SPECIFICITY.

endogamy the custom of mating or marrying within a kinship or residential group. *Cf.* EXOGAMY.

ethical centralization the development of a single ethic that is regarded as applying to all situations. *Cf.* SITUATIONALISM.

ethnocentrism the interpretation of native behavior from the viewpoint of the observer's society rather than from the viewpoint of the native's society.

evolutionary theory a conceptual scheme designed to expound how systems develop in determinate directions through persistent processes of change.

exogamy   the custom of mating with or marrying individuals from outside one's own kinship or residential group. *Cf.* ENDOGAMY.

extended family household   a residence unit composed not only of a couple and their offspring but of additional relatives as well. *Cf.* NUCLEAR FAMILY HOUSEHOLD.

formal pattern   a pattern regarded by members of a group as defining the only proper way to behave. *Cf.* TECHNICAL PATTERN.

functional pattern   a pattern of conditions and consequences formulated by the analyst with reference to a given society. *Cf.* LOGICAL PATTERN.

ideal pattern   a conception of morally desirable behavior formulated by members of a society but not necessarily paralleled by their actual patterns of behavior. *Cf.* ACTUAL PATTERN.

incest   culturally prohibited mating or marriage between kinsmen.

invisible functions   consequences or implications (of sociocultural patterns) not consciously perceived by natives of the society.

irrigated agriculture   a system of farming whereby crops are watered by artificial means.

kinsman   a person related to another by ties of common descent. *Cf.* AFFINE.

lineage   a relatively small unilineal descent group. *Cf.* CLAN.

logical pattern   a pattern formulated by the analyst with reference to a given society, in which he relates to rules of behavior practices he sees as derived from them. *Cf.* FUNCTIONAL PATTERN.

matrilateral cross-cousin marriage   a pattern that allows or encourages a man's marriage to his mother's brother's daughter, but prohibits or discourages his marriage to his father's sister's daughter.

matrilineal   pertaining to descent traced solely or primarily through the mother and her female relatives. *Cf.* PATRILINEAL.

matrilocal residence   the settling of the newly married couple in or near the household of the wife's parents. *Cf.* NEOLOCAL; PATRILOCAL.

neolocal residence   the settling of the newly married couple in a domicile separate from the households of both the husband's and the wife's parents. *Cf.* MATRILOCAL; PATRILOCAL.

nuclear family household a residence unit confined to a couple and their offspring. *Cf.* EXTENDED FAMILY HOUSEHOLD.

parallel cousin a child of one's parents' siblings of like sex, *e.g.,* one's mother's *sister's* daughter, one's father's *brother's* daughter. *Cf.* CROSS COUSIN.

particularism the pattern of evaluating individuals on the basis of their inherited status or kinship relationships rather than on the basis of their merit, skill, or accomplishments. *Cf.* UNIVERSALISM.

patrilineal pertaining to descent traced solely or primarily through the father and his male relatives. *Cf.* MATRILINEAL.

patrilocal residence the settling of the newly married couple in or near the household of the husband's parents. *Cf.* MATRILOCAL; NEOLOCAL.

personality the system of behavioral components of an individual person.

polygyny the custom of marriage between one man and two or more women simultaneously.

rationality the tendency to justify or explain actions by emphasizing their efficient contribution to ends. *Cf.* TRADITIONALISM.

ritual of rebellion culturally permitted symbolic expression of hostility and ambivalence toward institutionalized authority.

ritual of social relations stylized ceremonials in which participants play the same roles toward one another that they play in ordinary life, thereby insuring that supernatural processes will tend to desirable ends for the society—purification, protection, prosperity.

silent pattern a pattern that the natives of a society follow but cannot or do not verbalize.

situationalism the practice of applying different ethical rules to different situations. *Cf.* ETHICAL CENTRALIZATION.

slash and burn agriculture a system of farming entailing the cutting and burning of forest cover in order to prepare fields for planting and to increase their fertility.

social differentiation the separation of social units from one another.

social system a system of interacting roles and groups.

specialization the concentration of efforts toward a limited end.

specificity the tendency to define explicitly the rights and obligations entailed by a given social relationship. *Cf.* DIFFUSENESS.

syncretism the blending of historically distinct traditions.

technical pattern a pattern regarded by members of a group as defining one of several possible means to achieve some designated goal. *Cf.* FORMAL PATTERN.

teleological fallacy the assumption that every pattern which serves a given function was deliberately designed by someone to serve that function.

totem an object, often a plant or animal, identified with, and venerated by, an individual or group.

traditionalism the tendency to justify or explain actions by emphasizing their conformity to accepted and long-standing patterns. *Cf.* RATIONALITY.

unilineal descent group a group composed of individuals who trace common kinship through either maternal or paternal lines exclusively.

unilineal kinship a relationship established according to a pattern of tracing descent more or less exclusively through either paternal or maternal lines. *Cf.* BILINEAL KINSHIP.

universalism the pattern of evaluating individuals on the basis of their merit, skill, or accomplishments rather than on the basis of their inherited status or kinship relationships. *Cf.* PARTICULARISM.

Index